D1604071

Gay Identity

NOV 3 1988

RBCL 1988

Gay Identity

The Self Under Ban

by

William H. DuBay

CONTRA COSTA COLLEGE
DISCARD
LIBRARY
SAN PABLO, CALIFORNIA

McFarland & Company, Inc., Publishers
Jefferson, North Carolina, and London

NOV 3 1988

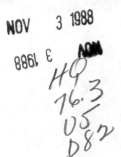

Library of Congress Cataloguing-in-Publication Data

DuBay, William H., 1934–
  Gay identity.

  Bibliography: p. 163.
  Includes index.
  1. Homosexuality — United States — Psychological
aspects. 2. Identity (Psychology) — United States.
I. Title.
HQ76.3.U5D82   1987   306.7′66   87-42505

ISBN 0-89950-269-5 (acid-free natural paper) ∞

© 1987 William H. DuBay. All rights reserved.

Printed in the United States of America.

McFarland   Box 611   Jefferson NC 28640

*Dedicated to the victims of AIDS and their families,
who have felt the full force of the ban.*

Contents

Introduction

This work is the result of an attempt to make sense out of my own "coming out" as a homosexual, a revolutionary experience for me as, I suspect, for a number of others. When I decided that I was a homosexual, a great switch was thrown in my brain, causing my life to take a quite sudden turn, starting me off in a direction for which I was completely unprepared.

Within a few weeks, my life was transformed. I informed all my relatives that I was gay and became rapidly involved in gay political activities. I woke one day to find myself living an all-gay lifestyle, spending all of my time with other gay males.

The psychological changes that I went through in becoming gay began to intrigue me. It had to do with a lot more than sex and pleasure. I noticed other people going through the same reorganizing experience in coming out. There appeared to be a uniformity here, a uniformity that seemed to override the great diversity found within the sexual lifestyles of the gay community.

When I began looking into this phenomenon, the information I found was confusing and contradictory. On the one hand, Alfred Kinsey and the sociologists were saying that "there is no such thing as a homosexual," and on the other hand, our whole manner of speaking refers to "homosexuals" as if they were a different *type* of human being. Definitions were lacking and terminology was difficult. There seemed to be a conspiracy to avoid any kind of scientific accuracy when dealing with whatever it is that makes a person gay.

Nothing made much sense until I revealed this problem to a young friend of mine, a paralegal VISTA worker in Fairbanks. "Oh! It's all in Becker!" he said, referring to Howard Becker's *Outsiders*. "It's called secondary deviance. The behavior is one thing. The role is something else."

Nothing had prepared me for Becker's book or the interactionist theory it represented. It hit me like a ton of bricks. The more I delved into interactionist thought, the more it seemed to fit both observation and experience as an explanation of sexual behaviors. As a theory, it seemed to hold its own better than all other theories. It is the only theory, in fact, that offers an explanation of gay identity that is consistent with current sociological thought.

Supported by the encouragement of friends, I began to follow leads, track down distant books and papers, and badger other writers and editors who had anything to say about the effects of labelling on homosexual behavior.

I wish to acknowledge and thank the many people who have helped and encouraged me along the way, including the venerable Lester Kirkendahl, one of the deans of sex research; Al Germann of Long Beach State; Wayne April (thanks, Wayne, wherever you are!); Ron Roizen of Berkeley; Dennis Kelso of the University of Alaska; Brendan Nagle of USC; Alan Cooke of Montreal; Dr. Fred Hillman of Anchorage; and my good friends Jon and Thelma Buchholdt. This does not exhaust the list of all the friends and lovers who have patiently listened to me hold forth on gay labelling, hoping I would get to the point.

If the conclusions reached here portray gay identity as a Trojan horse loaded with its own dangerous surprises, I ask my audience's indulgence for not completely answering the question, "Where do we go from here?" We are still in the grip of darkness, and it will be some time before we come into the full light of day. But we must follow the glimmers of light wherever we find them, wherever they might take us. The meanings of our lives are never created alone, and nothing binds us together more than discussing the possibilities of what we can become.

I. The Homosexual Myth

Deep within every individual and society can be found — as a sign of hope, judgment, or contradiction — eroticism, the crossroads where love and sexuality converge without always meeting. And deep within eroticism, the ultimate sign of scandal or supreme stimulus to thought, lies homosexuality (or as cautious people describe it, homophilia), the love of boys for boys, of girls for girls. — Raymond de Becker

Men in masses are gripped by personal troubles, but they are not aware of their true meaning and source. — C. Wright Mills

In 1984, the Alaska Department of Fisheries closed the crab-fishing grounds near Kodiak Island and in Bristol Bay. They were worried by the sudden decline in the population of several species, including the Alaska King crab. Crab prices immediately escalated. Some scientists believed that the decline was caused by an infestation of *Briarosaccus callosus*, a parasitic barnacle that attaches itself to the crab's internal organs.

When infested with this parasite, the female crab's ovaries, which occupy more than a quarter of the carapace, disappear completely; the male's gonads are greatly reduced and may disappear. Deprived of hormones, male crabs develop female characteristics. The barnacle's rootlets penetrate all of the crab's major organs including the nervous system. When the parasite is pinched, the crab actively responds. The parasite cannot be removed without endangering the host's life.

The barnacle transforms both male and female crabs into protective nursemaids, and the now-domesticated crabs assist in the delivery of the barnacle's young and tend them as if they were their own.

There is another parasite, also well adapted, that takes control of human behavior in much the same way. It is not a physical or biological organism, but one that infects our brain nonetheless. Like the parasitic barnacle, it establishes control over the manner in which we experience reality, often casting our social interactions in bizarre and contorted configurations.

The parasite is not sex, promiscuity, veneral disease, drugs, alcohol, nor the frightening scourge of AIDS. It is the myth of gay identity, the belief that homosexuals are a different kind of people.

1

Gay identity is one of the great working myths of our age. Even though it is based on ideas of gender and sex that have more to do with folklore than science, it occupies a central position in the beliefs and principles that govern our behaviors. It is a significant element in our social organization of gender and sexuality. They myth holds us all in thrall, not just those who have adopted the gay role.

We begin with the premise that there exists an evident distinction between (1) homosexual feelings, (2) homosexual behavior, and (3) the homosexual role. The argument presented here is that homosexual feelings play a minor part in becoming gay, which chiefly is the result of adopting the homosexual role.

Being gay is always a matter of self-definition. No matter what your sexual proclivities or experience, you are not gay until you decide you are. The decision to adopt the role and be gay is often followed by the need to share the decision with others, a process known as *coming out*.

While we have been taught to regard coming out as process of *acceptance* or *admission* of a condition we call *sexual orientation*, it is more accurately the result of *labelling oneself as a member of the homosexual community*, i.e., *adopting the homosexual role*. The former perspective puts the emphasis on the acceptance of an internal difference. The latter perspective, described in this book, puts the emphasis on the *process of adopting a socially constructed role*.

Although we cannot deny the underlying physiological basis of gender behaviors, *how we define and construe them* overlies our clinical understanding of them. Only by peeling away, one by one, these social overlays that surround our sexual behaviors will we be able to understand the psychological and physical needs of human development.

Our use of the term "role" probably corresponds more accurately to Talcott Parson's "status." In his paradigm, roles are combinations of norms, or expected behaviors; status is a combination of roles; and an institution is a combination of statuses. "Head of the house" is obviously a status, made up of the roles of parent, wage-earner, spouse, house-owner, etc. The gay status also incorporates a number of "roles," but we shall use the term "role" or "identity" here in the singular in the sense of "status."

For the purpose of this work, we use the terms "role" and "identity" interchangeably, with "role" referring to the set of meanings and norms constructed by society, while "identity" refers more to the subjective adoption and experience of that role by the individual. "I have a gay identity," means "I have adopted the gay role," "I have labelled myself as belonging to that group called homosexuals," and "I am a homosexual."

The gay myth is responsible for the creation of the gay community, which is an assemblage, not of people who share the same sexual orientation (they don't), but of those who have adopted the gay role. Underlying the many facets of gay life is an overriding concern with the gay role. The conversation and behavior of gay-identified individuals reveals that what distinguishes them from others is not their sexuality but their identity, their consciousness of being a people set apart. And what sets them apart is their joint commitment to a role created by society solely for the purposes of controlling and isolating the behaviors.

A feature of any myth is its ability to serve as a principle of organization for a number of social and personal beliefs, including those related to sexual behaviors and gender roles. Unravelling the myth is tedious work because of its involvement with our cherished beliefs about gender, sexuality, and our perception of ourselves as an enlightened, modern society. Rather than threaten those beliefs, we prefer to make comfortable accommodations with the parasitic myth.

Another feature of a hard-working myth is its *universality*. The more spurious and unlikely its origins, the more it pretends to be one of the world's eternal verities. To work at all, it must be seen as absolutely valid for all people of all times. The universal claim of the gay myth, trying to separate the world into gay and straight camps, runs into formidable opposition, especially in countries not used to such divisions.

Even in the United States, the myth frequently meets stiff opposition both inside and outside the academic world. One of the most vocal opponents of the myth was Alfred Kinsey. It is surprising how many people are heard to say, "According to Kinsey's homosexual-heterosexual scale, one out of ten persons is a homosexual," a statement that must have the world's most important sexual authority spinning in his grave. He was careful to point out that his "homosexual-heterosexual scale" represented ranges of sexual behaviors and experiences, *not* sexual orientation as commonly believed. Nor was it even meant to designate *types of people*. On several occasions, Kinsey went out of his way to explain:

> The classification of sexual behavior as masturbatory, heterosexual, or homosexual is, therefore, unfortunate if it suggests that only different types of persons seek out or accept each kind of sexual activity. There is nothing known in the anatomy or physiology of sexual response and orgasm which distinguishes masturbatory, heterosexual, or homosexual reactions. The terms are of value only because they describe the source of sexual stimulation, and they should not be taken as descriptions of the individuals who respond to the various stimuli. It would clarify our thinking if the terms could be dropped completely out of our vocabulary, for then socio-sexual behavior could be described as activity between a female and a male, or between two females, or between two males, and this would constitute a more objective record of the fact (1953:446–447).
>
> Males do not represent two discrete populations, heterosexual and homosexual. . . . Only the human mind invents categories and tries to force facts into pigeonholes. The living world is a continuum in each and every one of its aspects . . . (1948:639).

It is amazing to observe how many psychologists and psychiatrists have accepted this sort of propaganda, and have come to believe that homosexual males and females are discretely different from persons who merely have homosexual experience, or who react sometimes to homosexual stimuli. . . . Instead of using these terms as substantives which stand for persons, or even as adjectives to describe persons, they may better be used to describe the nature of the overt sexual relations, or of the stimuli to which an individual erotically responds (1948:616-617).

In regard to sexual behavior, it has been possible to maintain this dichotomy only by placing all persons who are exclusively heterosexual in a heterosexual category and all persons who have any amount of experience with their own sex, even including those with the slightest experience, in a homosexual category. . . . The attempt to maintain a simple dichotomy on these matters exposes the traditional biases which are likely to enter whenever the heterosexual or homosexual classification of an individual is involved (1948:468-469).

One of the factors that materially contributes to the development of exclusively homosexual histories is the ostracism which society imposes upon one who is discovered to have had perhaps no more than a lone experience. The high school boy is likely to be expelled from school and, if it is in a small town, he is almost certain to be driven from the community. His chances of making sexual contacts are tremendously reduced after the public disclosure, and he is forced into the company of other homosexual individuals among whom he finally develops an exclusively homosexual pattern for himself (1948:663).

Exclusive preferences of behavior, heterosexual or homosexual, come only with experience, or as a result of social pressures which tend to force an individual into an exclusive pattern of one or the other sort (1953:450-451).

Although Kinsey was clearly against the practice of labelling people gay or straight, the practice is taken for granted and even defended by the press, professionals, and the gay community itself. Kinsey was perhaps naive in ignoring the force of social stigma — society's disapproval — in maintaining the practice of gay labelling and even using his sexual scale in doing so.

Even less could he have expected that his own successors in the Institute of Sex Research that he founded would be leading the pack. After Kinsey's death, the Institute sponsored a series of studies on, of all things, "homosexuals" based on interviews with gay-identified persons rounded up at gay institutions. Just what identified their subjects as "homosexuals" the authors failed to make clear.

In one of these volumes, the authors revealed that the sexual outlet of their homosexual subjects covered a range from 2 to 6 on the Kinsey scale, a range that is meaningless *since it covers at least one-third of the white male population in our society*, indicating that there is more variety in sexual orientation within the gay community than outside it. We could only conclude homosexual orientation is *not* the significant factor that determines gay identity. Kinsey held that sexual experiences, sexual orientation, and the sexual roles are separate and in a way independent of one another. One's homosexual experiences, no matter how extensive, do not determine one's sexual orientation. Neither does one's orientation determine one's adoption of the gay role.

While sexual orientation may be an important factor leading to the adoption of the gay role, it is not necessary. We can also question whether recognition of homosexual feelings is necessary for the adoption of the role, as several authors have suggested. There have been many people who in some societies would have been regarded as transvestites and transsexuals but who in the United States have adopted the gay role because of confusion of homosexuality with violations of gender norms.

In the United States, there are many persons of significant homosexual outlet (2–6 on the Kinsey scale) who have not adopted the homosexual role. And there are many of significant heterosexual outlet (2–4) who have adopted the role. What makes a person homosexual? Whatever it is, it is not sex. It is the role.

British sociologist Mary McIntosh was one of the first to blow the whistle on scholars doing research on "homosexuals" and supporting labelling behaviors. In her now-famous article on "The Homosexual Role" published in 1968, she called on investigators to consider the influence of the role itself on the behaviors of those identified as homosexuals. She wrote:

> The vantage-point of comparative sociology enables us to see that the conception of homosexuality as a condition is, itself, a possible object of study. This conception and the behavior it supports operate as a form of social control in a society in which homosexuality is condemned. Furthermore, the uncritical acceptance of the conception by social scientists can be traced to their concern with homosexuality as a social problem. They have tended to accept the popular definition of what the problem is and they have been implicated in the process of social control. . . .
>
> It is interesting to notice that homosexuals themselves welcome and support the notion that homosexuality is a condition. For just as the rigid categorization deters people from drifting into deviancy, so it appears to foreclose on the possibility of drifting back into normalcy and thus removes the element of anxious choice. It appears to justify the deviant behavior of the homosexual as being appropriate for him as a member of the homosexual category. The deviancy can thus be seen as legitimate for him and he can continue in it without rejecting the norms of society.

The universal claims of the gay myth have seduced otherwise careful scholars to reinterpret history and anthropology in the same way, applying our peculiar explanation of homosexual behaviors to other cultures and other times. Works on "Homosexuality in Ancient Greece," for example, have attempted to explain the homosexual habits of the Greeks in terms of sexual orientation, an explanation the Greeks themselves would have found eccentric and probably offensive (along with our concept of "sexuality"—another concept of quite modern origins).

Similar descriptions of the *berdaches* found among American Indian societies as "a common institutionalized form of homosexuality" are also a mistake. There is no indication that sexual orientation had anything to do with choosing the life of a berdache. North American Indians had a tolerance for gender ambiguity that provided for more than one gender role without reference to sexual orientation.

The sexual practices of other societies are frequently similar in appearance but express quite different beliefs and social priorities. As anthropologists have told us, no human behaviors are more flexible, more malleable, or more expressive of the social structure of society than sexual behaviors, and it does no good to impose the sexual meanings of one society on others.

The gay myth also strives to universalize the oppression. Modern preachers would have us believe that the current suppression of homosexuality comes down to us in a straight line from ancient Hebrew or Roman times. As a matter of fact, the ancient laws against sodomy were vaguely defined and rarely invoked. The Roman church lumped *all* sexual behaviors, including homosexual ones, into the same bag, considering them as corrupt but unavoidable, the result of original sin. The church would have outlawed marital intercourse if it could have gotten away with it, so much did it despise sexuality.

In spite of the ancient proscriptions, a high degree of sexual tolerance developed during the Middle Ages, from which Western Europe emerged with a regard for personal and sexual freedoms that to today's Americans would be considered very sophisticated. The trouble started with the rise of the modern nation-state that began in the seventeenth century to enact new codes of law extending the power of the state into the families and private lives of its citizens.

A whole new definition of sex and the family was forming, one that would support the industrial and military ambitions of the new rulers. The new states began imposing a rigid standard of conduct that the ancient church would have thought impossible. They hit upon the spurious revelation proposed by the medical profession that sexual anomalies were the results of "mental illness" and incorporated the concept into their new laws. "Homosexuality" was but one in a long list of proscribed "abnormalities." Historians have described the sexual repression that descended on Western Europe and North America as a result of those laws as the "worst of any time, any place." Unlike the church, the modern state, armed with a whole array of terrifying medical technologies, no longer made the humane distinction between the sinner and the sin. From now on, the sinner *was* the sin. For over a hundred years, respected members of the medical profession have hacked away at gray matter and gonads attempting to remedy mythical sexual disease.

There seemed no limits to the rage of the modern state in stomping out defiant expressions of human love. Nazi Germany's extermination of a half-million gay-identified persons in European gas chambers is a crime we have witnessed but still refuse to recognize. No, the monster we face today is not the creation of antiquity, but is the child of our own times.

The concept of homosexuality as a disease has given way to the concept of homosexuality as a *condition*. Either way, the myth serves the purposes of social control by placing the cause of the emotion somehow beyond the experience itself, underlying it as an inherent condition, somehow permanently set in early childhood and remaining stable throughout one's life. This inherent condition we sometimes call "sexuality," "sexual orientation" or "sexual preference," but the meanings we give it are much more substantive. It is much more than a liking or a preference in the sense of a choice. It is rather the *explanation* of why we prefer. Many people refer to this condition as "my sexual identity," clearly indicating the sense of having a condition that sets them apart from others.

Gay-identified persons carefully cultivate and cherish this sense of having a differentiating condition. They tend to reinterpret their own biographies and give new meanings to their accomplishments, disappointments, and failures in the light of this perception. "I always knew I was different," some people say, "long before I experienced any homosexual feelings." For many people, the condition of being gay occupies a major part of their self-concept. The process goes from feeling gay and doing gay to being gay.

Why this tendency to reify a sexual feeling and make it the centerpiece of one's personality? The answer is found, as McIntosh suggested above, in the need to reduce the element of choice and anxiety related to socially proscribed behaviors. Adoption of the gay role is essentially a conversion, an affirmation of the belief that homosexual behaviors are the result of an internal condition that cannot be changed. Such an explanation grants the individual a warrant to proceed in the behavior in spite of the general proscriptions against it.

It is as if society says to those individuals who continue to defy the norm: "If you wish to proceed in this behavior, you have to undertake the burden of the gay role." The only way they can envision themselves pursuing the activity is to adopt the label/role: "It's less offensive to engage in homosexual behaviors if I *am* a homosexual." A certain amount of innocence is thereby preserved.

In spite of the fact that the recognition of one's sexual feelings remains relatively stable throughout life, commitment to the gay role undergoes remarkable variation. Scholars have observed that this commitment exhibits the characteristic of a *career* with a beginning, middle, and (for some) an end. The view that being gay is for life ignores the constant fluctuations in the population of the gay community itself, which is like a box into which, at one end, a new supply of neophytes is continually being added and from which, at the other end, others more experienced are rapidly exiting. Far from being a stable condition, one's commitment to the gay role undergoes constant revision, adaptation, attenuation, and even abandonment.

One of the most bizarre effects of the gay myth is the manner in which it ascribes the same "cause" to male and female homosexuality, as if they were simply male and female versions of the same thing. This confusion has led to some unfortunate difficulties and misunderstandings in the political relationships between the gay male and lesbian communities. Males and females experience their homosexuality as two different things. They may share the same oppression, but it is construed differently by society and is expressed quite differently.

Homosexual behaviors are important, as Kinsey said, because of what they tell us about the differences between male and female sexuality. Our modern fascination with homosexuality as something which lesbians and gay males have in common has obscured these important lessons. Male homosexuality is a way of being male and lesbianism is a way of being female. Each has more in common with its respective gender than with the other.

The enthusiasm of the gay community for the concept of homosexuality as a "normal, healthy" condition is all the more surprising when we consider that it is but a hair's breadth away from the concept of a diseased condition. The new liberalism that defines homosexuality as a permanent condition called sexual orientation is not very liberal at all, especially when we consider the high level of stigmatizing behavior it evokes. Anything which tends to label persons as a breed set apart puts them at enormous risk. The problem is not whether the condition of being gay is diseased or not, but whether it is a condition at all. Close examination will reveal that it is but a set of norms, meanings, symbols, and values that we apply to certain people called gay.

The "new homosexuality" is not new at all, but rather a sophisticated attempt to maintain control over sexual behaviors in an age that regards itself as sophisticated and liberal. After all, how can we regard ourselves as happy if we do not regard ourselves as free? We blind ourselves to the many ways in which the myth constricts our freedoms.

The gay myth has given much support to the belief in latent homosexuality. The idea that the cause of homosexuality is rooted in an underlying condition that is external to the experience itself has led many people to fear that they could "be gay" without having any gay feelings and that one's gayness might be easily triggered to actuality if sufficient precautions are not taken.

More than anything else, this concept of gayness residing as an unperceptible entity with a life of its own has, in itself, been a cause of a great constriction of male behaviors and emotions. One can never be too sure about one's masculinity. The question is no longer one of just retaining the visible appurtenances of masculinity, but one of being constantly on guard for internal signs of softness, tenderness, or erotic feeling that might actualize one's hidden gayness. Feelings once valued as central to social relations have been relegated to a set of persons banished to the periphery of society. What was once regarded as an emotional/sexual option for anyone is now confined to an isolated sexual lifestyle.

The antidote to all the fears about homosexuality is, of course, heterosexual orgasm, which has become the ultimate test of masculinity. Males, never secure enough about their heterosexual status, can never have enough of orgasm. Insecure males regard women more as instruments of asserting masculinity than as objects of love. Women, more like men now than ever, have also latched on to the connection between orgasm and self-worth. By supporting the new concern with orgasm, the gay myth heightens and radicalizes the importance of orgasm and the differences of gender, making the relationships between men and women all the more difficult and manipulative.

The absolute claims of the gay myth have radically altered the whole nature of social interaction in our society. The physical expressions of normal human interaction and affection have been suppressed because of the fears that one might be considered homosexual. Even feelings of affection for members of the same sex of any age, including children, are cruelly brought under suspicion.

This isolation has led to a great loss of human talent, sensitivities, and creativity, and not just in gay people, but in all others who have to hide their special talents for fear of appearing "different" to others. Other societies have more room for the expression of those ambiguous gender behaviors that we reject outright. Persons whom we confine to back rooms and bars other societies have honored as tenders of children, astrologers, dancers, chanters, minstrels, jesters, artists, shamans, sacred warriors and judges, seers, healers, and weavers of tales and magic.

Those special roles were often characterized by their ability to perceive and express the child's mystical world of spirit, symbol, liturgy, fantasy, nature, and life itself. As each society is continually being recreated in the minds of its young, such roles contributed directly to the formation of culture and the manner in which the society understood itself. The elimination of those mystical roles was necessary before the industrialized state could get on with the work of plundering our planet without the irritations of those who speak for its children.

Another facet of the myth is the isolation of gay-identified persons from children. No matter what their qualities of soul or how skilled they are in teaching children, gay-identified persons are perceived as different, and this difference must not be allowed to contaminate children. As a result of this educational policy, all teachers are required to maintain strict heterosexual standards, supporting the cultural constrictions of gender behavior and robbing their students of the chance to learn something about the ambiguities of life. What is worse, many people with special talents and skills in working with children are kept out of teaching altogether.

Fears of sexuality have grossly distorted the teaching profession by bringing into suspicion the natural emotions that normally exist between children and adults. As educator Paul Goodman said, erotic affectivity is an important component of the learning experience and it is cruel to bring those feelings under suspicion.

It is not just in the classroom, however, that the myth does its damage. Fears of homosexuality suppress the love, tenderness, affection, and physical sensuality of family life. Genital primacy has appropriated all forms of erotic contact into orgasmic behaviors, resulting in the sensual deprivation of children. By relating love to orgasm instead of touch, the status of children and those who tend them has been systematically reduced. Our high levels of wife-and-child battering, often attributed to the low levels of affective contact in our society, find much support in a system that defines sex in terms of orgasm and genital orientation.

Nowhere are the constrictions of the gay myth more dramatically expressed than in the exclusion of gay-identified persons from heterosexual relationships. Upon coming out, a person eschews the possibility of all future heterosexual relations, no matter how many or how successful such relationships may have been in the past. Belief in the gay difference imposes a new ethic which dictates that function follow form, rendering sexual relations with the opposite sex henceforth as "inauthentic."

This unquestioned compliance with the myth was illustrated in the film *Making Love,* in which the young doctor's wife questioned whether her husband's coming out had somehow invalidated the marriage. He obviously thought it did and promptly left her. The decision to adopt the gay role brought into play a new ethic which seemed to absolve him of any commitments he might have made to the marriage.

While we can understand his desire to explore his newly discovered sexual opportunities, we also wonder why he and his wife did not consider alternatives that could have salvaged what had up till then been a successful relationship. Others in the same situation have been able to experience their gay affair as any other extramarital affair: It certainly brings a strain to the marriage, but does not necessitate its end.

The concept of "being different" also leads many gay children to leave home unnecessarily — if their families have not already thrown them out. As a result, many young people, convinced they are different, leave home and make their way to the anonymity of large cities. Through this ongoing migration, the gay communities of our urban centers are constantly renewed. Gay-identified youths constitute a significant proportion of runaways and others separated from their families. The myth of the gay difference contributes much to the splintering of family strength and unity.

The myth of the gay difference has finally found its justification in the AIDS virus. Here is the physical marker for homosexuality that the doctors have sought for so long to identify homosexuals and separate them from others. There is little doubt that AIDS (Acquired Immune Deficiency Syndrome) has already influenced the gay role and the way society regards homosexual behavior. The stigma of this puzzling and treacherous disease has been juxtaposed on the stigma of being gay. There is no gay-identified person in this country who has not already felt this added burden.

This development lends new urgency to the study of gay identity and the manner in which social factors contribute to infectious diseases. As we have learned from the experience of colonized classes in developing countries, oppression leads to the depression of the social requirements of health. The populations of Third World countries have been afflicted with rapidly rising rates of promiscuity, prostitution, extramarital pregnancies, abortions, drug and alcohol abuse, and infectious diseases — often in societies where these elements were once absent.

In all societies, the single male is at great risk, more vulnerable to disease and mental stress, physical harm, and earlier death. This is exactly the situation into which our society places gay-identified males. Casting them out of their families, prohibiting them from bonding relationships of their own, and keeping them from the meaningful contacts with children, society does its best to victimize the health of gay-identified persons.

With the appearance of AIDS in our country, our society may no longer be able to afford the luxury of its ancient myths, which now come at a terribly high price. The public health industry has contributed subtly to the oppression by addressing infectious disease in terms of individual treatment instead of community response. The social history of infectious diseases shows us the extent to which the social meanings we attach to those diseases affects our responses. Social conditions and attitudes, environmental phenomena, and stigma are generally discounted as causes of disease. Ignoring these factors has made the medical profession in our country uniquely unqualified to deal with this complex phenomenon.

We will never get a handle on AIDS or other infectious diseases without addressing the social requirements for health. The gay myth attempts to isolate homosexual experience within the gay community, setting it outside the influence of social protections and restraints, creating a fertile ground for infectious diseases that otherwise would be absent. The myth demobilizes society's capacity for moderating and socializing the behavior. Only by coming to grips with the social dynamics of gay behaviors can we effectively deal with the real causes of AIDS.

Anti-war journalist Randolpf Bourne wrote during the First World War that the first task in abolishing war was to learn to think and act in such a way as if war did not exist. This book is directed toward that exercise: "How would we construe and express homosexual feelings in a society in which the oppression was absent?" It is one thing to say that homosexuality is normal, but nobody is talking about the gay-straight world not being divided on sexual lines. So massively has the gay myth insinuated its tendrils into our brain and our society that we hesitate to examine it too closely, much less attempt to extricate it.

But the risk must be taken. As a strategy for coping with oppression, the adoption of the gay role is not an effective choice for the individual or society. Let me make a qualification. The gay role now construed is not an effective choice for individuals or society. There will always be gay people, but the role should not be defined on sexual lines — it is meaningless.

Gay people there are, and some are indeed different, but it is not their sexuality that makes them different. Their real differences, as significant as they may be, are now submerged in the emphasis of the gay myth on sexual difference. If anything, it is their sexuality that they have most in common with all humans. We can end this introduction with one more appeal added to countless others, an appeal almost totally ignored by the academic and medical establishments: Gayness, unlike the medical term "homosexuality," has nothing to do with sex or sexual orientation. It concerns a wide range of divergent behaviors that set some people apart from others in their appearance, gender behavior, emotional sensibilities, intellectual powers, and their perspective of the world.

On the other hand, if homosexuality (sex) is good and normal, it must be good and normal for everyone, and not just for gay people. Such a solution has already been realized by many persons who have come to enjoy their homosexual capacities without having recourse to the gay role. We have to go further than that, however, and create a rationale that integrates homosexuality and gayness back into the family and relates them to the health and development of children. Unless they are seen as contributing to the pleasure of infants, the joy of mothers, the health of children, and the strength of youth, society will continue to suspect them and keep them under its powerful ban. It is only in the context of familial love that we will find the answers to the contradiction we call homosexuality.

II. The Identity Imperative

If you can't be yourself, why be anybody? — Jim Pierce, female impersonator

Having taken a look at Kinsey's position that homosexuals and heterosexuals are not two different kinds of human beings, we have to recognize the fact that society did not take him seriously. We continue to regard gay-identified persons as different, and that perception deeply affects their own behaviors and others' as well. Not only does gay identity play a major role in the behavior of gay-identified persons, it also plays a significant part in the general beliefs regarding gender and sexuality. The gay role has an important effect on the sexual behaviors of everyone.

Our agenda here includes first of all looking at the social construction of these basic elements: *personal identity*, (Chapter II), *sex* (Chapter III) and *gender* (Chapter IV). Chapter V takes up the central position of the family in the construction of the gay role.

Chapter VI discusses *the homosexual discourse*, the political and social background of the concept of "homosexuality," the medical philosophy it represents, and its usefulness to the state. While the homosexual discourse defines the content of the gay role — the concept of homosexuality — Chapter VII defines the form of the gay role: the political process of *stigma* that converts the concept of homosexuality into a deviant role. Chapter VIII defines how an individual comes to adopt that role for himself. Chapter IX examines the dynamic character of gay identity and how people go about maintaining, altering, and abandoning the gay role. Chapter X reviews the alternative theories of gay identity.

The significance of *identification* in the creation of the homosexual will not be clearly understood or appreciated without first understanding the nature of identity itself. There has been a tendency among writers on the subject of gay identity to shy away from any examination of the "identity" factor. They also ignore the meanings that gay-identified persons themselves place on their "identity," a term they frequently use in connection with their "sexuality." They often assume that there are two kinds of sexual orientation "identity," homosexual and heterosexual, just as there are two kinds of gender identity. Now we know that gender identity has some basis in the real world. Is there any basis for a distinct identity based on sexual orientation? To examine this question, we must look at identity itself before we can understand the meanings that gay-identified people give to it.

Becoming gay — adopting the gay role — is the expression of two important social achievements, our modern concepts of the self and of sexuality. In a very unique process, gay identity transforms these central concerns, sex and identity, into a unified concept. With the adoption of the gay role, one's sexuality rapidly moves to the center of one's self-concept, where it serves as a pivot around which one can organize one's world and personality.

In this chapter we take up the process of *identity maintenance*. The process of maintaining identity has several systems to rely on, including (1) a physiological one that establishes the sense of connection with one's body-space, (2) a social one that establishes one's space in society and history, and (3) an intellectual or mystical one that establishes one's connection with the physical universe.

The self-concept establishes our place in society. If the "self" can be regarded as the knowing subject, the self-concept is that collection of ideas we have about ourselves. How people think about themselves and assemble a self-concept is crucial in the understanding of gay identity.

One of the important correlates of the gay myth is the *myth of personality*, which, like the gay myth, attributes much of behavior to an internal set of instructions that is fixed early in life and comprises a pattern for behavior. We are taught to be true to ourselves in the sense of behaving in a manner coherent with that internal program. The myth of personality offers us an easy explanation for many characteristics such as being shy, aggressive, outgoing, or violent.

We can illustrate the nature of this belief by contrasting it with the beliefs of more traditional societies who believed that much of human behavior is caused by influences from *outside* the body such as spirits, spells, bewitchments, and the influence of the gods. Modern medicine has tended to reverse this belief by ascribing more and more of human behaviors to factors within the body, which we have come to identify with our personality.

We accord the same supernatural significance to internal conditions that we once ascribed to spiritual, outside influences. We believe in these internal roots of behavior so strongly that we attribute to them an almost divine infallibility. If these internal and subconscious sources could be directly perceived, we feel that they would become an unfailing source of direction, inspiration, and wisdom. Although we are limited to perceive them "darkly, as through a mirror," we are reminded that ignoring one's internal mandates is fraught with serious consequences. Aptitude tests confirm this belief, even though they often direct us toward occupations for which we have no liking. We must constantly placate the gods within for fear of bringing down some terrible retaliation.

The gay myth supports this belief with its emphasis on sexual orientation as a component of personality to which the individual must accommodate himself to be "authentic." To ignore one's homosexual feelings, for example, and proceed with a marriage is believed to be courting disaster, even though there is no evidence to support such a claim.

There is much evidence, however, showing that what we call "personality" is nothing more than our self-concept, a collection of ideas we have about ourselves. Not only is our self-concept constantly undergoing change, but it also seems to be directly related to our perceptions of what others think about us.

We are accustomed to regard personality as an internal fixed condition rather than a mental image of a complex social interaction. Personality, like being gay, is not the result of something inside *or* outside the individual, but rather of a social process, that is, the results of a *dialog* between the individual and society. Internal characteristics—such as body type or sexual experiences—are certainly *involved* in the formation of the self-concept, but they do not *determine* it. Personal characteristics such as body height, appearance, temperament, digestion, and the like provide the raw material that is fed into the mill of social interaction to produce our self-concept.

George Herbert Mead is regarded as one of the founders of symbolic interactionism. In *Mind, Self, and Society* (1934), he did much to illuminate the internal process of how the mind constructs the idea of the self. Beginning with the observation that the infant at first knows *persons* and only later comes to know *things*, Mead held that thought is essentially *pragmatic*, that is, it is based on the model of two people discussing the way to solve a problem. In one swoop, Mead gives us a theory that unites both culture and thought into a coherent and continuous process.

According to Mead, thought is nothing more than imaginary conversation conducted inside our head with an imaginary audience concerning whatever practical problem is at hand. Even in our most private activities, such as reading a book, we are engaged conversationally, sharing our reactions internally with some imagined audience. While we tend to be amused by those who lip-read or "talk to themselves," the only difference between them and others is that they apparently haven't mastered the art of keeping their mouths shut and have let their internal conversation leak out. They are not really "talking to themselves." Just as you and I do internally, they are talking to an imaginary audience.

Society and thought are complementary, directly reflecting and creating one another. Human behavior, accordingly, is the result of the

meanings and understandings (symbols) created by the social interaction
of conversation, both real and imaginary. Thought is radically social,
rooted in the way we interact with others. What we call culture—the
distinctive features of each human society—is the product of the social
meanings given to behaviors and objects in our real and imaginary
conversations.

McCall and Simmons (1966:39–40) stated, "The most important
thing about man's situation is that he lives simultaneously in two different
worlds. In the first place he is a mammal of quite ordinary properties, yet
at the same time he lives in a symbolic universe." Lindesmith and Strauss
(1968:7) went on to say that our social groupings depend on how we construct those symbols: "The central position [of symbolic interactionism]
is that the features of human behavior that distinguish it from the
behavior of other animals are derived from the fact that man is a symbol
manipulator, the only symbol-manipulating animal and the only animal
whose social groupings depend upon and are pervaded by complex symbolic process." Not only is thought based on an interactive exchange of
symbols, so is society.

This interactive and social explanation of thought, perhaps the most
important development in the philosophy of behavior since Plato, provides a remarkable coherence between the worlds inside and outside our
heads. It also provides us with the capacity of self-recognition and objectification. We are able to perceive and talk about ourselves as objects, explaining ourselves to imaginary or real audiences as we go along. What
we are in the habit of calling "personality" derives much from the collection of ideas we have gathered from real and internal conversations about
ourselves. On closer examination, we see that our self-concept is mostly
comprised of our own assessment of how others regard us. It is an *interactive* and reflective process: "What I think others think about me explains
to me who I am." Because there is no other way of thinking about
ourselves, we can begin to understand the intensely social and interactive
nature of our self-concept.

But the process of forming a self-concept is only one part, the social
part, of identity maintenance. There are reasons to believe that conversation and human interaction, as important as they are, are but social expressions of a dynamic *biological* process that goes back to the very roots
of life. As a biological process, identity maintenance has to do with pro-
tecting the *separation of the organism from the rest of the world.* This
task answers the most fundamental question of life: "Why does an organism act at all?" Every living organism is dedicated to the goal of maintaining the organization of its parts as a single, living unit different from its
separate parts and different from the rest of the world. Death consists in
losing that element of unity and organization, allowing the parts to
reassume their separate status, again joining the "rest of the world."

Webster's dictionary uses the terms "oneness" and "individuality" to define identity. Identity is also used in a broader and generic sense, not to denote oneness or singularity, but as belonging to a certain class. In this latter sense we "identify" a certain plant or animal as belonging to a certain genus and species. But in its strict and philosophical meaning, it precludes any sense of belonging to a group. It means just the opposite: self-sameness, absolute uniqueness, separate from all others, occupying a space taken up by no other.

Identity comes from the Latin word *idem* meaning "the same thing." The meaning of identity is twofold: to establish something's self-sameness and at the same time its separateness from all other things. We use the term this way when we "establish the identity of stolen goods." It is in this meaning that philosophy establishes the most basic rule of thought and nature, the principle of identity: "A thing cannot be and not be at the same time and in the same respect." This leads to the necessary corollaries that no two things are really the same or "identical," and "nature never does the same thing twice." A thing can be identical only with itself. When we refer to "identical" twins or "identical" sets of silver we use the term only by way of analogy: "These two sets of silver would almost seem to be identical."

The Greek philosophers, in their concept of "entropy" — the tendency of all matter and energy in the universe to degrade to a homogenous state of chaos and uniformity — saw in living organisms the ability to reverse that tendency and to bring order out of chaos, to organize matter into more and more complex forms that became more and more successful in maintaining those crucial barriers between selfhood and chaos. They recognized the special way in which all living things as "subsistent individuals" participate in the maintenance of their own selfhood. In living objects, self-sameness is not just an objective fact, but also a subjective process.

Another element of the animal world is sensation, which creates the possibility of *subjectivity* and the knowledge of oneself as the sensor or knower. This subjectivity should not be confused with the self-concept. While the self-concept is composed of ideas about ourself, we have no ideas about ourselves as subjects. We perceive our own subjectivity in the act of knowing but not as an object of that knowing. When we use the term "I" or the "self," we are referring to our subjectivity as the source of knowing and doing.

Nor should we confuse the self with what is called the soul. As Thomas Aquinas said, "I am not my soul." For centuries, philosophical questions of human identity centered on the problem of change. Aristotle, puzzled about how organisms can change and yet remain the same — how the hen's egg turns into an embryo and then a chicken — deduced the existence of an internal biological "plan" carrying the whole process through from beginning to end. He called this plan "form" because it informed shapeless matter and made it a living thing. Our whole language is thoroughly impregnated with this ancient theory of "hylomorphism," matter-and-form. Scholastic philosophers in the middle ages "baptized" this formula by saying the Christian soul is identical with Aristotle's form.

Newtonian physics for a time eclipsed Aristotle's doctrine on *formal cause* by emphasizing instead *efficient causes* and dazzling the world with its display of machines, clocks, and steam engines, an emphasis which has come to characterize modern industrial societies.

Darwin, whose *The Origin of Species* did much to validate the ancient idea of the formal cause, took much inspiration from Aristotle. He once remarked, "Linnaeus and Cuvier have been my two gods, but they were mere schoolboys compared to old Aristotle."

The discoverers of DNA were fond of pointing out the relevance of Aristotle's hylomorphism to their historic discovery: Within each cell of the living being there is not a passive pattern but an active information system that not only passes on information from one generation to another and provides for adaptation to change, but creates an enormous capacity for learning and the storage of information outside the body. Living organisms amazingly participate in the shaping of their own behaviors and destinies.

But while DNA fills the bill for Aristotle's *forma*, it is hardly a substitute for life itself, which has so far escaped the gaze of science. Life is much more than the instructions used in organizing the body, just as a computer is much more than information contained in its hardware and software.

Matching the discovery of DNA in significance was our new knowledge of the immune system, the most dynamic and ancient system within the body. Going back millions of years to pre-life organic forms, the body's ability to attack and destroy foreign elements is based on its ability to read the protein coding of the cell membrane that is unique to each living body. Not only does the body manufacture special defenses for each intruding substance, but it retains those defenses for more efficient mobilization in case of future attacks.

Probably nowhere in the physical world do we find such a clear presentation of an organism's struggle to maintain the separation between the self and the not-self. To miss one trespassing microorganism can mean the difference between life and death. The various elements of the immune system throw themselves into the task of destroying the intruders with an apocalyptic fury.

So formidable are these defenses, they sometimes work against the body's best interests. Through what seems to be cruel misreadings of information, they can turn against the body's own tissues, causing a variety of allergies and other auto-immune diseases, even death. In the case of

Rh-factor incompatibility between a mother and infant, blood escaping from the infant during childbirth into the mother's sytem can cause her defenses to mobilize antibodies so rapidly as to kill the child as it is being born. Such tragedies would continually overwhelm us if the body did not also possess other, equally powerful systems that monitor and check the immense force of its defenses.

But the immune system is not the only biological system involved in the maintenance of human identity. The biological defenses of the organism are expanded in vertebrates to the functions of the brain and the senses. In the higher mammals, the maintenance of the individual's identity becomes a social task: The individual mobilizes the aid of others in the maintenance of identity. A by-product of this aggressive organization of the self is the phenomenon we call society.

Sigmund Freud drew the attention of science to the significance of the sense of touch in the maintenance of identity. He found that tactile stimulation is one of the most important needs of the human being, more important in fact than nutrition and reproduction. The child has a developmental need for pleasurable stimulation during critical periods of its development, without which the child can suffer physical impairment that can even cause death.

Doing work on the sexuality of human beings, Freud found that human identity was a developmental *process*, which begins soon after birth. He summarized his views concerning sexuality in his *Outline of Psychoanalysis* (1940:152):

> a. The sexual function does not start with puberty, but begins soon after birth with clear manifestations.
> b. It is necessary to make a sharp distinction between the concepts sexual and genital. The first is wider and includes many activities which have nothing to do with the genitals.
> c. Sexuality is defined as the function of gaining pleasurable gratification from specific bodily zones. This function is placed in the service of procreation only secondarily. Often both functions do not completely fuse.

Science is only beginning to understand and unravel the significance of Freud's observation, which gave us the handle needed for the study of human development by providing a connecting link between behavior and identity, between the experience of the child and the behavior of the adult. Freud's recognition of the generalized, nongenital sexuality found in the physical contact between mother and child was to be the foundation of his doctrine on identity. He wrote (1908:198): "The sexual behavior of a human being often *lays down the pattern* for all other modes of reacting to life." Without physical contact, babies die and adults are driven to despair, depression, and acts of suicide and violence.

Subsequent research has shown how the sense of self is intimately related to the sense of touch, and the ability of the other senses to maintain identity is related to their ability to emulate and enhance the sense of touch.

The pleasurable contact between the nursing infant and mother lays the foundation for all those experiences embraced in our concepts of love (*eros*), touching, physical affection, affective contact, fondling, petting, caressing, stroking, pleasuring, tenderness, cutaneous stimulation, sensuality, loving friendship (*agape*), tactuality, dearness (*philia, caritas*), desire, trust, veneration, feeling, closeness, intimacy, and familiarity.

Diverse societies throughout the world have long regarded the pleasures enjoyed between mother and child as the model for the tender, loving relationships between other individuals throughout the rest of society. Freud suggested that not only does infantile tactual experience set the pattern for one's later responses to life, but that the sense of touch, being the most proximate sense, is the model for the other senses. Later research has confirmed that even our most sophisticated accomplishments — art, language, music, mathematics, and the exploration of space — are derived in some fashion from the spatial discernment learned through the pleasurable experiences of touching.

Others have attributed almost every expression of human neurosis and unhappiness — from picking one's nose to genocide — to the deprivation of pleasurable contacts with others, giving much support to Freud's concept of the *libido* — the general need for pleasurable stimulation — as the most basic human need. If there is any truth at all to the concept of a sexual drive, it is in our need for cutaneous stimulation as a basic condition of human development.

The feeling of identity and selfhood stems from the feeling of contact with one's body. The healthy person has an image of himself that largely depends on the way his body looks and feels — to himself and to others. Losing a sense of one's body is one of the first symptoms of schizophrenia, where one's mind takes leave of an uncomfortable body (and situation) and mentally takes refuge in the body of another. All of what we do "to stay healthy" — work, play, exercise, sports, athletics, music, entertainment, touching, making love — is related to the tactual confirmation of identity, the continual reaffirmation and redefinition of the space occupied by our bodies.

The infant comes into the world invisible to itself. It possesses a capacity for sensuality and perception. Outside the womb, it will be unable to hold everything together for long without quickly coming to a recognition of itself. Sensations arrive at the nerve centers totally disorganized, scrambled, meaningless, without codes, cues, or symbols offering value to the organism. A ghost to itself, the infant briefly lives in a weightless, homogenized world much like the womb from which it has just emerged. To the infant, objects are as indistinguishable from one another as they are from itself.

Propelled by forces of instinct, it loudly demands and takes preliminary nourishment. The first swallows of milk from the mother's breast are charged with antibodies which the infant will need until its own immune system is fully developed. But the baby needs more than biological defenses. Unless it quickly learns to recognize itself, it will die. Coded DNA information no longer suffices. Its capacity to gather information from outside its own body must be turned on.

The newborn infant is helpless to turn on its own learning systems, but his suckling activities stimulate pleasure in the mother. Catching up to what humans have known for thousands of years, science has now documented the manner in which the mother's response of pleasure now identifies the infant to itself. Her pleasurable response to its needs enable it to identify its own feelings and needs. It soon learns of its capacity to give pleasure to others and win its own pleasure in return. In this exchange, the infant apprehends itself.

At the beginning of the century, it was a medical fad not to touch or fondle infants. They were to be left by themselves in their cribs until it was time for feeding. This radical and perverse procedure could be enforced only in foundling homes for abandoned babies, where it proved disastrous. A 1915 report on children's institutions in ten different cities in the U.S. made the staggering disclosure that in all but one institution every infant under two had died. The conclusion of pediatricians was that the children were victims of marasmus, a refusal to take nutrition, which was the result of "hospitalism," the deprivation of maternal, loving care. Unloved and untouched, the infants took their own lives. Commenting on this development, Dr. Rene Spitz (1945) wrote that newborn infants "can die, or not develop, because nobody has taken the interest to seduce them to live."

In the nourishment of the mother's breast, the smile in her eyes, the tactility of her skin, the joy in her voice, and the caresses of her hands, learning is learned. The erotic touch of skin upon skin brings one's body and all the other bodies of the world into existence. The boundaries between the "me" and the "not me" come into focus. Sensory information becomes unscrambled as faces are separated from one another and from the self and are indelibly etched in the brain.

The erotic touching that first takes place between an infant and mother remains an important source of identity support throughout life. Freud said this "nongenital sexuality" is "self-sublimating," incapable of excess, and able to "prompt and dominate the unfolding of all the other functions." It is the "exemplary function" upon which human social systems are built. Freud's "pleasure principle" established the importance of erotic contact between the mother and infant in the formation of the recognition of the self that is the foundation for the individual's taking command of his world and becoming, as Ortega y Gasset (1949) wrote, "a vital program which . . . overpowers environment to lodge itself there."

While some writers have criticized Freud for emphasizing the sexual nature of infantile pleasure, it was an association he could not avoid. He pointed out (1940:151) that the whole body is an erotic zone, and that if the child did not receive enough pleasurable stimulation, its sexual interests would become excessively isolated in the genitals, "demanding full gratification on their own account and thus disturbing sexual integration" (1949:24).

Freud also saw the continuity that exists between the generalized, unfocused sexuality of the infant—which can also be retained and enjoyed by adults if society encourages it—and the genital experience that emerges in adolescence. The foundation of Freud's theory of sexuality came from his observation of the activity of the infant's lips at the breast (1905:182):

> It was a child's first and most vital acitivity, his sucking at his mother's breast, or at substitutes for it, that must have familiarized him with this pleasure. The child's lips . . . behave like an erotogenic zone, and no doubt stimulation caused by the warm flow of milk is the cause of the pleasurable sensation. . . . No one who has seen a baby sinking back satiated from the breast and falling asleep with flushed cheeks and a blissful smile can escape the reflection that this picture persists as a prototype of the expression of sexual satisfaction later in life. The need for repeating the sexual satisfaction now becomes detached from the need for taking nourishment—a separation which becomes inevitable when the teeth appear and food is no longer taken by sucking.

The need for bodily contact among older children and adults is more easily expressed in those societies that are still able to distinguish between the affectionate contact and mating behavior. In our society, there has been a steep decline in the physical expressions of sociability, even within the family. These new inhibitions are attributed to the fact that all forms of tactile affection are associated with intercourse.

While in some societies "love" refers first of all to the pleasurable physical contact with children, in the United States it refers either to (1) internalized and privatized emotions of affection, or (2) marital intercourse. Physical intimacy is acceptable to most people in the United States only as it is considered as a prelude to part of adult intercourse, and therefore subject to the usual range of sexual taboos. As Ashley Montagu (1978:166) stated, ". . . in the Western world it is highly probable that sexual activity, indeed the frenetic preoccupation with sex that characterizes Western culture, is in many cases not the expression of sexual interest at all, but rather a search for the satisfaction of the need of contact." For this reason, many women, especially, submit to intercourse in order to enjoy the physical satisfactions of being held.

In Freud's "Repetition Principle," he noted that one of the most basic patterns in human life was the need to repeat pleasurable actions. He was led to conclude, in *Beyond the Pleasure Principle* (1920), that this repetition is essentially a restoration of an earlier existing state. It is not enough that mother and child interact physically and pleasurably in order to elicit the infant's participation in the establishment of identity: The activity must be repeated.

The need for repeated recognition and identity reinforcement is the necessary response to the "ravages of time" and the high metabolic rate of the human organism. It may be that repetition is needed to counteract the irreversibility of the flow of time and to dampen the impact of a constantly changing universe upon an organism which must retain the sense of *sameness* from one moment to the next.

Once a certain order of complexity has been achieved, the infant begins to participate in the organization of environment and identity. Using the mother as a base for security, the toddler begins to explore the world around him. George Herbert Mead recognized the importance of *vocalization* as a means of nonphysical contact and self-affirmation. Animals that vocalize hear themselves in the same manner that they hear others and thereby are able to sense themselves as separate objects. Vocalization is not only a means of communicating, a remote way of acting upon other things and noting their response, but a manner of listening to oneself as an object.

The physical world of sensual experience is not the only arena of establishing and maintaining selfhood. There is also a symbolic world made up of the words, meanings, roles that we use to organize our behaviors and endow the world of other persons with meaning. It is in this symbolic world taking shape inside our head that each person creates society anew and carves his own space in it.

Erik Erikson (1959:113), in *Identity and the Life Cycle*, described the way the individual marshals the social world in which he lives: "Identity formation . . . is dependent on the process by which a *society* . . . *identifies the young individual*, recognizing him as somebody who had to become the way he is, and who, being the way he is, is taken for granted. . . . The community, in turn, feels 'recognized' by the individual who cares to ask for recognition."

"The business of childhood is play," Piaget wrote. Through the rough-and-tumble years of childhood, the individual develops an inward image of society. The fundamental social element of identity is the *role*, which is a *set of expected behaviors sanctioned by society for the performance of certain functions*. We all know how the plumber is supposed to conduct himself during a service call. We grow up learning everyone's role—what people do all day with their time.

Much of play and other childhood activity is directed toward internalizing social roles. Children learn society by practicing roles in play, trying them out, posing. In a society in which male violence plays a significant part in the maintenance of social boundaries, it is not surprising that boys dedicate themselves assiduously to games involving cops and robbers, cowboys and Indians, and military battle. Such pastimes are not just physically satisfying, but they are an important part of the child's reconstruction of society within his own head.

Society is like a great closet full of thousands of costumes, which children rifle through at lightning speed, stopping only momentarily to try one on, perhaps alter it a bit, mimic and prance, and quickly discard it before seeking another. The fantastic speed at which children can assemble complete roles from a few vague clues and act them out is indicative of the great importance of roles in human life. We are born natural imposters, and by imagining ourselves in the roles of others, we create a model of society in our minds, within which we construct our own place in society. Hundreds of roles are considered, picked through, and filed away. By the time the child reaches adulthood, an impressive collection of roles and institutions has been carefully analyzed and classified.

We are not passive recipients of roles, however. It is especially in the mocking behavior of children that we see their special capacity to modify roles through new subtle distinctions and comparisons. We never use a role without tailoring it to our own likes, and it will never be the same once we have employed it. In his magnum opus on identity, *Young Man Luther: A Study in Psychoanalysis and History* (1958:254), Erikson goes on to explain the manner in which each society is created anew in the play of children:

> Each new being is received into a style of life prepared by tradition and held together by tradition, and at the same time disintegrating because of the very nature of tradition. We say that tradition "molds" the individual, "channels" his drives. But the social process does not mold a new being merely to housebreak him; it molds generations in order to be remolded, to be reinvigorated, by them.... In describing the interdependence of individual aspiration and of societal striving, we describe something indispensable to human life.

In effect, each new generation creates society anew, bringing along some new values and some old, in a complex, rapid-fire manufacture and exchange of symbols, roles and beliefs.

When we speak of having "a positive self-image," we refer to the comfortable assessment of successfully playing one's role in the eyes of significant others. While most of us play several roles—each of which is supported by a different referent group of people—people vary tremendously in the number of roles they play and also in the importance they attach to each of the roles.

Some writers have discounted the importance of the gay role with the argument that most children do not have any gay role models and are not taught how to be homosexuals. Therefore, they conclude that gay identity is simply the recognition of a sexual desire.

The answer to this objection is found in the many ways in which roles are transmitted to each generation. It is not always necessary to have a flesh-and-blood father on hand to learn the meanings of fatherhood. Neither is it necessary to have a live homosexual role-model on hand to learn the role. To the contrary, our society clearly defines the homosexual role, which these days is learned early by children. There are few children who grow up without learning the term "homosexual" and what it means. Schoolyard and locker-room banter fill in all the negative details and connotations. Children may not have an accurate or complete idea of what homosexuals are, but they have no doubt about the existence of the role, the negative esteem attached to it, and its gender-related meanings.

Erik Erikson (1959) supported Freud's contention that outside the needs for bodily contact, our most important source of identity support comes from our work role. In Henry Miller's *Death of a Salesman*, we see the extent to which a person can become encapsulated in a work role, so much so that his job becomes central to his self-concept. On the other end of the scale, we all know of people whose work role is of little importance. While we often tend to envy the freedom that such persons seem to enjoy, we attach great importance to work roles, which for most of us remains a central feature of our self-concept.

When young people have difficulty finding their place in the working world, they experience real identity crises. They are not without resources, however, and may revert to other, more basic identity support systems, and even create new social groupings supportive of identity. Young people today who have not secured a satisfying work role in society will find identity support in the more physical pleasures of drugs, sexuality, rock music, and the emergency identity groups attached to them. When one of our identity-support systems fails, emergency support groups can sometimes be mobilized.

Adolescence and the emergence of genital sexuality bring into play a whole new dimension for the maintenance of identity. New roles and new pleasures attached to courtship and marriage open new dimensions of identity maintenance. The arrival of children brings not only new role responsibilities and satisfactions, but also new opportunities for tactile support. The concern with genital satisfaction often subsides with the advent of children and the tactile pleasures they provide. The luxurious pleasures of children reinforce the selfhood of the parents, making the child truly the father of the man and the mother of the woman.

The social world in which we take our place is always quite constrained and limited, perhaps a function of the limited number of people who can inhabit a certain space. Our repertoire of roles is impressive, but it does not express all the possibilities of human culture. No matter how sophisticated and cosmopolitan our upbringing, we are never able to become human beings in a global sense. Our social world is limited to much smaller, tribal units. The survival of tribal, extended family-type social units may be an indication of an inherent need to guarantee a secure source of tactuality and affection. Human bonding has proven highly resistant to the state's efforts at constricting it.

Adam Curle (1972) calls social identity "belonging identity," because it is concerned with "what we belong to" in terms of professions, groups, communities, and the like, and also with "what belongs to us" (i.e. property) which also helps to establish standing in the community. Belonging identity makes community life possible as well as the achievements of political and economic organization. But it is also responsible for war, mob violence, colonialism, and racism. The identity of each society demands the creation of enemies, the "not us," against which the society pits and recognizes itself as distinctive.

Erik Erikson (1968:41) wrote about the mischief cause by our tribal limitations:

> Man as a species has survived by being divided into what I have called *pseudospecies*. First each horde or tribe, class and nation, but then also every religious association has become *the* human species, considering all the others a freakish and gratuitous invention of some irrelevant deity. . . . This projection, in conjunction with their territoriality, gave men a reason to slaughter one another *in majorem gloriam*. If, then, identity can be said to be a "good thing" in human evolution—because good things are those which seem to have been necessary for what, indeed, has survived—we should not overlook the fact that this system of mortal divisions had been vastly overburdened with the function of reaffirming for each pseudospecies its superiority over all others.

In spite of our modern pretense to transcend tribalism, we may not be able to do without it altogether, and rather than trying to act as if we have overcome our tribal limitations, it might be better to first recognize tribalism's function in the course of human development.

A third support system for the maintenance of identity arises from our mental capacity to transcend the cultural limitations of our tribe. We first observe this capacity in the manner in which gifted children construct roles for themselves quite unlike any in their society. We see such constructions in the French poet Rimbaud, whose early poetry enabled him to escape the limitations of the small village in which he was raised.

Exceptional psychic powers are often associated with persons of ambiguous gender. Such a gifted child emerged in the last moments of Ingmar Bergman's film *Fanny and Alexander* to frightfully resolve the conflicts besetting the children's family.

This metaphysical ability to transcend and set oneself apart from the "normal" definitions of reality is not limited to psychic children, however. Even quite ordinary citizens at times enjoy rare moments of insight that enable them to transcend what they have learned from others, to stand "over and against" their community, in a sense bringing judgement against it.

All societies have recognized the importance of change for survival and generally make room for those who have special insights into the future, the past, or the hidden influences in human behavior. Most societies have institutionalized those functions within the roles of seers, prophets, and shamans that allowed them to adapt and change to meet new situations.

Modern societies tend to generalize these mystical functions in the democratic belief that inspiration can come to anyone: "All people will be taught by God." We now believe that we all possess this higher reason that preserves the independence of the individual and a certain separateness from the rest of the community. Although we are not called upon to use it very much, Adam Curle (1972:31–32) wrote that this capacity produces an "awareness identity" that functions to keep our other identity systems in balance: "It derives from general awareness and contributes to the more or less organized self-image by which we define ourselves. It can be recognized by its relative unpretentiousness. Whereas belonging-identity is somewhat grandiose, albeit with moods of depressed uncertainty and self-doubt, awareness-identity begins to recognize the contradictions and limitations of our nature."

Curle (1972:34–35) also observed that some people are endowed with more awareness capability than others. It can also be attained artificially through religious practice, meditation, ritual, fasting, drugs, and other mind-altering techniques. He wrote that we often move rapidly from one level of awareness to another, observing the same situation first from a standpoint of society and then from a more objective standpoint. This higher awareness, he claims, is hard to maintain for any length of time, because our social awareness is "an exceptionally powerful, natural force to which we are all subject" (1972:33), and it can overwhelm us in spite of efforts to resist.

One of the most prominent features we note about our systems of identity maintenance is their complementarity: When one fails, others are there to back up. When a businessman is absent from the luxurious contacts of family, often his need for genital contact will reemerge and become more demanding than usual. Professors, police, doctors, and judges derive a heightened sense of identity from the very special roles they play. An individual who is suddenly deprived of his being able to function in an esteemed role always experiences a painful crisis and will quickly mobilize the support of other roles and loyalties among friends and family.

Equally important is the need of society to provide enough roles to satisfy the needs of all. The influence of the modern state has constricted the range of roles available, creating the "identity crisis" of our age, as Lichtenstein (1977:258) explained:

> Cultures are storehouses, collectively maintained, for the accumulation of available identities. The storehouse offers to most but not all individuals within a given culture realistic or symbolic options of identity implementation. If the number of individuals for which the available supply of identity configurations is out of reach or inapplicable increases, sooner or later a great cultural crisis tends to occur. . . . Thus, there remains the fact that for each individual it is the historical situation in which he lives that will either provide or fail to provide the real or symbolic prerequisites which could enable him to find an implementation appropriate to his personal identity theme.

Among modern writers, William Butler Yeats expressed the clearest understanding of the dynamic nature of identity and struggled with it constantly. More than other lights of his age, he eschewed popular beliefs in progress for society and sincerity for the individual. For Yeats, there was no self to be "true to." On the contrary, self was constantly in the making. He saw it as a process by which identities were constantly *exchanged* between the individual and society. We don one mask or *daimon*, as he called it, and then quickly doff it for another. In this constant creation of *antithetical* selves, one's identity and selfhood grows. For Yeats, in fact, all growth, all knowledge was identity. He poses and answers these mysteries in his poem "Among School Children" (1963:242–245):

> Labor is blossoming or dancing where
> The body is not bruised to pleasure soul,
> Nor beauty born out of its own despair,
> Nor blear-eyed wisdom out of midnight oil.
> O chestnut tree, great rooted blossomer,
> Are you the leaf, the blossom or the bole?
> O body swayed to music, O brightening glance,
> How can we know the dancer from the dance?

Novelist Andrew Holleran took his inspiration from Yeats' teaching that identity is constant reincarnation, and in *Dancer from the Dance*

(1978) wove a story about Malone, who one day gave up the struggle to keep his sexuality "in its place." Abandoning his lucrative attorney's practice, he became an "antithetical self" and abandoned himself to his sexual fantasies in the fast lanes of gay New York. If we can look beneath the extravagance of his sexual excesses, we see the struggles of identity. True to Yeats' formula, Malone disappears at the end of the book, perhaps with another identity taking shape some place else.

Yeats saw in these identity conflicts the source of all biography, history, and culture. He wrote in his introduction to *The Resurrection* of the way in which we pick out roles, try them on, use them and modify them for our own needs, and then pass them on to others: "We may come to think that nothing exists but a stream of souls, that all knowledge is biography, and with Plotinus that every soul is unique, that these souls, these eternal archetypes, combine into greater units as days and nights into months, months into years, and at last into the final unit that differs from that which they were at the beginning."

Role-making not only connects us with our society, but with history's past and future as well. The individual roles we choose and modify become merged into archetypal and communal identities, a common heritage that will continue to have a rippling effect down through history. Through these roles, our lives and actions are liberated from our individual selves to be returned to a communal and historical matrix of values, beliefs, and expectations. Roles are the medium we use to create society.

As Yeats wrote, "Man is nothing till he is united to an image." Alaskan Eskimos, who frequently use ceremonial masks in their dances to depict the influence of the spirit world in their lives, have a saying that "masks do not conceal; they reveal," reminding us of the Greek origin of the word "person," the actor's mask, which both created and projected his character.

Yeats saw the significance of history not in the improvement of economic conditions but in its revelation of personal identity, a strategy for carving out one's space in the world. The outcome of such an incredible enterprise is always problematic. Along with Ortega y Gasset (1939:174) we will always be astonished by "the tremendous fact that, unlike all other beings in the universe, man can never be sure that he is, in fact, a man, as the tiger is sure of being a tiger and the fish of being a fish. . . . Being man signifies precisely always being on the point of not being a man, being a living problem, an absolute and hazardous adventure."

III. The Sexual Self

Moreover, sexual orientation is only one aspect of homosexuality, which is a personality, a sensitivity. A spirit. It cannot be ignored like a pimple or repressed like the urge to eat a chocolate-covered cherry; it cannot be isolated from one's personality. It is an inexorable part of what makes one an individual. — Richard Friedel, in *The Movie Lover*

The three complementary arenas of identity maintenance—touching/pleasure, society, and intellect—often compete. While people attempt to agree on the acceptable limits on all behaviors, sex and the transcendent capacities of the intellect can be especially troublesome, causing nearly all societies to establish special roles and institutions for their control. In our society, those roles and institutions are found in the family, religion, and the professions.

In the last chapter, we looked at the social construction of the self. In this chapter we will look at the social construction of sexuality. Actually, sexuality is a very recent invention. It probably did not exist before the beginning of the nineteenth century. Sure, people have always engaged in sexual behaviors, and most societies have developed a wide range of norms, roles, and taboos governing them. But that is not what we are talking about.

What we have here are two different things: the behaviors and our explanations of them. It is likely that people of all races and times have thought about sexual behaviors and have attempted to explain them. But it was left to nearly our own age to contrive a *scientific* explanation of these behaviors. Many other societies have developed an *ars erotica*. Ours was the first to come up with a *scientia sexualis*.

As we will see, this new science is eminently political, a product of government's need to develop ever-new sources of power and control. When speaking of "government," this author certainly does not mean to imply an conspiratorial or intentional policy of a particular agency or program in charge of sexual behaviors. No, we understand government in the sense of the modern nation-state, with its multiplicity of centers of power divested in numberless agencies and programs, along with its ability to mobilize law, taxes, the military, personnel, property, and resources.

There is a dialectic between government and sex (with the family, perhaps, someplace in the middle) that over the years has imperceptibly but powerfully influenced how we experience sex. Closely assisting institutions of the state (law, corrections, education, public assistance, etc.) in shaping our perceptions of human sexuality have been the professions, including medicine and the academic professions.

One of the most notable results of this transformation has been the progressive *internalization* of sexual behavior. In other times and places, sexual behavior was thought of something external that took place between people. Now it is something that takes place in the individual. We are no longer so apt to engage in rapturous praise of our beloved. The whole thought of one being the lover and the other the beloved, in fact, seems foreign to us. We somehow demand that love be reciprocal, perhaps because we regard loving as originating in the lover rather than the beloved.

The consummation of love depends no longer on the acquiescence or seizure of the beloved so much as the careful negotiation of two equal parties who have carefully cultivated and groomed their capacities for love. Previously, people negotiated wealth and property in the arrangements of marriage. Today we negotiate interests: leisure activities, financial potential, beauty, health and fitness, and sex itself. While marriage originally was directed to something outside the individual — the extension of the family — today it is mainly considered a means of self-fulfillment.

The internalization of sex has resulted in *the myth of the sexual drive*. It is easy to see how it fits in with the myth of personality as a fixed concept: Genital sexuality, whether gay or straight, is somehow fixed early in life and all that we can do is express or repress it. We cannot deny that there is a certain *stability* in our recognition of sexual pleasure throughout life. If this were not so, sex would hardly be useful for the day to day maintenance of identity and the affirmation of the self.

But, while it is one thing to claim that we *recognize* our sexual feelings as being the same from one day to the next, and from one year to the next, the explanations and meanings we attach to those feelings vary considerably, as do their external expressions over time.

We have little appreciation of how novel our ideas of sex are and how strange they would have appeared to our ancestors, who were more comfortable with the "exteriority" of sex. The Christian church, perhaps under the influences of neo–Platonism, came to condemn nearly every form of genital activity, making it legitimate for married couples only under the most constrained conditions. But the church was loath to ascribe these passions to anything inherent in human nature itself. Such a position would defile the image of an all-good and omnipotent creator. Genital behavior was not thought of so much as a human drive as the result of the manipulation of the devil, "who wanders about seeking whom he may devour." There was not so much here of the idea of an instinctive "drive" as there was of some outside interference. The church Fathers did not see human sexuality as the result of an "animalistic" urge so much as an external, demonic one. As St. Paul claimed, "Our struggles are not with the princes of this world."

The incorporation of monasticism within the church, the developing doctrine of celibacy for the clergy, and the appreciation given virginity among those dedicated to the work of the church further demonstrated the church's view of genital activity as a truly malleable behavior, responsive to religious beliefs.

Theologians would have been confused by our attempts to lump all homosexual activities together under the umbrella of "sexual preference." The penitentials, those manuals that helped uneducated confessors in the dispensing of penances, distinguished between same-sex practices in ways that would make us feel uncomfortable, including some that gave heavier penances for heterosexual versions of the same acts committed by same-sex partners. According to Boswell (1980), homosexual offenses during the Middle Ages were generally treated the same way as heterosexual ones. What offended our forebears was not the sexual orientation or affection implied in sodomy but the violation of gender roles: using another man as a woman. Affective relationships between members of the same sex were regarded quite differently and were highly valued in many European societies until quite recent times.

With the advent of the Enlightenment, society came to reject the idea of the devil as the source of genital excess. The study of anatomy and physiology clarified the physical aspects of sexual expression. Those first anatomical discoveries made a great impression on the minds of investigators, who concluded that sexual infractions, like normal sexual behavior, must have physical explanations. With the later impact of the Industrial Revolution and rapid advances in science, professionals became more interested than ever in looking for physiological explanations of deviant human behavior. They thought that correction would merely be a matter of removing a gland, administering some hormones, or slicing out some portion of the brain.

During the nineteenth century, specialists were intrigued with the phenomenon of posthypnotic suggestion, and no one more so than the young Sigmund Freud. He had witnessed demonstrations of this during a visit to Nancy in 1899 and had translated two of Bernheim's books on the subject into German. It was to be for Freud the source of a revolutionary insight.

What struck Freud in posthypnotic suggestion was the fact that the subjects of the demonstrations, who had been told to do strange things after coming out of their hypnotic trance, were quick to give—and apparently believe—"common sense" explanations of their strange behavior. Freud related this phenomenon to the ability he observed in everyone to continually give reasons for what they do—even though the real reasons for their behavior are unknown to them.

He became intrigued with the idea that our behavior can be motivated by purposes not known to us. These "hidden purposes" became his "subconscious ideas" that result from modern society's suppression of infantile sexuality to which we long to return. The neurosis of industrialized man, and the whole concept of psychiatric analysis, is based on the resistance of the individual to conscious awareness of this repressed desire.

Freud's doctrine of repression of the generalized libido, which can be said to include both nongenital and genital sexuality, was later misinterpreted to mean only genital sexuality. This constriction has contributed to the perception of the troublesome urges toward anger, aggressiveness, domination, and sex as independent forces demanding periodic release like the steam in a steam engine. Instead of having a life of their own, emotions are cyclic and static, coming and going in response to stimulations from a variety of internal and external causes. They often disappear without any release at all but in response to a change in one's circumstances.

Freud's doctrine of *latency* was also distorted to support the homosexual myth. This doctrine originally referred to the period of life between seven and eleven when previously active touching needs were temporarily dormant or "latent." We wonder if Freud's observation of this matter was culturally limited to the behaviors of older children in his Austrian/Jewish society where touching satisfactions are suspended until puberty. Prepubescent children in many other societies exhibit a great deal of touching behavior, much of it coming from the care they provide infants and younger children as well as from adults and one another. It is likely that incest taboos had been extended to include the touching of preadolescent children by Freud's time (they now prohibit a great deal of affectionate contact with children).

In any case, Freud's theory of prepubescent latency came to be generally understood as any disordered state that is unrealized and dormant but has the potential of becoming active and conscious. It is this second meaning that Sagarin (1975:148) described as "scientifically unsound, conceptually useless, and socially pernicious," contributing substantially to the reification of homosexuality. Because of this concept, he wrote, "social scientists and laymen alike think, speak, and write as if homosexuals really existed."

The doctrine of latent homosexuality puts everybody, males especially, into an impossible situation. Even the person who has never been touched by the slightest homosexual impulse is in jeopardy, always scrutinizing his feelings, never knowing when the beast within will actualize and overtake him. Incredible as the scenario is, it has come to exert a considerable influence on our sexual beliefs.

The post–Freudian interpretations of libido and sexuality have contributed to what Kenneth Plummer (1975:6) called the "myth of sexual power" by which we believe that the sexual drive is the most dominant force in human life. Plummer said there are left-wing and right-wing versions of this belief: "While the right wing sees sexuality as the demon within and the left wing sees sexuality as the great liberator, both credit sexuality with enormous — almost mystical — powers in contributing to social order. Sex becomes the central force upon which civilizations are built up and empires crashed down."

John H. Gagnon and William Simon (1968:121) also claimed that much of folklore and public policy is shaped by the belief that sexual behaviors are the result of a standoff between immense social sanctions and the biological forces of the sexual drive: "Thus the act of freeing the sexual impulse is thought of by some persons as increasing human freedom and by others as creating the conditions of social collapse. In this sense, we have overlooked the meanings and power of sexual acts, and what is likely to be discovered is that the significance of sexuality is exactly in proportion to its perceived significance; that is without the imagery of power and danger, the sexual impulse is no more potent that any other biological component."

While Freud's successors were going off the deep end speculating about clinical causes of sexual behavior, cultural anthropologists working in foreign lands were making significant discoveries about the great variety of sexual practices throughout the world. It was Kinsey's achievement to draw our attention to the great variety of sexual practices within the United States.

From within the chapters of Kinsey's surprising data on the incidences of extramarital sex, masturbation, and homosexual outlet, there emerged overwhelming evidence that the diversity of human sexual behaviors cannot possibly be explained by physiological differences, including the behavioral differences between males and females. Kinsey (1953:567–641) pointed out that the anatomical differences between male and female do not account for the pronounced differences in their sexual responses, including the earlier development of sexual responsiveness in males and the earlier decline of the male response in middle age.

He went on to attack (1953:761) hormonal theories of sexual behaviors: "Within limits, the levels of sexual response may be modified by reducing or increasing the amount of available hormone, but there seems to be no reason for believing that the patterns of sexual behavior may be modified by hormonal therapy."

In attacking physiological explanations of sexual behavior, Kinsey also questioned common beliefs of what makes a "normal" or healthy sex life. At a time when it was popular to deplore celibacy or abstinence of any kind as unnatural, repressed, and even unhealthy, Kinsey scrutinized the data to find little evidence for such beliefs.

He stated (1953:526) that 3 percent of married females never reach orgasm and that 30 percent of unmarried females have never experienced orgasm. What is even more significant, 28 percent stated that they not only didn't have sex, they also didn't need it. Among males, some 3 percent (Kinsey et al., 1948:206) rarely if ever have sex and some 11 percent of males under 31 have frequencies as low as once in two weeks or lower, with that percentage growing in later years. But he also noted (1948:205) that there is no reason why a large proportion of the human population could not enjoy orgasm *at least* once a day if social values were set aside, since nearly everyone has the physical capacity for such frequencies.

Considering the social importance still attached to abstinence and the large numbers of people who practice it, Kinsey was understandably disturbed about how little scientific information existed regarding this important sexual pattern. He challenged two assumptions about abstinence: first, that it is unhealthy, and second, that it is a form of sexual sublimation. In his section on nocturnal emission in the *Male* volume (1948:526–530) Kinsey put down the sexual-release theory by noting that nocturnal emission is not always related to lack of sexual activity and is frequently, in fact, linked to other forms of sexual conduct preceding sleep. He suggested that nocturnal emissions, being dream-related, are influenced more by one's daytime experiences and desires. He also suggested that boys have often learned from others and from literature about nocturnal emissions beforehand and this may in itself be a causative factor. He debunked physiological explanations as unscientific and untenable, claiming that there is no build-up of seminal fluid or any other physiological change observed as a result of abstinence. He admitted there might be some neurological disturbance arising from a lack of sex, but it has not been demonstrated. The tension that is often experienced as a result of abstinence can be more easily attributed to role conflicts and social expectations.

Kinsey also criticized (1948:205–213) the idea that sexual "energy" can be sublimated into "higher forms of expression" through abstinence. Kinsey wrote that in order to prove the sublimation theory, it would be necessary to find individuals of previously known and proven sexual capacities whose erotic responses have been reduced or eliminated, *without nervous disturbance*, as a result of an expenditure of nonsexual activities.

Kinsey (1953:195) was also convinced that the incidence of one's sexual outlet is clinically insignificant:

There is a tendency to consider anything in human behavior that is unusual, not well known, or not well understood, as neurotic, psychopathic, immature, perverse, or an expression of some sort of psychological disturbance.

There is an inclination among psychiatrists to consider all unresponding individuals as inhibited, and there is a certain scepticism in the profession of the existence of people who are basically low in their capacity to respond. This amounts to asserting that all people are more or less equal in their sexual endowments, and ignores the existence of individual variation. No one who knows how remarkably different individuals may be in morphology, in physiologic reactions, and in other psychologic capacities, could conceive of erotic capacities (of all things) that were basically uniform throughout a population. Considerable psychiatric therapy can be wasted on persons (especially females) who are misjudged to be cases of repression when, in actuality, at least some of them never were equipped to respond erotically.

It is only recently that many of these findings have been reaching their way into popular literature. Gabrielle Brown, in *The New Celibacy*, traced the historical connection between celibacy and the growth of consciousness. She stressed (1980:139–140) the manner in which successful marriages often progress from genital behaviors to more satisfying forms of eroticism: "This growth from expressed sexual union to a perhaps more intimate physical union is a common experience of marriage but one our society tends to overlook in the face of the popular, if misguided, desire to hold on to the success of concrete sexual activity as the most significant expression of physical marital union."

One of Kinsey's best contributions was his documentation of the great diversity in both the incidence and nature of sexual outlet in the United States, a phenomenon he referred to as the great *discrepancy* between physiology and sexual behavior. While many sexual differences can be explained by physiological difference, they go far beyond the inherent differences of physiology.

Referring back to his work as a biologist, Kinsey (1948:195–196) explained:

> One of us has published data (Kinsey 1942) on individual variation in the population of insects. The populations represented individuals of single species, from single localities. There were many characters which varied. Extreme wing lengths, for instance, varied between 10 and 180 micrometer units. This difference of 18 times probably represents as extreme a linear variation as is known in any population of adults of any species of plant or animal. But differences between the extreme frequencies of sexual outlet in the human range far beyond these morphologic differences. Calculation will show that the difference between one ejaculation in thirty years and mean frequencies of, say, 30 ejaculations per week throughout the whole of thirty years, is a matter of 45,000 times. This is the order of the variation which may occur between two individuals

who live in the same town and who are neighbors, meeting in the same place of business, and coming together in common social activities.

Kinsey went on to say that this sort of variation — which is liable to occur within the histories of any 100 people — is a significant factor in our attempts to understand sexual behaviors. In many schools, there has been a failure to recognize the sexual incongruities which exist between different persons, families, and ethnic groups. Sex education programs are predicated on the idea that persons reach sexual maturity at the same time, and that the beliefs and mores regarding sex and related pleasures are the same in all families. Kinsey pointed out that the development of physical maturity has little to do with the onset of sexual activity — often surprising parents and teachers who assume that the two go together.

Wardell Pomeroy, who assisted Kinsey in his mammoth study of 18,000 subjects, gave a good example of the biological/behavioral discrepancy in his biography of Kinsey. It seems that Kinsey had heard of a man who had kept an accurate record of his sex life. Kinsey and Pomeroy hopped in a car and drove from Indiana to the Southwest to conduct an interview with the man that took 17 hours. Pomeroy (1972:122) wrote that his history "astounded even us, who had heard everything."

The man recounted details of homosexual relations with 600 preadolescent males, heterosexual relations with 200 preadolescent females, intercourse with countless adults of both sexes and animals of many species, and his elaborate masturbation techniques. His first heterosexual relationship was with his grandmother and his first homosexual relationship with his father. He had had sex with 17 of his known 33 relatives. At one point in the interview, after Kinsey and Pomeroy expressed some scepticism about his claim to be able to masturbate to ejaculation from a limp start in ten seconds (he was 63 at the time) he calmly proceeded to demonstrate his talent.

"If that sounds like *Tobacco Road* or *God's Little Acre*," Pomeroy explained, "I will add that he was a college graduate who held a respectable government job." The history of this quiet, self-effacing man provided a fair part of Kinsey's chapter on child sexuality in the *Male* volume.

Because of Kinsey's strong distaste for the psychiatric discussions about the etiology of sexual behavior, he rarely addressed the causes of this discrepancy. There were occasions, however, when his opinions on the subject slipped into the text and carried much of the flavor of symbolic interactionism. He noted, for example, that the different outlets for masturbation and pornography in different cultural groups must reflect the differences of beliefs and principles within those groups.

In the followng extraordinary statement, Kinsey (1953:165) indicated his views on the social influences on human sexual behaviors:

The record suggests that the physiologic mechanism of any emotional response (anger, fright, pain, etc.) may be the basic mechanism of sexual response. Originally, the preadolescent boy erects indiscriminately to the whole array of emotional situations, whether they be sexual or nonsexual in nature. By his late teens the male has been so conditioned that he rarely responds to anything except a direct physical stimulation of genitalia or to psychic situations that are specifically sexual. In the still older male even physical stimulation is rarely effective unless accompanied by such a psychologic atmosphere. The picture is that of the psychosexual emerging from a much more generalized and basic physiologic capacity *which becomes sexual as the adult knows it*, through experience and conditioning.

In spite of this venture into the realm of sociological thinking, Kinsey's attempt to record behavior without any interpretations or judgements cost him dearly in terms of opposition, not only of the churches, but also of other scientists. Taking a purely "scientific" position that we should observe what the human animal *does* before we make any moral judgements about its behavior, Kinsey tended to ignore not only the *moral values* attached to the behavior but also the social causes. Unlike the sexual behaviors of other animals, human sexual behaviors, like all human behaviors, are the products of socially constructed meanings.

Within today's polycultural society, we each construct for ourselves sexual worlds in which we perceive differently the occasions and opportunities for sexual contact. "What do you do when you find a naked lady in your hotel room?" will be answered quite differently, depending on whom you ask. Within polite society and in public presentations such as TV newscasts, Americans maintain a polymorphous ignorance about sexual behavior, as if everyone was observing the most rigid norms. This blind spot obscures the tremendous differences, not only the behavioral differences noted by Kinsey, but differences in awareness of sexual opportunities and signals. As we will discuss later, one of the functions of affiliating with the gay community upon coming out is learning "how to cruise," that is, the construction of new perceptions and signals for increasing sexual opportunities.

M.H. Kuhn, writing in *Social Problems* (1954:123) soon after the appearance of the *Female* volume, summed up the criticism of Kinsey's tendency to reduce sexual learning to physiological, Pavlovian nerve conditioning:

> Sex acts, sexual objects, sexual partners (human or otherwise) like all other objects towards which human beings behave are *social objects*; that is they have meanings because meanings are assigned to them by the groups of which human beings are members for there is nothing in the physiology of man which gives any dependable clue as to what pattern of activity will be followed toward them. The meanings of these social objects are mediated to the individual by means of language just as in the

case of all other social objects.... In short, the sexual motives which human beings have are derived from the social roles they play; like all other motives these would not be possible were not the actions physiologically possible, but the physiology does not apply the motives, designate the partners, invest the objects with preformed passions, nor even dictate the objectives to be achieved.

The interactionists developed the idea that society provides not only for the distribution of sex (who gets what) but also for its organization (how we perceive and experience it). Peter Berger and Thomas Luckman (1966:49) wrote in *The Social Construction of Reality* that human sexuality has a very high degree of pliability:

> It is not only relatively independent of temporal rhythms, it is pliable both in the objects towards which it may be directed and in its modalities of expression. Ethnological evidence shows that, in sexual matters, man is capable of almost anything.... At the same time, of course, human sexuality is directed, sometimes rigidly structured, in every particular culture. Every culture has a distinctive cultural configuration, with its own specialized patterns of sexual conduct and its own "anthropological" assumptions in the sexual area. The empirical relativity of these configurations, their immense variety, and luxurious inventiveness, indicate that they are the products of man's own socio-cultural formations rather than of a biologically fixed human nature.

This proposition stays clear of any "sociological determinism" that would have society exerting a totalitarian control over individual sexual behavior. One of the first tenets of the interactionist view is the voluntary nature of the social process: It is always the result of negotiations between real persons. As Kenneth Plummer (1975:40) explained: "Man, then, is born into a pre-existing 'sexual world' with its own laws, norms, values, meanings.... This 'world' exists independently of any specific factor, confronts him as massively real, and exerts a tacit power over him.... Each society develops its own configuration of sexual meanings, but actors do not rudely encounter them. Rather, they are built up by actors in a highly intricate process over a life span. An important set of constraints on sexual manipulation will thus be the interactive ones."

The major determinants of human sexual behavior come partly from biological and psychological limits, partly from the objective values and sanctions of culture itself, but mostly from the *choices of the individual negotiating a sexual lifestyle* that is able to reconcile identity needs with social constraints.

Undeniably, genitality is rooted in biological process, capacities and needs. But admitting this in no way provides for a greater degree of biological determinism than is true of other areas of corresponding interaction. Indeed, the reverse may be true: Genitality may be precisely the realm wherein the superordinate position of the sociocultural over the biological is most complete. In orgasm, we may be less ourselves as individuals and more the observers of social imperatives than we realize.

Sexual identity is the result of a process as problematic as the development of social identity: It cannot be taken for granted. The outcome is always unpredictable, the result of a constantly renewed negotiation, a bargain between the individual and the community conducted on the level of symbols and meanings.

Finding little evidence for physiological explanations for the differences in sexual behaviors, Kinsey rejected theories holding that homosexual behavior was the result of inherent hormonal, physiological, or psychological differences. He was also aware of the social and political forces at work in sexual behaviors. His was the more obvious explanation:

> The inherent physiologic capacity of an animal to respond to any sufficient stimulus seems, then, the basic explanation of the fact that some individuals respond to stimuli originating in other individuals of their own sex — and it appears to indicate that every individual could so respond if the opportunity offered and one were not conditioned against making such responses (1953:447).
> Exclusive preference of behavior, heterosexual or homosexual, comes only with experience, or as a result of social pressures which tend to force an individual into an exclusive pattern of one or the other sort. Psychologists and psychiatrists, reflecting the mores of the culture in which they have been raised, have spent a good deal of time trying to explain the origins of homosexual activity; but considering the physiology of sexual response and the mammalian backgrounds of human behavior, it is not so difficult to explain why a human animal does a particular thing sexually. It is more difficult to explain why each and every individual is not in every type of sexual activity (1953:450–451).
> I think that much of human sexual behavior is no more complicated than a person's likes or dislikes for particular foods, books, amusements, or anything else. Through it all, association is a very important factor. This means that what a person happens to do one time is avoided or repeated another time, depending upon the pleasure derived from the first experience (in Pomeroy, 1972:324).

In this sense, Kinsey's explanation is consistent with that of the interactionists: Behavior is the result of the individual's encounter with an interactively constructed reality, a phenomenon intimately shared by physical experience and the meanings attributed to it.

Society is ambivalent about orgasmic sexuality: It is both an end and a means, both an opportunity and a problem. Insofar as it is a direct source of affirmation for the individual, it is capable of social mischief, but insofar as it is a human behavior, it can be manipulated to serve the more general purposes of society. It is in this latter sense that we say that society is responsible for the distribution and organization of sexuality. Sex is socially possible because it serves the overriding aims of society.

If the American and British writers have been foremost in establishing the *social* construction of sexuality, the ranks of the French have demonstrated the *political* sources of sexuality. Led by Michel Foucault, the French are more comfortable with concepts of power as a sociological given and have been better prepared to show us how intimately power enters into our experience of sexuality.

American sociologists, on the contrary, suffer from a political puritanism that regards manifestations of power and domination as evil and a call to action. It is hard to be objective under such a constraint. They prefer to treat the macrosocial issues in terms of demographic changes and to see microsocial and individual issues in terms of adjustment and the management of tension and conflict. Power is a significant sociological reality that enters everything, especially our experience and knowledge of sex.

Basically, Foucault argued that today's sexual habits are not the result of a repression coming down to us in a straight line from ancient times. Rather, they are the result of dramatic changes that have taken place in the last few hundred years, mainly the result of the collaboration of citizens in the development of the new nation state. In appropriating the domain of sexuality from the older kinship societies as a means of gaining power and influence, the modern nation-state has contributed to an endless *sexual discourse* made up of new laws, prohibitions, studies, and the emergence of a *scientia sexualis*.

Foucault (1978:103) gave us an important description of the manner in which society uses sexuality for its own purposes:

> Sexuality must not be described as a stubborn drive, by nature alien and of necessity disobedient to a power which exhausts itself trying to subdue it and often fails to control it entirely. It appears rather as an especially dense transfer point for relations of power: between men and women, young people and old people, parents and offspring, teachers and students, priests and laity, and administration and a population.
>
> Sexuality is not the most intractable element in power relations, but rather one of those endowed with the greatest instrumentality: useful for the greatest number of maneuvers and capable of serving as a point of support, as a linchpin, for the most varied strategies.

The great difficulty of authors in defining "sexuality" testifies to its political usefulness. As Germaine Greer (1984:236) wrote: "Sex is actually a magical, suggestive and utterly undefineable idea. It includes gender, eroticism, genitality, mystery, prurience, fertility, virility, titillation, neurology, psychopathology, hygiene, pornography, and sin, all hovering about actual experiences of the most intractable subjectivity, and therefore an ideal focus for religion." The state could now teach religion a few things about the exploitation and obfuscation of human reproductivity.

The political confusion that surrounds sex has been incorporated into our concept of homosexuality. Both have become part of the varied strategies of power that determine how our society is constructed. But the element of exploitation that enters most strongly into the sphere of human reproductivity is not sex but gender, the subject to which we must now turn.

IV. The Syntax of Gender

It's because th' men aren't *men, that th' women have to be.* — D. H.
Lawrence in *Lady Chatterly's Lover*

The social construction of gender — like the social construction of the
self and of sexuality — is intimately involved in the construction of the gay
role. The proposition that gender is a social construction is apt to raise
eyebrows. What is more obvious than the biological nature of gender or
its independence from the caprice of culture? Don't all societies recognize
the obvious differences between male and female? Even if we recognize
the manner in which society exploits and exaggerates the differences between male and female, don't the facts of reproduction *naturally* put
women at a disadvantage? If our perceptions of the differences between
male and female seem much more rooted in nature, it is because of the
great importance that our society attaches to the maintenance of those
perceptions.

The widespread beliefs surrounding homosexuality have become
an intimate part of the social construction of gender. The gay myth
has become a kingpin in the norms we apply to gender behaviors, eliminating once and for all any ambiguous middle ground between male
and female. How the gay role — and the structure of sexual orientation
on which it rests — neutralizes this ambiguity to protect gender boundaries is an important contribution to the sexual history of the Western
world.

Until quite recently, the gay role stood for a greater tolerance for
gender ambiguity. In his *Symposium*, Plato taught that each of us is born
with two halves. Those who are endowed with one half male and the
other half female were considered whole human beings, and those her-
maphrodites exhibiting the physical characteristics of both genders were
considered favored by the gods. Today's gay community, unlike the
modern concept of homosexuality, can probably be traced back in a
straight line to those institutions, baths, and brothels in ancient Rome,
where transvestites, eunuchs, male prostitutes, and catamites gathered
for business and sociability. The clear distinction we maintain between
the sexes was not so clear in former times.

Since the middle of this century, however, the gay movement has joined the movement to eliminate gender ambiguity, turning the focus from the physical concepts of gender to the internal concept of sexual orientation.

This new paradigm, however, has produced some very bizarre results, not the least of which is the confusion of male and female homosexuality. As Evelyn Blackwood (1985:6) complained, "Because of the importance of gender roles in homosexual behavior, no analysis can be complete without adequately evaluating both female and male gender roles. . . . Past research on homosexuality reflects the implicit assumption that lesbian behavior is the mirror-image of male homosexuality. Yet, the act of having sex with a member of one's own sex may be culturally defined in rather divergent ways for men and women." Lesbianism and male homosexuality are two completely different phenomena, but the emphasis on an internal sexual condition as the source of same-sex behaviors has clouded our perception of the differences.

In order to understand how fully gender concerns dominate our beliefs about homosexuality, we should appreciate the manner in which they are constructed. Our gender myths employ the same strategy as our beliefs about personality and sex, namely, the attribution of gender behavior to some inherent condition. What we usually think of when we are speaking about gender is not anatomical differences, but a whole range of social beliefs encapsulating those differences. As science has pointed out, the anatomical differences between male and female are quite insignificant when compared to what we make of them.

Anatomical differences act as *symbols* for what we believe are the basic underlying reasons for what we define as "normal" gender behavior. The structure of our society is built around maintaining our mythic beliefs in the differences between male and female. Those beliefs, in turn, offer much support for the male values of genitality, competition, and domination. We perceive vaginas and penises not just as anatomical facts but as meaningful signs representing basic beliefs about human nature. In short, our beliefs in the differences between male and female go far beyond the visible cues offered by human physiology.

Comparative, cross-cultural studies discovered that societies often configure gender behaviors very differently. Some societies have more than two genders, for example, and some up to six. It seems there are few restrictions on how a society can define gender roles. In all cases, each society takes to the business of defining and enforcing gender behavior with the same amount of seriousness. It appears that instinct is not enough. Unless society attaches importance to the bearing and raising of children it might not get done. Human nature being as mischievous and adventurous as it is, people might otherwise get too involved with other projects. We might not be able to take reproductive behaviors for granted.

Margaret Mead's famous studies of seven remote societies of the South Seas offered descriptions of gender behavior that made people in our country very uncomfortable: "Here the Tchambuli women (of New Guinea), brisk, unadorned, managing and industrious, fish and go to market: the men, decorative and adorned, carve and paint and practice dance-steps, their headhunting tradition replaced by the simpler practice of buying victims to validate their manhood" (1949:54).

Subsequent studies have confirmed that there is no evidence that females are more social, more suggestible, have lower self-esteem or less achievement motivation than males, that males are more analytic, or that females are more compliant than males or less involved in assertions of dominance. There is some evidence that females are superior in verbal abilities and that males are superior in spatial and quantitative ability.

Cross-cultural studies also have indicated that boys differ from girls in the direction of greater egoism and greater aggressiveness, though the amount of this difference varies from one society to another. Because these differences are universally taught, it is difficult to say whether they are the product of genes or culture.

For a long time, people have suspected that the presence of the "male" hormone, testosterone, produces aggressive and violent behavior. Castration has been used to reduce aggressiveness in both animals and men. The question that remains is not *whether*, but *how* testosterone does this. Scientists now believe that it acts on nerve receptors in the limbic system, which affects sexual and aggressive behavior. Estradiol and progesterone seem to have corresponding effects in producing maternal and nurturing behavior in women.

The problem faced by scientists was that differences in behavior are seen in boys and girls long before puberty, long before enough hormones are circulating in their blood to make a difference. John Money was able to state in 1965:

> The hormones that bring about sexual maturation do not, according to all the evidence available, have any differential determining influences on the psychosexual, male-female direction and content of perceptual, memory, or dream imagery that may trigger or be associated with erotic arousal. On the contrary, there is strong chemical and presumptive evidence . . . that the libido hormone is the same for men and women and is androgen. Psychosexually, the androgenic function is limited to partial regulation of the intensity and frequency of sexual desire and arousal, but not the cognitional patterns of arousal (1965:14).

Other studies found that the further up a species is on the evolutionary scale, the less sexual behavior is determined by hormones and the more by learning. New questions about the influence of hormones arrived when G. Raisman and P.M. Field (1973) discovered subtle differences in the brain patterns of male and female rats. More, they found that the differences in the male brain were *caused* by the circulation of testosterone during a certain period of their development. If they were castrated just after birth, their brains retained the female pattern. If females were given an injection of testosterone right after birth, they would develop the male brain pattern.

The possibility that preadolescent gender differences in aggressiveness were biological in origin was further confirmed with work on andrenogenital syndrome, which is caused by a defect in the adrenal cortex of females and results in large amounts of testosterone and tomboyish behavior. Scientists have concluded that the presence of masculinizing hormones acting on the brain near or shortly before the time of birth makes lasting changes on the brain.

Endocrinologist Juliane Imperato-McGinley (1979:1233–37) found a similar syndrome in three Dominican Republic villages which afflicted 38 individuals from 23 interrelated families over a period of four generations. Nineteen of the subjects appeared at birth to be normal females and were reared as such by relatives. At puberty, they failed to develop breasts and instead underwent a spontaneous sex change, developing primary and secondary male characteristics including penis and testes, deepening of the voice, and a muscular masculine physique.

The study showed that the subjects were born genetically male—with the XY chromosomes—with normal amounts of testosterone circulating in their blood at birth. Because of a defect of a single gene, an enzyme was lacking for the production of dehydrotestosterone, the hormone responsible for the external male sex characteristics at birth. The presence of testosterone was able to produce normal masculine puberty.

The amazing thing about this phenomenon is that 17 out of the 18 subjects were able to make a successful adjustment to their new male roles, though not without difficulty and even years of confusion and anguish. This led Imperato-McGinley and her colleagues to write: "These subjects demonstrate that in the absence of sociocultural factors that could interrupt the natural sequence of events, the effect of testosterone predominates, over-riding the effect of rearing as girls. . . . Our data show that environmental or social factors are not solely responsible for the formation of a male-gender identity. Androgens make a strong and definite contribution" (1979:1233, 1236).

The effects of hormones upon *development* are indeed impressive, but we are only beginning to understand the effects of hormones and other physiological factors upon *behavior*. Edward O. Wilson and other sociobiologists were impressed with the ability of Darwinism to explain the brain's function in causing consistent behavior among species. They cited evidence pointing to the existence of "meta-grammars" of basic human behaviors that are passed on in our genes, within which individual cultures and individuals are allowed immense varieties of options.

While the effects of hormones and the brain upon the bodily differences of males and females are known, it is possible that the observed differences in the male and female brains serve only physiological and reproductive functions and have little or nothing to do with behavior.

D.H. Lawrence understood well the influence of social norms on gender behavior. If Yeats was the prophet of the exterior self, Lawrence was the prophet of the exteriority of gender. For Lawrence, the modern crisis of identity was the crisis of sexual roles. He saw human sexuality as totally dependent upon roles. He rejected the modern concern with the individual as the source of sexuality. He saw the weakness of the identity produced by our democratic, industrial, and individualistic culture. As a British champion of genital primacy, Lawrence held that there is no genuine and selfless sexuality that does not result from a complete abandonment to our defined roles of man and woman. Without that, there is the individual urge to dominate and injure, and the sadomasochistic need to control. Only by complete faithfulness to the ancient roles of manhood and womanhood will true relationships emerge. In modern society, there is a split between the self and these roles that makes a collision of different egos, each out to exploit the other as instruments of sexual gratification. As Langbaum (1977:259) noted: "In *Women in Love*, he [Lawrence] portrays a twentieth-century world in which all identity structures are split, both within themselves and from the universe, and all sexuality is consequently sadomasochistic." There is hope only if we can again make some connection with the universe and with sexual roles, without which there is no sexuality. Lawrence found true identity in this abandonment to traditional gender roles (a position embraced today by the fundamentalists, to everyone's surprise). He sensed that there is no personality separate from the roles played and that alienation from roles is alienation from both feeling and identity. Lawrence blamed industrialization for the breakdown of sexual roles.

Later studies have confirmed Lawrence's perception of the exteriority of gender roles. Anthropologist Harriet Whitehead (1981:83), writing about the social construction of gender, mentioned the way societies construct gender out of meanings:

> When I speak of cultural constructions of gender, I mean simply the ideas that give social meaning to physical differences between the sexes,

rendering two biological classes, male and female, into two social classes, men and women, and making the social relationships in which men and women stand toward each other appear reasonable and appropriate. A social gender dichotomy is present in all known societies in the sense that everywhere anatomic sexual differences observable at birth are used to start tracking the newborn into one or the other of two social-role complexes.

Is it possible even to conceive of a society without gender roles? Salvatore Cucchiari traced the beginning of gender roles to a hypothetical prehistoric and pre-gender society, starting with the supposition that gender and connected family-related values were instituted at some point in time. Beginning with the position of Freud (1923) and Money and Tucker (1975:6) that humans are born into the world bisexual, Cucchiari (1975:45) concluded that pre-gender society was bisexual in the sense of general abandonment to polymorphous eroticism, and that:

(1) Anatomical differences were not systematically categorized. Not only was the connection between heterosexual sex and pregnancy not important, it may have been important to suppress. All children had full juridical rights by virtue of being born to any woman of the group. In a system that supported common rights and responsibilities toward children, it may have been important *not* to know lineage, filiation, or descent.

(2) Sexuality was not a part of self-identity.

(3) Sexuality was not an important aspect of interpersonal bonds.

(4) For all these reasons, intense and unrestricted sexual expression within the group was compatible with harmonious social relations.

As in contemporary foraging societies, women and men were both viewed as part of the same social milieu, with some people providing for children by tending them, others providing by foraging for food. Although women tended to do more of the child tending and men more foraging, there was no strict division of labor as seen in gender societies. At one time or another both sexes were expected to fill different roles. As Cucchiari explained: "Pre-gender society was as cognizant as any society of the facts of reproduction: who gets pregnant, for how long, who suckles children, and so on. But the question is what do these facts mean? . . . In short, are the facts of reproduction also gender facts? I have argued that biological facts do not speak for themselves."

As new ideas about women began to appear, a separate role was first constructed for them. Cucchiari wrote, "Indeed, the category 'men' emerges later as a latent category in opposition to the category 'women.'" Cucchiari saw the distinctive role arising in three related developments.

The first was the increase in competition among males themselves for prestige: the arrival of individualism. It was at this point, Cucchiari claimed, that heterosexuality arrived. Women became objects of competition, trophies, and status symbols. Sex became genderized as a woman's anatomical differences were employed to serve the emerging competitive social situation. Sexual attractiveness and conquest was an integral aspect of this new competition. "But sexual competition tends to skew sexual preference into one of two exclusive directions: intragender homosexuality or intergender heterosexuality," according to Cucchiari.

The second reason for the emerging dichotomy was the repressive division of labor imposed on women. In the pre-gender society, child rearing was an open communal responsibility. Women began to regard their ability to have children as a competitive resource to attract males and express their own gender identity. The "maternal bond" appeared as males appropriated the tasks of hunting and foraging more to themselves, leaving the task of child-tending to women.

The new division of labor created new problems in raising male children, who were now required to fashion their identity in *opposition* to their most immediate gender model:

> In a world of different activities, personality types, and aspirations to which the human infant is exposed, he/she must reject some in favor of others with hardly the ability to know why. This must lead to a sense of loss. Thousands of years of androgynous myths and folk tales testify to the unconscious need to be reunited with a repressed part of ourselves. This is another powerful force behind heterosexuality. Repression not only leaves each of the genders with a sense of incompleteness, but tends to fetishize the opposite gender (1981:58).

The third reason was found in the human need to construct a symbolic explanation for the competitive dichotomy. The new symbolization of women as objects of competition introduced the idea of sexuality as dangerous and something to be *controlled*. Cucchiari wrote (1981:59): "Exclusive heterosexuality and sexual possessiveness tend to lead to a more defined method of mate selection and to further restraints on sexual relations in the horde—what is called 'pair bonding' by the ethologists." From this pairing arose the need to seek mates in other hordes and the eventual development of the family, marriage, incest taboos, and the need to keep records of genealogy to distinguish siblings and horde mates from future spouses.

The need to acquire mates from neighboring hordes was first accomplished by the exchange of children. It was a small step from the exchange of child brides to the exchange of adult women in daughter and sister exchange. This last development represented the final step in the domination of some adults by others, a principle totally antithetic to pre-gender societies. Male domination is responsible for all the conditions for the family as a stable social institution: gender, pairing, division of labor, exogamous exchange of women, incest taboos,and exclusive heterosexuality.

Cucchiari (1981:52) echoed Freud's feeling about the connection between gender roles and male domination: "Racial categories are close analogues of gender categories. As with the gender system, people are assigned to them at birth (determined by parentage) and often tagged for life by certain phenotypic markers. Like the gender system too, racial categories seem to always be set within a hierarchical social system. . . ."

Cucchiari's hypothesis that the attempts of the patriarchs to exploit gender for the purpose of making favorable alliances with other kinship groups were responsible for the prohibition of same-sex behaviors is a position held by some feminists. This is not a position well supported by the anthropological record, however, which shows numerous kinship societies in which heterosexual and homosexual behaviors are equally regarded.

But Cucchiari's hypothesis of a society without the concepts of gender is not so farfetched when we consider the late origins of the conjugal family itself, parents living under the same roof with their children. In Europe the replacement of the extended family with the conjugal family began around 700 B.C. As a result of Roman colonization and commerce, this pattern of kinship began to spread. By the tenth century A.D., the conjugal family had replaced the kinship families of Northern Europe (Goody, 1983).

Although the ancient Romans and Greeks were familiar with our modern concepts of "family" and "child," these meanings were lost in Europe after the sixth century until the late seventeenth century. For a long time, "family" referred to property and meant the household of servants, wives, and children. There was no word referring to a child as a member of a family. Life was simply divided into infancy, youth and old age (Rossiaud, 1976:68).

"Babee" or "enfant" both originally meant the child in the womb or the newborn infant. By the Middle Ages, however, laws making parents accountable for the behavior of their offspring extended the meaning of childhood to include any dependent person under 16–18 years of age, including soldiers in the army (from which we get our word "infantry"). Youth ("jeune") comprised the ages of 16–18 to 45–50 years of age and was followed by respected old age or ridiculed senility.

Childhood as we know it was practically unknown. After weaning, the children were often raised by others "with the least trouble and the most pleasure." At the age of five or six, they were thrust out into the adult world, most often farmed out to other households, where they apprenticed as servants. They dressed as adults and were depicted by artists of the time as small adults, not with the sentimental features we have come to associate with children. Our current concepts of both "child" and "family" — and the relationship between the two — did not begin to emerge until the arrival of the modern nation-states in the middle of the seventeenth century (Aries, 1962).

These developments accompanied corresponding refinements in the definitions of gender and the relationships between men and women. The arrival of the Industrial Revolution put women to work in the factories from the very beginning, causing them to delay marriage by several years. This event by itself exaggerated the distinctions between men and women as administrators had to justify the intolerable conditions under which women were expected to work. As we will see, the *potestas patria*, the patriarchal right over the life of spouses and children, was usurped by the state in its attempt to redefine the family and the relationships between male and female.

In "The Myth of Male Superiority: Rise and Demise" Seymour and Hilda Parker (1979) rejected both the theory that male superiority is based on the physical superiority of males and the "conspiracy" theory that males consciously plot and contrive to preserve male hegemony. They admitted that there are certain phylogenetic differences *which aid boys and girls in fulfilling cultural role expectations in distinctive ways.* They also claimed that different societies respond to these differences in different ways. This sexual division of labor is important in the ways in which it is sometimes used (in agricultural and industrial societies more than hunting societies) to support the myth of male superiority.

It is in the sexual division of labor that male superiority finds its greatest support. There is little evidence in any society that the work done by males is any more important or necessary than that done by women. But the type of work done by males "entitles" them to greater power and prestige in the community. The authors wrote (1979:299), "The data clearly do not permit us to make any statements about general biobehavioral superiority or inferiority. Females were adapted to assume a central role in reproduction and socialization in human sociality, while male adaptations were particularly suited to agonistic, exploratory, and strenuous responses. We categorically reject the reductionist explanation of the ideology of male superiority or power in social systems as being a direct function of the male biological endowment."

The Parkers borrowed the concept of *social exchange theory* from economics to explain male superiority. According to this concept, people enter into relationships and contracts in order to exchange and maximize values. The particular culture defines and determines the "exchange value" of the exchanged commodities. If one party to a relationship is seen to be contributing more, he is given more power and prestige as a means of stabilizing and continuing the relationship. Relating this to male dominance, the Parkers (1979:300) explained that "The requirements for male-role activities are elicited with greater difficulty or cost both to the individual and, therefore, to society. The more traditional and routine tasks of women do not require as high a level of achievement, special effort, etc. . . . " The conclusions of social exchange theory have supported the campaign in our country to gain "equivalent pay" for equivalent work by women. The reason women don't have the more taxing jobs is that they have purposely been kept out of them.

The Parkers (1979:301) saw males more than females affected by the losses incurred in the gendered society. Accordingly, more effort was given to their training. "Male vulnerability" may be another factor contributing to the greater prestige given. It seems that males are not so well equipped for their tasks of strength and derring-do as are women for their more civilizing tasks. They are much more prone to neurological disease, deviant behavior, learning and reading difficulties, sex-role identity problems, lower life expectancy, greater difficulty in adapting to long-term stress — all of which suggested to the Parkers (1979:301) that "vulnerability in male-role performance, deriving from innate genetic programming and exacerbated by the division of labor, compounds the problems associated with male-task performance."

We could assume that if gender behavior were biologically programmed, we would be able to take it for granted. But, while we leave a good deal of freedom in our society for differences in sexual behaviors, we radically constrict gender behaviors. Gender is the object of our greatest pedagogic attention, all of which leads us to suspect the importance of gender to society as an instrument of power.

Gagnon and Simon (1973:29), in their work on the social sources of sexual behavior, stated: "The decision whether to raise a child male or female is probably based on the most significant labeling experience that the child will receive. Once a parent or doctor has identified a child, always by the anatomic conformation of his genitals (perhaps this is the meaning of 'anatomy becomes destiny,' anatomy in conjunction with social attribution) as male or female, there are released the separate cultural syndromes that are related to the rearing of male or female children."

John Money and Joan and John Hampson (1955:285), describing the social elements in the development of gender role, wrote: "A gender role is not established at birth, but is built up cumulatively through experiences encountered and transacted — through casual and unplanned learning, through explicit instruction and inculcation, and through spontaneously putting two and two together to make sometimes four and sometimes five."

The influences of the home environment set the stage for these sex roles, which mirror our attitudes and mimic our relationships. Sex roles ensure that lifestyles and stereotypes are passed from parents to children as inexorably as blue eyes or small feet. Money and the Hampsons

(1955,1956) showed how gender role is usually set by a little after two years of age and any attempts after that to change the role of children who have been somehow placed originally in the wrong category have severe negative psychological consequences for the child. How gender-role teaching goes on during the first two years is not clear. It is mostly informal and subliminal information conveyed by parents who are convinced the child is of one gender or another. The type of play engaged in, the attitudes toward the child, and the manner of addressing the child in all interactions have a very definite effect.

Once the child acquires language, however, the process becomes much more observable and definite, going beyond the realm of gestures. Gagnon and Simon (1973:31) wrote:

> It is during this period that the child comes under the control of the communicative process, no matter how primitively at first, for it is in the naming and organizing of experience in scripts that the child begins to organize his plans for dealing with the world. Two salient experiences dominate the post-verbal years until puberty, all of which are influential in the development of an ultimate sexual identity. The first of these is the pattern of naming the child's behaviors in general and the specific adult reaction to behaviors that are conceived to be sexual. The second is the continued building of conventional gender identities based on preverbal social decision about the maleness or femaleness of the child.

The distribution of sexual behaviors is largely regulated on lines of gender. The fear of homosexual behaviors has become a major concern in gender compliance and training. Not being homosexual is central to the modern concepts of being male and female, so much so that parents feel that the appearance of homosexual behaviors in their children reflects upon their effectiveness as parents. Perhaps nowhere do we find so clearly illustrated the role of the family as an institution of social control than in their responsibility to "prevent" homosexuality.

Ann Jacobsen in "A Woman's Place—Her Natural Destiny," (in Gordon and Libby, 1976:46) pointed out the influence of homosexuality in this process: "The big concern is often homosexuality. Having a son turn out gay haunts nearly every father. Having a lesbian daughter isn't nearly so threatening. Keeping girls feminine is more a matter of keeping them attractive, alluring, and marriageable."

In all the areas of interaction with children, gender roles are taught as master roles into which all other roles must fit. All other efforts—in sports, competition, love, business, education, and "achievement"—are evaluated in reference to playing out the role of being male or female.

With adolescence, there arises the need to manage sexuality because of the new sense of having a sexual status and the increasing role that genitality assumes in social conduct. Even though the onset of sexual experience varies from one individual to another,adolescence is a special period of development because, as Gagnon and Simon (1973:51) state, "it is at this time that society at large (and, more approximately, parents, peers, schools, and media) recognizes and, in part, imposes on and invents the conventional sexual capacity of the individual. Even though the capacity for orgasm ... is available far earlier in life and even experienced by some infants and children, there is no sense in which the society promotes the utilization of or organization of this capacity into preadolescent experience."

It is during adolescence that the male focus on genital concerns becomes most dominant. The masculine commitment to genitality is reinforced by frequent masturbation and orgasm in middle and upper classes, while males in lower classes have more opportunity for coitus. Females meanwhile become more committed to maternal forms of sexuality. As a result, by the time courtship arrives, males and females frequently have two completely different ideas of sex. Thus much of the time of courtship and early marriage is taken up in mutual education as these differing sexual activities are explored and exchanged.

Gagnon and Simon (1973:58-60) wrote that the general absence of masturbation among women is usually explained by asserting that (1) masturbation is universal and women just suppress their memories of it, (2) women are more inhibited and repressed than men, or (3) women have a weaker biological drive. The authors attack these views as ill-founded and leading to "endless confusions and misunderstandings about female sexuality."

They hold to a learning explanation instead: Women are simply not taught to be sexual in a focused, genital way until later in life.

While they admitted that it is "both difficult and dangerous for a female to become too committed or too sexually active during adolescence," they reject the usual explanation that most girls successfully repress an elementary urge.

As an alternative to the "repression" theory, the authors wrote (1973:60), "It is not women's sexual drive that is inhibited, for the language of 'drive' and 'inhibition' are both faulty; it is that women receive little training in sexual activity that is not prohibitory, while at the same time being positively trained in docility." For females, masturbation is rarely linked to important social values. For boys, on the other hand, any kind of bodily manipulation is linked to the male values of achievement, control, aggression, dominance, and the violation of social norms.

Young males of all groups find in genital activities support for their vulnerable and fragile status as males, while young women, whose roles are worked out within the home, are more confident of their feminine status and receive abundant identity support from their attachment to mothers and other women. Boys must leave home and find their place in life to win the hand of a bride.

While our society regards same-sex behaviors as a form of gender betrayal, there are some societies that regard them as a form of gender enhancement. In *Guardians of the Flutes*, Gilbert Herdt (1981:2–3) gave us an example of a traditional society, the Sambia tribe of the Highlands of New Guinea, in which young males pursued their masculinity in the context of same-sex genital behavior:

> Seven-to-ten-year-old Sambia boys are taken from their mothers when first initiated to the male cult, and thereafter experience the most powerful and seductive homosexual fellatio activities. For some ten to fifteen years, they engage in these practices on a daily basis, first as fellator, and then as fellated. Elders teach that semen is absolutely vital; it should be consumed daily since the creation of biological maleness and the maintenance of masculinity depend on it. Hence, from middle childhood until puberty, boys should perform fellatio on older youths.
>
> Near puberty the same initiates become dominant youths. Ritual helps remake their social and erotic identity, the bachelors becoming the fellated partners for a new crop of ritual novices. And at the same time, youths and boys alike must absolutely avoid women, on pain of punishment. For not only must secret homoeroticism be hidden from women but females are also believed to be contaminating—their menstrual blood polluting, and worse, lethal. This dual pattern—prescribed homosexual activities and avoidance of women—persists until marriage. So all heterosexual relationships, intrigues, and even casual conversations among boys and girls are blocked, and forbidden.
>
> Whereas homosexual practices begin with initiation, they become far more than a ceremony. All boys are forcibly initiated. They scarcely have choice. For long afterwards, ritualized homosexuality becomes the center of their existence. Born from the deepest trauma of maternal separation and ritual threats, homosexual fellatio is dangerous and exciting, powerful and cruel. And from such experiences is born a boy's sense of masculinity . . . . Yet, in spite of this formidable background, the final outcome is exclusive heterosexuality.

From a Western perspective, with its belief in the sexual drive, it is unimaginable that any society would thus risk universal homosexuality among young males without endangering its survival. Yet this homosexual act is for Sambian males an expression of manliness, not femininity, the royal road to manhood itself. As throughout the rest of the sexual world, what determines the behavior are the meanings attached to it: "And from such experiences is born a boy's sense of masculinity."

From the universal use of words referring to "male" and "female," we can too easily assume that they mean the same things and are loaded with the same connotations of gender with which we are familiar. The degree to which they diverge from Western assumptions about gender can sometimes be measured in the acceptance given ambiguous gender roles. Charles and Cherry Lindholm (1982:78–80), writing about "The Erotic Sorcerers," stated that while the effeminate male is provided a sanctioned role in other societies, he has been the "unhappy scapegoat for Western culture's horror of sexual ambiguity, a horror intensified by Judeo-Christian moral values. But while our society views cross-dressing with strong distaste, other societies have different attitudes and may offer the cross-dressing man an accepted and even respected role."

In Tahiti, where heterosexuality comes easily to all males, each village has one—and only one—mahu, a man who dresses as a woman. He may stay a mahu all his life, or abdicate his role and raise a family, in which case another mahu is chosen. The status of being a mahu is considerable, and the village makes sure there is no lack of candidates. Men in the villages engage in casual homosexual relations with the mahu. Our authors suggest that the role of mahu is basically symbolic, in that it serves as a symbolic demarcation between maleness and femaleness in Tahitian society.

The authors concluded: "The presence of such a symbolic marker permits a wide range of male behavior. Even extreme effeminacy does not disqualify someone from being regarded as a normal man, and there are many such men in Tahiti with wives and children. Other cultures, our own included, are not so tolerant of effeminate behavior in men. Some anthropologists have suggested that this very intolerance in fact pushes men who are 'womanlike' into homosexuality, since they have no place within the narrow boundaries of the culture's traditional male image."

The emergence of the new gay role based on sexual orientation was, in fact, in response to not only the need to eliminate ambiguous gender roles but also new demands to tighten up already restricted definitions of male and female. The new role now serves as a catch-all not only for gender inverts but also for anyone else having difficulty fitting into our constricted definitions of gender. Plummer (1975:135–136) explained that we now are required to interpret a wide range of gender events as homosexual:

> For example, some actors may well find a base created for subsequent homosexual interpretation though gender confusions—a child coming to see his bodily self as in some ways inappropriate to the cultural definitions of his gender: a small, frail, fragile boy may come to perceive himself as 'not like other men,' and go from this belief to build up a definition of being homosexual. Others may develop a sense of 'differentness'—which cuts them off from everybody else: the boy who prefers to be alone, or the boy whose interest is in the arts and literature finds himself distinguished markedly from his 'football crazy' peers. As one respondent to Ross commented: 'I thought I was different because I wanted to become an artist and not because of homosexuality.' This sense of 'differentness' is a fairly

common experience in homosexual case histories. As a simple example, four working-class homosexuals interviewed revealed a highly sensitive childhood — playing violins, visiting art museums, developing taste in the arts, literature, and music, taking an interest in fashion and clothes to an extent that seems strangely at odds with the traditional working-class male culture in which they were brought up. They were incidentally characterized by very slender frail physical frames. I am *not* saying here that 'homosexuality' gives rise to these interests or physiques. Quite the contrary: the interests and physique may well provide a subsequent base for interpreting oneself as homosexual. They provide clues for retrospective interpretation. In each of these early *social* experiences, a potential base is created for a subsequent *sexual* interpretation.

Similar observations were made by Richard Troiden, in his study on 150 gay-identified males. Troiden separated these sensitizing experiences into preadolescent and adolescent phases. He stated (1979:36) regarding the childhood years: "The references to alienation and gender inadequacy show that childhood *social* experiences played a greater role in sensitizing a person for subsequent self-definition as homosexual than did preadolescent experiences gained in the spheres of *genitality* (same-sex relations) and *emotionality* (warmth and excitement). . . . What is suggested here is that homosexual and heterosexual males may differ in terms of the *meanings* they later come to attribute to a childhood sense of apartness."

Similar observations about gender behavior and homosexual motivation were made by Bell, Weinberg, and Hammersmith in their *Sexual Preference: Its Development in Men and Women.* From their study of 1,500 gay-identified persons conducted in San Francisco, the authors concluded that both male and female homosexuals did report greater alienation from their peers than did heterosexuals. While they admitted that confirming studies of this evidence regarding lesbians are in short supply, they wrote (1981:84):

> A number of empirical investigations have supported the notion that the peer relationships of prehomosexual boys differ from those of their heterosexual counterparts. Several studies have reported that prehomosexual boys are more likely to have been loners and to have been rejected by other boys. Another study found that during childhood, prehomosexual boys were more likely than preheterosexual boys to have spent most of their time with girls and less likely to have had any male buddies. Finally, psychiatrists have described their homosexual male patients as more likely than their heterosexual male patients to have been social isolates during childhood and adolescence, to have played mostly with girls, to have avoided competitive group games, and to have been clinging children, afraid to venture out beyond the safety of their households.

The authors say that, while their research gives confirmation to the theory that prehomosexual boys are less likely to be socially involved with

male peers than preheterosexual boys, indications were that "social isolation is more likely to *reflect* the differences between homosexual and
heterosexual males than to *contribute* to such differences" (1981:85).

We see here the manner in which the gay myth has been able to
resolve a wide range of personal gender conflicts. The slightest difficulty
in managing today's bizarre and rigid gender roles can propel a person
towards the gay role. We thereby are able to eliminate a whole world of
nonconforming gender possibilities by putting them into the same
blender called "homosexuality," after which they all look alike.

For some persons, the homoerotic response that validates the male
individualism, aspiration, and hero-worship inherent in our society
becomes more than a source of pleasure and personal fulfillment. It also
becomes the means of salvaging their gender by offering an explanation
for their own personal conflicts with the model. As one gay person's father
told him, "I was relieved when you came out as a homosexual. I was
beginning to think there was something wrong with you." As bad as it is
to be gay in our society, it is worse to defy one's gender. The new
hyphenated gender terminology (gay male, straight female, etc.)
eliminates the need in our society to confront any gender ambiguity.

We should not be led to conclude that feelings of alienation from
one's gender always or automatically trigger a homoerotic response.
Neither should we conclude that alienation is the only trigger. There are
many persons secure in their gender identity who also enjoy same-sex
pleasures. Clarence Tripp (1975:80–82) explained:

> Very young boys frequently associate what is male with what is sex-
> ual in such a way as to arrive at a powerful homosexual thrust before
> realizing that heterosexual possibilities even exist. Not that these and a
> host of other sexual starts are only beginnings of homosexuality; it can
> begin from sources far away from sex. In fact, eroticism often arrives late
> as a guest at its own banquet: a high degree of affection or rapport be-
> tween two people, especially if they see each other across an otherwise un-
> bridgeable barrier of age or of status, can easily generate sexual feel-
> ings.... A high-intensity admiration very easily becomes eroticized,
> especially when it is focused on a particular individual—a result all the
> more likely when a youngster is sexually precocious or has still other
> reasons for welcoming a sexual contact.
>   It has often been thought that boys who have "identity problems" or
> who feel inferior in some sense are the ones who are inclined to admire the
> masculine attainments of others enough to eroticize them. And by exten-
> sion, a host of other insecurities, as well as low aggressiveness in general,
> have been thought relevant. Sometimes these descriptions do fit, though
> by no means as neatly or as often as one might suppose.... Evelyn Hooker
> has noted (with a careful eye to aspirations) that a boy who sees him-
> self apart from a nearby group often views other boys as having a certain
> prized alliance—a situation that can breed envy, desire, and the inven-
> tion of an erotic solution to his problem, particularly if he finds an

especially admired group member with whom a sexual bridge is possible.

The results, however, can be the same without any social misalignment. Even a boy who is near the top of his group and knows it, especially if he is somewhat idealistic, is quite capable of having his aspirations continually soar ahead of his own achievements. Much like a musclebuilder who is fired ever more by each bit of improvement, it is as if his whole concept of maleness and the very encouragement he gets from what he has already accomplished lead him to constantly raise his sights. In the spirit of this abounding appetite, he may be quite ready not only to glorify an admired male, but to search for one and often, then, to engineer a sexual contact.

Males secure in their gender identification engage in extensive homosexual contacts with less need for the gay role to explain their behaviors, yet even they may find certain saving advantages in it. Because of increasing competition from women, many males today find in homosexuality a refuge for a threatened genital primacy. Gay identity allows them to pursue an untrammeled masculinity that would be much more constrained in a modern heterosexual relationship.

But other people, especially among the young, see the gay role as a cop-out, a collaboration with the state's rigid definitions of gender. The theatrics of the hippies of the 1960s paved the way for the radical gays who assaulted the dogmas of gender with their outrageous "genderfuck" presentations. (Gorilla Rose and Tomato DiPlenty of a once-popular Seattle gay theater group called the Whiz Kids come to mind.)

More recently, the cause has been taken up by the advocates of punk and new wave, who are even more forthcoming in their commitment to gender ambiguity. In attempting to sever the connection between androgyny and homosexuality, they are doing an end run around the whole issue of sexual orientation, a play that is guaranteed to further confuse and upset their families.

In the creation of gender, society writes in much larger script than do the needs of biology or nature. As Cucchiari (1981:34) explained: "But the point has been demonstrated: physical or biological features, even the most prominent, are not inherently meaningful. To become markers or referents of race or gender, these features must be welded in categories, given a broad range of meanings, and in the case of racial categories the very features themselves must be maintained by cultural sanctions." And nowhere is the social scripting of gender more obvious than in the regulation of homosexual behaviors.

V. Family Matters

There has been so much action in the past, especially sexual action, a wearying repetition over and over, without a corresponding thought, a corresponding realization. Now our business is to realize sex. Today the full conscious realization of sex is even more important than the act itself. —D.H. Lawrence

I met him while drinking coffee at McDonald's in downtown Anchorage, a fourteen-year-old Eskimo male who had just arrived in the big city from his village in Northwestern Alaska. I listened with some astonishment as he told his sad tale of his father's ordering him out of the house for being gay. The traumatic confrontation that follows announcement of a person's gay identity to his parents occurs quite frequently in the United States, but for an Eskimo family to banish a youngster for being gay seemed unthinkable to me at the time. Strong kinship bonds and a high tolerance for individual differences were once characteristic features of Eskimo life. What was going on here? I offered the young man some names and phone numbers to call for assistance, but he was on his way out of the state. I never saw him again.

The relationship with one's family is of great significance to those who have adopted a gay identity. The question of whether to declare one's gayness to the family is also a matter of concern. In most cases, the declaration of one's gayness is accompanied by a great deal of trauma, though not always followed by the disruptive conclusion observed in the above incident.

Family matters and the relationship to one's family are the subjects of the everyday conversation of gay-identified persons. New acquaintances often share with one another the details of when and how one broke the news of one's "gayness" to the family and how they reacted.

In many cases, young people voluntarily leave the family without any announcement, avoiding a scene and imposing on themselves the anticipated punishment. Those families that offer a high level of acceptance usually do so after a tense period of adjustment, and the relationship afterward is often never the same.

Why is it that so much of the proscription of homosexuality is enforced on the family level? What is the role that the family plays in the creation of the gay role? In other times and in other cultures, there may have been high levels of social disapproval coming from the church or state, but sexual variations such as homosexuality hardly bothered one's kin or associates. The family itself has become the state's agent for controlling this behavior. To see how this came about, we must first understand the new social role played by the family itself.

It is something of a cliché to say that the "family is the basic unit of society." The truth of that statement is difficult to discern in any universal sense. The conjugal family as a living arrangement is very much a product of the state. The human race got along without the family for a very long period of time, and many societies still do without it. In most societies, men and women do not live together, and weaned children are not raised by the parents but by the whole community.

In our own society we give lip service to the primacy of the family, but it is not even mentioned in the Constitution. Our legal rights devolve upon the individual, not the family. The modern nation-state has taken over many of the functions of kinship depending on what sector of society you happen to live in. The autonomy of "good families" is relatively intact, while the state frequently intervenes in the family matters of those families in the "social sector," who are the clients of social workers. Within all sectors, beliefs regarding the family provide the state its most effective mechanisms for social control.

The lack of continuity between traditional kin groups and the modern family is quite significant. The family is not just a kin group reduced to simplest reproductive function. Contrary to folklore, the functions of kinship were not passed on to the family but to the state. The family, as a creation of the modern nation-state, has its resistance to homosexuality built in. As a political artifact, the family is hardly "natural" in the sense of being designed to meet the developmental needs of the human being. It is, instead, a political compromise arranged between numberless and shifting sources of power.

As political science has shown us, all power begins not at the top but at the bottom, in the relationship between parent and child. Described as a "strategy of inequity," power is first experienced in the parental relationship. That power than becomes a bargaining chip for alliances and strategies outside the family, first with other families of equal status and later with more powerful families who are in a position to offer protections and advantages in return for the father's control of the family.

Power acts in a uniform and comprehensive manner from top to bottom according to the endlessly reproduced mechanisms of law, taboo, regulation, and censorship: from state to family, from president to father, from Congress to the school principal, from all the agencies of domination to the subject himself. However multiple the sources of power, one defines power always in a juridical form and sees himself in relation to power as one who obeys. It is a mistake to think of power only in terms of restrictive laws and regulations. We, the state, also deploy sexuality and other rewards for political purposes, usually reserving them for members of good families.

We do not create norms and roles willy-nilly, but in response to these shifting conflicts of power beginning with the family. Power bubbles up from the family collecting and enlarging as it goes, finally bursting forth in the official pronouncements of laws and sanctions. Because of its intimate contribution to power, the modern nuclear family has played a key role in the shaping of its own destiny and structure.

The reader should be warned that what follows is a grossly generalized theory of the development of the modern nuclear family. The study of the *history* of the family is about where nuclear physics was in 1850. Social history becomes very difficult or impossible before the period when modern statistical records were kept. Accounts from one country cannot be applied to neighboring countries, nor from one part of a country to another. Promulgated laws often had little to do with the everyday practices of people. In olden times, private behaviors were not conceptualized at all as topics for literature. People felt little need to report them or write about them.

Anthropological evidence was and is often clouded by colonialistic influences and cultural bias. The terminology used by anthropologists is difficult, and different reports from the same area are often difficult to reconcile. Even when reports are reliable, different societies may attach quite different meanings and values to the same observed behaviors. What is regarded as innocent in one tribe may be considered quite offensive in a neighboring tribe.

Even today, when it comes to medical history, the problem persists. It was recently determined, for example, that 50 percent of all cases previously diagnosed as senility were, in fact, Alzheimer's disease. Until quite recently, pathologists and epidemiologists could not distinguish between influenza and pneumonia.

How little we have to go on when it comes to investigating the private lives of families! We have even less when it comes to understanding how people perceived and explained those behaviors. Until Kinsey's time, there was no attempt to assess the private sexual experiences of individuals, and there has been damn little since.

But, in spite of the paucity of information, the first reports coming in suggest to us broad patterns of the family's development. And from these patterns of development we can propose theories for future investigation.

The general configuration of kinship societies (which vary greatly in spite of some universal similarities) always emerges as the background for the study of the modern family. Whatever we say about kinship, it was eminently successful as a model of social organization, enabling human societies to successfully explore and settle all the inhabitable areas of the world by the thirteenth century A.D. In spite of the encroachments of modernity, kinship retains its dominance in most societies of the world, posing a constant problem — if not a threat — to the developing nation-states, against which kinship stands as a powerful and ancient rival. The modern state has developed Oedipally in relationship to kinship: It must kill its parent in order to survive.

What is remarkable about all kinship societies is the universal evidence of gender divisions, the incest taboo, and exogamy (marriage outside the group). Another notable feature is the higher level of sociability and affectivity in most kinship societies. In many ways, sex performs the same function in the modern family as consanguinity and bonding did in traditional societies. Our idea of sex was invented by the modern state to be the glue that holds the modern family together, a function that provides us with a key to the origins of the homosexual role.

To appreciate the meaning of sex in our society, we should first look at affectivity in kinship societies, as they share similar social functions. In his famous work on the human significance of skin, Ashley Montagu (1978) saw the connection between the amount of affectivity (which he calls "tactuality") afforded infants and children with a community's level of aggression or cooperation. Societies with low levels of contact, such as the Japanese and Northwestern Europe societies, characteristically exhibit higher levels of aggression, while those with more bodily contact exhibit higher levels of cooperation and harmony.

While there are differences in the level of affectivity between families of the same society and between individuals of the same family, each society specifically trains its young to respond differently to tactile stimulation, thereby modifying and accenting the biological and temperamental characteristics of the society (L. Frank, 1957:241).

Anthropologists have noted that the primary relationship in traditional societies is not found in the sexual relationship of husband and wife but the relationship *between the child and the rest of the community*. While Americans regard themselves as a "child-centered" society — usually measured by the amount of money spent on children — they are often surprised and even shocked at the high level of pleasure derived from children in traditional societies where "babies are the fun." As Germaine Greer (1984:257–58) put it:

> Most of the pleasure in the world is still provided by children and not by genital dabbling. Most of the women in the world still spend long hours in close body contact with their babies and many men can be seen with

64   Gay Identity

their sons or daughters standing between their legs as they gossip on their
charpoys or under the trees or squatting by the house wall. There is an un-
shaven guerilla leader who was found by a journalist who came to interview him, with a baby on his knee, letting little fingers stretch his lips
while he uttered the words that strike fear into the heart of nations. The
eroticism of most of the world still includes the vast store of sensuality that
radiates from children, whose deliciousness is more obvious to people
grown old and snarled by a life of bitter toil and hard rations than it is to
our smooth-skinned, overfed selves, but the attack has been mounted
(1984:257–258).

Montagu (1978), beginning with the traditional practice of keeping
infants in constant contact with the body of the mother during the period
between birth and weaning (exterogestation), mounted impressive
evidence of the benefits of physical intimacy for both children and adults.
In kinship societies, the sensual pleasures enjoyed by children are often
extended to the rest of the community. Jules Henry (1964:18–19), writing
of the highly tactile Kaingang tribe of Brazil, described the children as
lying "like cats absorbing the delicious stroking of adults." Male and
female children — sisters, brothers, inlaws, and cousins — sleep together in
great lumps, side by side, embraced and with legs crossed.

Margaret Mead (1952:40–41), describing the Arapesh of New
Guinea, wrote of the way in which infants were always being carried by
someone. A child's crying was always something to be avoided, and the
breast was immediately offered for comfort. As in many other societies,
breastfeeding was continued for three or four years, during which the
child slept in close contact with its mother. Nursing was a playful and
erotic experience for both mother and child, who teased and played with
one breast while nursing the other. Mead commented, "Thus the whole
matter of nourishment is made into an occasion of high affectivity and
becomes a means by which the child develops and maintains a sensitivity
to caresses in every part of its body."

A general feature of most kinship societies is the central position held
by children and those activities and persons dedicated to the pleasure,
health, and welfare of children. As Mead (1952:100) explained: "To the
Arapesh, the world is a garden that must be tilled, not for one's self, not
in pride and boasting, not for hoarding and usury, but that the yams and
the dogs and the pigs and most of all the children may grow. From this
whole attitude flow many of the other Arapesh traits, the lack of conflict
between the old and the young, the lack of any expectation of jealousy
or envy, the emphasis upon co-operation."

Konner (1982:307) reported that when a mother of the !Kung tribe
of Africa was read the passage from the 1976 edition of Dr. Spock's book
on child care regarding "not spoiling" fretful infants and letting them cry,
she reacted with a mixture of surprise, amusement, and contempt.

"Doesn't he realize it's only a baby?" she asked. "It has no sense, that's why it cries. You pick it up. Later on, when it gets bigger, it will have sense, and it won't cry so much." Like other mothers in all the societies where the development of children is a primary concern, she had confidence in the process of growth, and was not concerned about the possibility of "spoiling" the baby; also, she considered the "unspoiling" procedure ethically unacceptable.

Konner (1982:312), commented that most parents in the traditional nonindustrial world would place Dr. Spock's advice "squarely in the category of public advocacy of child abuse and neglect. There is no basis for the inference that the infant is crying from anger, and there is little basis for the inference that the procedure is harmless."

Konner (1982:309) also noted that the distance between sleeping infants and mothers is another indicator of the level of the status and care afforded children. In hunter-gatherer societies, infants always sleep in the same bed with the mother, often in direct physical contact. An infant sleeping alone would be subject to almost certain attack by predatory animals.

Even in other traditional societies, the same proximity is noted. In 90 nonindustrial societies other than hunter-gatherers studied worldwide, the mother and infant slept in the same bed in 41 cases, in the same room with bed unspecified in 30, and in the same room in separate beds in 19. In none of the 90 cases did mother and infant sleep in separate rooms.

Greer (1984:27–28) elaborated on the manner in which the socialization of children is carried out in kinship societies. "It is not easy to drive the wedge of professional care into traditional families," she wrote. "There is no need of a play group, because the play group is right there, nor for that matter of the nursery school. . . . Mothers are not so vulnerable to infantile ill temper because they do not have to take sole responsibility for it. Reward and punishment are doled out according to family practice. . . ."

In many ways, kinship societies offer an environment in which individual liberties seem extremely curtailed. But, as Greer pointed out, they offer "a sense and a context to mothering which two-bedroom ranch houses in the suburbs do not. . . . Perhaps the most important difference between mothering in traditional societies and mothering in our own is that the traditional mother's role increases in complexity and importance as she grows older."

In child-centered societies, the pleasures of children pervade the community like a great current, bringing everyone into close physical contact, adults and youth as well as children. Describing the sleeping patterns of the Kaingang tribe of South America, Henry (1964) wrote, "Married and unmarried young men lie cheek by jowl, arms around one another, legs slung across bodies, for all the world like lovers in our own society. Sometimes they lie caressing that way in little knots of three and four. . . . The basis for man's loyalty to man has roots in the many warm body contacts between them."

Clarence Tripp (one of Kinsey's associates), describing the erotic content of male bonding, drew this picture of the high level of affectivity observed between adult males in some kinship societies:

> Men everywhere have tended to cluster and affiliate with each other into tight-knit cliques, and into larger groups. Many observers have attributed the formation of such groups to what the members then do with their affiliation — be this hunting, the waging of war, or the exercise of political power. . . . Perhaps so; but it can be shown that the male bond is just as pronounced in situations in which men are relaxing as it is when they are engaged in some project (1975:48–49).
>
> In most societies the male bond involves a considerable amount of bodily contact. Americans, and to a lesser extent Europeans, are quite unusual in their avoidance of intimate physical contact. Both the amount and the kinds of such contacts in other parts of the world are thus a surprise and a shock to Western eyes: Men more than women tend to hold hands or place an arm around a friend's waist or shoulder as they walk along. And the detailed view an anthropologist gets is even more striking. In a number of tribes, the standard greeting is to reach out and gently grasp a stranger's penis, or to cup his testicles in hand. In others, (e.g., the Cashinahua) friends lie together in hammocks during the day, casually fondling each other's genitalia while talking (though it is considered embarrasing if one's friend, or the anthropologist, gets an erection).
>
> In perhaps three-quarters of all societies, the sleeping arrangements are such that men lie closely intertwined, legs and arms thrown over and around each other; even tight clasping and kissing are not at all unusual. . . . Whether there happens to be a taboo on overt homosexuality or not, the sleeping regulations remain about the same. . . . These body-contact examples are hardly homosexual in an erotic sense, least of all in the eyes of the participants. . . . And yet, the male bond clearly carries a considerable charge of affection — an urge for contact which is unquestionably bent more upon seeking a personal intimacy than a group identity (1975:50–51).

Some societies have been able to retain their affective practices throughout the transition to an industrial society. An acquaintance of the author's, an Australian aboriginal, is a social worker married to a white engineer. They live with their six children in a company town adjacent to a mining operation. Though not a tribal person, she retains many tribal customs, including subsistence hunting of the local varieties of kangaroo.

During a recent visit to the United States, she laughed as she told the author, "People here always ask me if we still walk around naked. We don't do that any more. We live in a modern house, but we — the whole family—have always slept together in the same bed. As you might guess, it is a rather large bed now and takes up almost the whole room. When my daughter returned from college with her new white husband, he was shocked at first—didn't know what he was getting into. She couldn't think of sleeping in a separate bed, much less a separate room. And neither could the rest of us! Her husband now enjoys it as much as we do." If authorities discovered such a practice in the United States, they would initiate an investigation and probably commit the children to institutions, especially if the family were poor.

In North America, the functioning of child-centered societies can still be observed in the Eskimo societies of the Arctic. The callous indifference toward children among ancient Germanic and Viking tribes has often been excused by noting the harshness of their Northern climate. Well, perhaps their environment was not harsh enough, because the Eskimos (who successfully colonized and absorbed the Viking society of West Greenland after 300 years of contact), who are the most renowned for their daring feats of bravery and exploration, have also exhibited an amazing sophistication in their practices of raising children.

Ranking among the oldest and most distinguished societies of our hemisphere, the Eskimos, or Inuit as they now prefer to be called, have clearly demonstrated the relevance of child care to the matter of human survival. A number of anthropological studies have documented the traditional child-rearing practices of the Inuit, but one of the best is Jean Briggs's portrait (1970) of family life among the Uktu Inuit of Chantrey Inlet, north of Hudson Bay.

My own contact with Inuit families of Alaska was largely limited to covering a few of the many town meetings they hold in which political and environmental issues are discussed. They attend meetings with great enthusiasm, always bringing their small children with them. Some mothers still wear their infants on their backs, scooting them around in front of their parkas to nurse, as older children look on with envious pleasure. In this world organized around children, rarely does one hear an infant cry.

Toddlers have the freedom of the meeting hall, quietly moving from one family group to another who snatch them up into their laps for some delicious fondling. The more adventurous are seen crawling between the legs of officials and distinguished guests on the speaker's platform, providing a lively counterpoint to the business under discussion.

Children over four are apparently emancipated and are seen outside roaming the neighborhood or playing at the homes of neighbors. Often losing a sense of time in the Arctic scheme of things, they sleep in the homes where they tire and are returned to mothers at a later hour.

During the recesses of the meetings, the older children appear out of the cold as if magically summoned to demonstrate their special capacity for play. They quickly seduce the toddlers away from their mothers' knee for some instant game, often utilizing for equipment anything not nailed down — ladders, tables, chairs, benches, gym carts. The adults, far from being disturbed, seem enchanted by the uproar. They return to the business of the meeting still chuckling, smugly reminded of what makes them so unique as a society.

The eloquent understatement of one of their leaders, "Our children are special to us," referred to the special esteem they have for children — so precisely tuned over centuries to the child's genetic program of development in response to the demands of a rigorous environment. The Inuit care of children is a remarkable social achievement that will continue to have a pronounced effect on child care practices throughout the world.

The higher levels of affectivity in kinship societies may be related to their tolerance for sexual behaviors. The use of reproductive behaviors for the building of alliances between kinship groups and limited to established heads of households may have allowed a higher tolerance for nonreproductive sexual behaviors. In most societies, where the greatest shame is attached to children born outside marriage, the emphasis is placed not on limiting sexuality so much as avoidance of pregnancy.

Historians are just beginning to understand the manner in which the emerging nation-states were to replace kinship societies. It is difficult for us to imagine a situation in which "society" was not the state and in which kinship groups constituted all there was of society. As primitive forms of kinship grew, some groups came to dominate others, creating new alliances and possibilities for power. This development eventually resulted in feudalistic societies in which local nobility traded military protection for fealty and service. The local patriarch would guarantee the loyalty and control of his group in return for his lord's military protection.

Out of these feudal-kinship alliances grew the monarchies, the immediate forerunners of the nation-state. Ironically, the Western monarchies found much of their strength in the laws of ancient Greece and Rome. While we tend to think of the monarchies as above the law (in many things they were), they also used the law and its traditions to expand their power and suppress rival lords, thereby developing many of the legal processes that we regard so highly. Ever so slowly, governments began to substitute law for war in the consolidation of internal control. But war remains the basic strategy for dealing with other national powers to the present day, providing the state its main reason for existence.

It was in the laws of the ancient republics that the family was first conceptualized, first in the rights of fathers over servants, slaves, and children. The Roman laws which made parents responsible for the acts of their children also formulated the laws against incest, inserting the power of the state into the relationship between fathers and daughters. This replacement of kinship authority by that of the state would continue until our own time, with its family and juvenile courts administering the relationships of the families in the social sector.

If it was law that gave birth to the monarchies, it was commerce and capitalism that gave birth to the modern nation-state. The monarchies learned from the republics such as Amsterdam and Venice how to greatly expand their war-making capabilities by borrowing money from the banks, forever sealing the close relationship between international finance and the state that has come to dominate the modern world.

Unfortunately for the monarchic families, the burgeoning agencies of government they spawned soon overwhelmed them. The possibility of the state operating quite well without the help of the sclerotic royal families quickly caught on. The revolutions either eliminated the monarchies or neutralized their power, marking the beginning of modernity: government beyond kinship.

Freed from the demands of kinship and faced with disruptive social changes that included massive dislocations of people from country to city, officials suddenly found themselves with the responsibilities formerly administered by kinship groups. We often assume that the overthrow of the monarchies simply meant that the vote instead of heredity would name the heads of state and that prerogatives of old-world kinship would be inherited by the family. Instead, it was the state that usurped the patriarchal *potestas patria*, the absolute right over life and death. The state often met resistance from the patriarchal families, some until our own times, as we see in the Mafia clans of Southern Italy.

Society no longer was to be a government of families, but a government through the family. The bourgeois, nuclear family (limiting the home to the simplest elements of father, mother, and children) provided a political *technique* that eminently suited the state's new agenda and the people's demands for personal freedom and economic advancement.

The conjugal family—first observed in the ancient city-states of Europe—was eminently fitted to the needs of the new nation-states. Overpopulation, wars, famine, disease, and land speculation in rural areas caused a tremendous migration of people to the large cities of Europe, where young men and women were put to work in the expanding textile industries (Braudel, 1982). The incidence of disease and crime that accompanied the hordes of unemployed and homeless who filled the cities brought a quick end to the social and sexual promiscuity characteristic of medieval Europe. In response to the sudden increase in infectious diseases including the plague and the impoverishment of unemployed and underpaid youths, new programs and agencies sprang into existence—public health, welfare, sanitation—giving shape to "big government."

The breakdown of the marital rituals of kinship raised the legal age of marriage by five or more years. Working women put their infants out to nurse or abandoned them in great numbers, resulting in mounting infant mortality rates.

From the seventeenth to the nineteenth centuries, a sexual repression descended upon Europe that was greater than at any time, anywhere (Flandrin, 1980). For the first time in history, society began to enforce the Christian prohibitions against sex outside of marriage. A new celibacy was imposed on adolescents and the unmarried; the luxurious freedoms of youth were eliminated and their flourishing associations such as the *abbayes joyeux* ("youthful abbeys") were disbanded (Rossiaud, 1976). The ubiquitous public baths (often operated by the Church in spite of their hedonistic reputations) were closed. Bodily affection everywhere suffered a severe decline as officials drew up new laws that contributed to the restriction of sexual activity to the home, or, more precisely, to the marital union.

This new sexual direction was the result of two important developments, an important theological break with the past and the reform of the schools. The theological break first appeared in the attempts of the church to assert its authority in the matter of marriage. The Catholic church had emerged in an old, established society whose forms of courtship and marriage it did not for the most part contest, and it showed a similar tolerance towards the customs of the nations it later converted (Gottleib, 1980:50). In the twelfth century, however, the church made its move in the canonical reforms of Gratian, who decided that the formal element in marriage was the *consent* of the contracting parties. This decree immediately began its work of dismantling the ancient traditions of courtship and marriage. By the late Middle Ages, the church had established its position as the final authority in establishing the validity of a marriage, vanquishing the ancient rights of kinship. Eventually, the state would move in and appropriate this power from the church.

The subtle changes in law were matched by a slow but evident change in Christian devotion, a change that first appeared in the writings of fifteenth-century mystic and pedagogue Gerson, who wrote the first treatise on sin. This "modern devotion," which eventually found expression in the writings of Alphonsus Ligouri, Thomas à Kempis and John Wesley, was highly introspective, focusing on one's internal states of emotion. Foucault traced this development in centuries of confession, where the idea of sex slowly took shape. Simply, the new devotion replaced the devil with the body itself as the source of evil. Examinations of conscience now focussed on the concupiscence of the body. The Reformation and the Council of Trent both gave official support to the concept of the sexual body.

If the idea of sex as an internal experience was conceived in the confessional, it came to term not in the family but the school. In confession, the new sexual discourse was lost in the telling. This was to change, however, with the state's new interest in the bodies of children. The new emphasis focused on removing children from the promiscuous adult world, first in the schools and later in the homes.

The Latin schools and colleges, outgrowths of the medieval university, were renowned for the promiscuity and uproarious conduct of the students. Boys as young as twelve attended ungraded classes in the company of youths as old as twenty-five, and often were completely unsupervised outside of class. One medieval wag commented that new students were apt to get the pox thrice before cracking the first page of Aristotle.

In the increasing demand for universal education, families were not about to send their sons, much less their daughters, to study under such riotous conditions in which swordplay and whoring were the most popular extracurricular activities. There were new demands for gradating classes according to age and for constant supervision. The church, in the writings of Francis de La Salle, who founded the Christian Brothers, and Ignatius Loyola, founder of the Jesuits, incorporated the modern devotion into their systems of education. Focussing on the capacity of children for mischief, they called for the closest scrutiny and surveillance of their behavior. The new curricula developed for gradated classes arose out of these concerns, giving birth to the new psychology of childhood (Aries, 1962).

Donzelot (1979) described how the schools solved many problems at once. Thomas Malthus ingeniously proposed that the schools would lower the rates of infant mortality by making it impossible for parents to count on a sizeable direct gain from their children's labor, thereby introducing an element of sexual restraint. Parents now had to support their children while the state educated them. The first public schools, run by religious communities for the benefit of the poor, suddenly became elegant institutions known for both discipline and scholastics. The wealthy became envious, withdrew their children from paying schools, and sent them to schools for the poor. Again, as in the case of the church's authority over marriage, the state moved in and appropriated this new form of education.

The foundation of modernity can be found in this attempt to reform the peasants who were being transformed into the working class. For centuries, the Western church had considered society not reformable, a *massa damnationis* as Augustine had claimed, and had graciously resigned itself to the sexual and marriage practices of the different peoples under its jurisdiction, as we observed in the high level of sexual tolerance in the Middle Ages of Europe. Society was regarded as corrupt but governable, baptized but not reformable. Suddenly, with the populations liberated from the traditions of kinship, the state, first in the ministrations of the church and later in its own institutions, saw its chance to mold society into its own image, beginning with the education of children. The idea of progress was born, and the old order, the *ancien regime*, was set aside with a new belief in the malleability of the child's body and mind.

The new technology of the child was later transferred to the home, where the medical profession focussed on removing children from the care of servants. The bourgeoisie characterized servants as being of a lower-class, coarser stock whose indulgence and neglect of their charges was apt to leave them malformed and capricious. In Europe of the Middle Ages, not only servants but also parents and relatives engaged children in sexual play, which was forbidden as soon as they reached puberty. As Aries (1962:106) pointed out, people then believed that the child before puberty was unaware of sex and incapable of either innocence or pollution.

The new pedagogues, vigorously promoting the new innocence of children, initiated a 200-year campaign against masturbation that brought all of one's emotions under suspicion and examination. The universal prohibition against playing with oneself promoted the conceptualization and intensification of the pleasure.

The burgeoning state took an immediate interest first in what Donzelot (1979) called the *preservation of children*. Reacting against the squandering of infant life in the cities, officials set up the first foundling homes for abandoned babies. At first, policy protected the identity of the donors, going so far as to install "turrets," turnstyles where mothers could deposit their babies without revealing their identity.

Donzelot (1979:26–30) wrote that the gimmick was such an overwhelming success that yearly admissions at the St. Vincent de Paul foundling home in Paris went from 3,150 in 1740 to 131,000 in 1859. Needless to say, the increase stirred a lot of official debate. The homes were so crowded that they began farming infants out to nurses. When word got out about this, mothers would deposit their babies in the homes, and then through third parties fraudulently retrieve the children and collect the nurse's allotment. Puzzled by the staggering rise in abandonments, officials appointed a series of commissions to investigate. In 1837, in response to the abuses, a report finally recommended that the foundling homes be replaced by a system of aid to *all* mothers at home, giving birth to the modern welfare system.

What also happened, according to Donzelot (1979:30–31), was the extension of state control over the rearing of the children of working-class families. A special, mother's branch of hygiene and family medicine created a special alliance between such mothers and the new branch of hygenic/preventive medicine. On the one hand, the new relationship transformed working-class mothers into state-supported nurses. On the other hand, this doctor/mother coalition gave women new status and support in their impoverished condition, further weakened the authority of fathers, laid the groundwork for women's suffrage and the feminist movement, and strengthened the alliance between the home and the state.

The new family became the focus of the state's interests in the social sector, made up of the working class and the uprooted, preindustrialized masses that flooded the cities and were a constant threat to the new industrial order.

On the one hand, the social sector was liberated from the constraints of the old regime but not yet committed to the new. Free to move from one city to another as they pleased, these yet-undomesticated hordes lived in rented hovels and wasted their wages at taverns and cabarets. They carried into the new age the promiscuous sociability of the Middle Ages, defying the standards for health and discipline demanded by an industrial society.

On the other hand, they were still committed to the values of the past. Because of the lack of dowries, males refused to marry, yet their patriarchal values caused them to beget countless children, who were abandoned at will or exploited for their labor. The state moved in to usurp jurisdiction over children.

Just as threatening to the new economy were the old kinship alliances and trade associations. The distinction between the old economy and the new state-supported economy was very clear. The social sector in the cities, along with the rural peasantry, offered formidable resistance to the new regime. When they were not threatening the new order with riots and uprisings, they provided the raw material for proponents of socialist and utopian schemes. In 1861, Louis-Arsene Meunier described the threat posed by "these families who people the suburbs of our great cities, the crests of our mountains, the environs of our forests, our seaports, mines, and factories, these entire races of bohemians, gypsies, or Egyptians who have preserved the customs of the barbarians in our midst, all these populations who have been weakened, dulled, and demoralized by the habits of vice and vagabondage" (in Donzelot, 1979:78).

The answer was, of course, moral education as applied in the schools, in the philanthropic efforts of industry and private associations of reform, and the ministrations of the church, the courts, social workers, and the medical profession. More and more, the close association of the family and the school was to be the focus of the new state's war on the ancient bonds of kinship.

As the rationales for the old patriarchy were set aside, new ones quickly took their place. The new definition of the home as the obligatory locus for sexuality created some unexpected problems. The breakdown of ancient communal restraints restored an almost absolute authority to fathers, who oftentimes exploited or neglected their children. The resulting concern of philanthropists and authorities resulted in a slew of laws passed in the 1900s regarding the protection of children, child labor, the contract of apprenticeship, the use of children by merchants and peddlers, the supervision of wet nurses, compulsory education, and so on. As Donzelot (1978:78) commented, these laws, ostensibly directed towards the welfare of children, resulted in the further weakening of the bonds of kinship, this time between parents and children.

The rigorous constraints of the new family brought an increased concern about *incest*. In the ancient scheme of things, the prohibition against incest was based not on the concern for children but on the concern for developing peaceful alliances between kinship groups. The tendency to marry closely among one's own kind and within one's village had long been resisted by church law, which in the Middle Ages went so far as to impede marriages to the seventh degree of consanguinity, which, if enforced, would have prohibited marriage to nearly everyone in the same county (Flandrin, 1979:28).

In the new scheme of things, however, the reasons for the incest prohibitions were not based on preserving alliances but on breaking them up, namely on weakening the authority of the father over children. The constriction of sexuality to the family, as Foucault (1978:109) remarked, made the home incestuous from the start. Incest is always there to be dealt with, an "obsession and an attraction, a dreadful secret and an indispensable pivot," making the family a hotbed of continual sexual excitement. The state moved rapidly to exploit the new laws against incest to wipe out the vestiges of kinship among the lower and working class homes. The prohibitions against incest are now directed at preserving the innocence and mental health of the child and punishing the perversity of the adult offender, but the courts still use these laws to intrude upon the families of the poor.

The concern about incest was accompanied by a century-long campaign to redesign the architecture of the homes, first of the middle class and then of the working class, to provide separate sleeping quarters for children. The first concern of the reformers was to get children out of their parents' beds. The second concern was not to remove children so far as to escape surveillance.

The effect of this new sleeping arrangement was both to intensify the sexual relationship of the husband and wife and to diminish the affectionate stimulation of children. The new doctrine of the innocence of children — and the new privacy afforded them — made them especially vulnerable to sexual abuse by adults. Exiled from the familial bed, children were deprived of the watchful protections of sociability and affection.

By desexualizing children and mystifying the sexuality of women, we reduced their status. Homes became schools of adult etiquette where infants were not treated as developing mammals but as undisciplined and wayward adults. In 1894, Luther Emmett Holt, Sr., published *The Care and Feeding of Children*, which was to dominate the rearing of children in North America with its last (fifteenth) edition published in 1934. The Dr. Spock of his time, Holt advised against rocking the infant to sleep, not picking it up when it cried, feeding it by the clock, and not spoiling it with too much handling.

John B. Watson (1928:83–87), then dean of North American behavioral psychology, published *The Psychological Care of Infant and Child* in which he advised treating children like young adults: "Let your behavior always be objective and kindly firm. Never hug and kiss them, never let them sit on your lap. . . . Shake hands with them in the morning. . . . In conclusion won't you remember that when you are tempted to pet your child that mother love is a dangerous instrument . . . which may inflict a never healing wound . . . which may make infancy unhappy, adolescence a nightmare . . . which may wreck your adult son or daughter's vocational future and their chance for marital happiness."

Much of this mischief was strictly enforced in the foundling hospitals, with the disastrous results as already noted. Unfortunately, it is still around, making its influence felt in the child care practices of our day. With medical experts and state agencies finally setting the standards for the care of infants and children, the most intimate claims of kinship over child care were finally vanquished.

The new alliance between the home and the state not only limited sexuality, but also affectivity, to the marital couple. The sexual focus of the new alliance — as the reward for the burdens of familial control and production — put more burdens on the sexual act than it was capable of bearing. Sex became the central concern of life and the touchstone of one's adjustment and performance in society. One can never have enough of it.

Germaine Greer (1984:237–238) noted: "Sexual activity, and by this is largely understood genital sexual activity, should begin early and ought to continue for the whole inordinately long lifetime of modern consumer man. The mass media are cooperating in a campaign to promote sexual intercourse among geriatrics, who now feel that they ought to be interested, just as definitely as people in peasant civilizations believe that to be interested in sex past the age of reproduction is comical." Deprived of familial powers of administration and the pleasures of children, the elderly have nothing left but orgasm. If genital activity decreases, steps must be taken "to rejig the circumstances," usually by way of fancy role-playing, sexual toys, pornography, wife-swapping, and the more intense spices of sadomasochism. Citizens shrink from no ordeal that their civic duty to orgasm might impose.

This concentration on orgasm brought a host of conflicts to the family, to which the medical industry was quick to respond. Doctors, priests, educators, psychiatrists, pastors, and other experts patiently listened to the long complaints of sexual suffering. It was, Foucault (1978:111) wrote, as if we had suddenly discovered a long-guarded and dreadful secret: The family was the source of all the misfortunes of sex. From the middle of the nineteenth century on, the family engaged in the most difficult confessions, "soliciting an audience with everyone who might know something about the matter, and opening itself to endless examination. The family was the crystal in the deployment of sexuality: it seemed to be the source of a sexuality which it actually only reflected and defracted."

Greer cited some of the immense social costs of our orgasmic priorities. The first and most obvious has been the highest rates of unwanted and illegitimate pregnancies in history: "No human society exists in which human beings may copulate at will; no human community has ever been organized around the principle of free love, or could be, as long as reproduction and sexual activity were inextricably connected. Marriage is a license to reproduce. Even in societies where sexual experimentation among young people is encouraged, the incidence of illegitimate birth is rare and disgraceful" (1984:84).

Unwanted and illegitimate children point to the rapid decline in the status of children in society. For mothers throughout the world working in factories, the bearing and rearing of children has been made a special burden. Unlike those kinship societies that celebrate pregnancy with a sense of excited anticipation that surrounds the expectant mother with the loving attention of friends, our modern world attaches no privileges to pregnancy and greatly limits the pleasures of motherhood. "From conception," Greer (1984:7–8) wrote, "pregnancy is regarded as an abnormal state which women are entitled to find extremely distressing . . . an illness, requiring submission to the wisdom of health professionals and constant monitoring, as if the fetus were a saboteur hidden in its mother's soma."

Orgasm has replaced the love of children as the social engine of the family. As Greer (1984:258) reminded us, "If all pleasure in babies has been destroyed, orgasm is the only alternative." The high incidence of violence and neglect visited upon children is but an expression of the new restrictions on familial affection. With affection so limited within the family, it is no surprise that people are now required to go to court to gain visitation rights with their grandchildren or that the pleasurable touching of children not one's own is regarded as child abuse. According to Greer (1984:7), "None of us thinks that one generation has a right to the children of the next generation, not only because it gives no help in raising children of the next generation but because in our view the exercise of such a right would represent an intolerable intrusion into the rights of the individual. Only two people have the right to want a child, its parents, and even then the father has no a priori right to want a child from an unwilling woman."

While Greer's description of the modern family seems bleak and overdrawn, she impressively stated the case of its own decadence. "The Caucasian race is nearing the end of a phase of unparalleled expansion," she wrote (1984:457). And the child-oriented societies are on the ascendancy.

The overcrowding of cities and the demands of industry caused the state to use the concept of the family as a technique for social discrimination and control. Those who were members of good families enjoyed a contract with the new state that guaranteed them health and pleasure along with material advancement, while those unable to maintain the good order of the family came under the state's direct tutelage as administered by the courts and social workers.

All of this contributed to the medicalization of sex and the psychiatrization of emotion. Foucault (1978:104–105) outlined the four political strategies in the new configuration of power:

(1) The hysterization of women's bodies, whereby women's bodies were considered saturated with sexuality, prone to illness, and confined to the domestic sphere of family and children.

(2) The pedagogization of children's sex, which held that practically all children are prone to engage in sexual activities of an unnatural sort, calling for the constant supervision by adults and the attention of the medical profession.

(3) The socialization of procreative behavior making couples now economically and politically responsible to a society that regarded birth control practices as pathogenic.

(4) The psychiatrization of sexuality that endlessly multiplied the aberrations of the sexual body (including homosexuality), creating new demands for technologies of correction.

What was involved here was the creation of sex itself. What began as the reform of the schools led to the desexualization of children and the creation of a new sexual technology. As a historical construct, sex was born as a great surface network of laws, pleasures, alliances, technologies, and science, all contributing to the sexual discourse and intensification of pleasure. The imposition of the repressions that began in the seventeenth century and their alleviation in the twentieth were all part of the same ongoing reorganization of society. Whether sex was being attacked by officials or being defended by the psychiatrists, the same thing was happening: for the first time people were talking about it.

The new state uses sexual differences as the basis for social differentiation, creating an aristocracy of sex. By the end of the eighteenth century, the upper and middle classes put their new sexual body up against the valorous blood lines of the nobles and the kinship of the peasants. The downfall of the *ancien regime* demanded a reexamination of all behaviors and the laws governing them. The localization of sexuality in the body demanded an intense review of the varieties of sexual experience by officials, doctors, and academics, who set about formulating laws, technologies, and therapies for their use and control.

By the end of the nineteenth century, the bourgeoisie put their pampered sexuality up against the "bad blood" of the lower classes and the degenerates. The criteria for social differentiation were not, as Marcuse (1966) and other Marxist commentators have thought, in the economic system, or, as North American sociologists have thought, in demographic changes, but in the state itself, which deployed the new sexuality first among the upper and middle class and later among the lower and working classes.

Foucault goes much farther than anyone else in saying that it is not just creation of the *meanings* of sex we are talking about but the reality itself. "All along the great lines which the development of the deployment of sexuality has followed since the nineteenth century," he wrote (1978: 152–53), "one sees the elaboration of this idea that there exists something other than bodies, organs, somatic localizations, functions, anatomo-physiological systems, sensations, and pleasures; something else and something more, with intrinsic properties and laws of its own: 'sex'." Always and everywhere, sex is an expression of the matrix of power that exploits both the restrictions of law and the promises of life and pleasure.

Following this line of thought, we can see that the major influences contributing to the homosexual role did not come down in a straight line from the oppressions of antiquity. The vestiges of Hebrew and Roman law that survived the liberality of the Middle Ages were among the first set aside in the age of revolution. The jurists of the modern age were interested not so much in preserving the laws of antiquity as in forming a new order of industry.

Neither can we fully accept the contention of Hocquenghem (1978) and other Marxist writers who claim that capitalism was to blame for the sexual constrictions of the modern family. Certainly capitalism was to blame insofar as it reduced the economic importance of the family. But more fundamental was a conflict between the modern state and the old order of kinship alliances, a conflict as much in evidence in Marxist countries as in capitalist ones.

We can now see why homosexuality constitutes such a threat to the modern family: It threatens the orgasmic integrity on which the family's contract with the state rests. As one of a number of sexual inadequacies, it represents a failure of duty.

In a more subconscious way, it also represents the values on which the new family depends. Itself a product of the new sexual discourse, homosexuality presents not so much a contradiction to the family as a reflection of its low regard for kinship, its suppression of affectivity, and its worship of orgasm. Homosexuality is feared not so much because it is a threat to family life but because it reflects its values so perfectly. What made the arrival of the gay role so very appropriate was the manner in which it supported the organization of the new state.

Foucault (1978:159) concluded the introduction to his history of sexuality by suggesting that one day in the distant future, people will look back and wonder how it was that we became so enraptured with "the shadow of sex" and dedicated all our skills to drawing out its truth and discovering its secrets. They will be even more astonished to learn that we did it all in the cause of personal liberation, not realizing that all the ruses employed down through the centuries to make us regard sex as important endowed the state with enormous concentrations of power.

VI. The Homosexual Discourse I: Kertbeny's Solution

There are practically no European groups, unless it be in England, and few if any other cultures elsewhere in the world which have become as disturbed over male homosexuality as we have here in the United States. — Alfred Kinsey

What was self-evident, natural, and not in the least sick did not re-quire an excuse through an explanation.... It was love just like any other love. Whoever could not or would not accept it as love was mistaken. — John Henry Mackay

The role of the family in the creation of the gay role was matched by the role of medicine. In the emergence of the modern nation-state, new intersecting lines of power, like a great matrix, descended upon our society, conveying new meanings and relationships on everything, en-titling them with a new social purpose. Unlike former alliances, the new state placed a much higher value on the human body as its most impor-tant resource, and much of its efforts at the realignments of power went into the redefinition of disease and the body.

Accompanying this intensification of power was the intensification of *abstraction*. Perhaps the most notable technique of power, abstraction renders an object *social* and *political* by making it a symbol of something else. We abstract the life and goodness from the earth and attribute it to God, while we attribute its death to the Devil, thereby rendering life and death more easily manipulated. The realities become the symbols, like variables in a computer program, pointing to that to which they have conveyed their significance.

If the primitive mind tends to project living spirits into objects, the modern mind replicates the process, symbolizing objects in a way coherent with the social and political order. Abstraction is always an act of power.

One of the most ancient forms of abstraction was the attribution of the woman's inferior status to her sexuality. The belief that attributed pollution to anyone tainted by menstrual blood was an important tool in the maintenance of patriarchal privilege. The church expanded its control over life by abstracting it, transforming the physical world into a symbol of the supernatural world. By abstracting the reproductive significance from marriage and referring it to the mystical union of Christ and his church, the church extended its control over the institution. By the Middle Ages, the church had successfully abstracted the main features of rural European societies: work, art, music, leisure, war, the seasons, the landscapes, the harvests, birth, illness, death, plants, and animals. As everyday material life became transfigured into a symbol of supernatural life, it was given unity and significance. It also came more easily under the control of the church.

The new states were quick to employ the techniques of abstraction. Under the old regime, wealth was represented in the display of livestock, wives, progeny, servants, land, and property. The new aristocracies of the commercial city-states such as Venice, Nantes, and Naples, however, were able to discard the trappings of wealth and often passed unnoticed on the streets among other citizens. They had effectively abstracted wealth from goods and referred it to their bills of exchange and bank balances, reducing their material possessions to the symbols of power. Wealth was also abstracted from labor, as Marx claimed. Labor was no longer esteemed for the utility or beauty of what it produced but for its ability to increase the productivity of money.

In the realm of human experience, behaviors became more and more abstracted and internalized. Love was abstracted from the practice of love and referred to the internal mystery of sex.

During the late eighteenth and early nineteenth century, doctors attempted to abstract disease from the diseased body and attribute it to the new concept of disease as a biological species somehow existing independently of the body. Previous to that period, health and disease were pretty much described as they were *experienced*, in terms of the symptoms of pain, fever, lesions, deformities, and disabilities. Except for a few common manifestations such as syphilis and the plague, all disease was considered the same; only the manifestations were considered different. The main source of the physician's diagnosis was the patient's own narrative description of his poor health. This narrative was then augmented by the physician's observation of the patient's general appearance and functions: skin color, urine, and stool. Only rarely did the physician bother to examine the patient's body or even ask him "where it hurt."

A thorough reorganization and rethinking of the body and disease accompanied the development of the new nation-states. In France, officials went so far as to close down all the hospitals and medical schools, which they felt were symbols of oppression, ancient dogma, and privilege. Everything was thought through and developed from scratch. In less than 200 years, diagnosis based on the patient's narrative and the physician's observations have been supplanted by judgments based on evidence provided by laboratory procedures and mechanical and electronic equipment. Technology itself—beginning with the microscope and stethoscope and coming up to computerized sonic scanners—was largely responsible for bringing about the possibility of directly "seeing" inside the human body. Technology appears to have taken over medicine, often affecting the physician's perception of the nature of an illness. The diagnostic tools chosen now select some aspects of the illness while excluding others (Reiser, 1978).

But technology tells us only one part of the story. Michel Foucault's account of the birth of clinical medicine (1973) described the mutation in the *discourse of disease* that was first necessary before doctors could look within the body to "see" the progress and function of disease. This did not take place until the end of the eighteenth century. Under the new regime, the emphasis was less on the health of the body than its *normality*, less on the internal organization of the body and more on the *medical bipolarity of the normal and the pathological*.

The medical reformers of the eighteenth century also looked upon diseases as distinct species and spent much energy in *nosology*, the classification of diseases, an activity borrowed from the field of botany. The doctors came to believe that each disease is a separate species with a life of its own, quite independent of the organs or body in which it resides.

Under this new paradigm, doctors were still classifying the diseases in terms of their perceived symptoms rather than their cause or function. For instance, there was a whole family of diseases named after different kinds of fevers, having nothing at all to do with the causes of the fevers. Not only that, but as Foucault (1973:117–119) explained, they reduced the diagnosis to the simplest terms, using as few symptoms as possible to identify the disease. This led to a belief in the *alphabetical* structure of the disease, in which the symptoms had to follow one another in a perceived order, like the letters of a word, in order to point to a specific disease. Psychiatry would later take up this reductionist approach to mental illness, eliminating all but the simplest symptoms, which had to relate to one another in the right syntactical order.

Disease resided in two spaces: one, its taxonomic position in a family of diseases, and the other its place within the body. Foucault (1973:18–20) said that the new states added a third dimension: the institutional spatialization of disease that distributes different diseases to different institutions. Some are taken care of in the family, some in hospitals, some in clinics of different sorts, some in public buildings, others in private offices. He noted that the more complex the environment, e.g. a city hospital, the more *denatured* was the disease regarded and isolated from its natural home, the family, which the medical profession came to regard as the new locus of the health of the citizens of the new order.

The institutional spatialization of disease corresponded to the political agenda and the new concepts of the family. If the home was to be the best place for the control and cure of disease, it became necessary to institute more controls over the home. The new medicine had to be integrated into the social space in its entirety. The political concerns with disease conspired to give doctors control of the structure of the family.

There developed a medical consciousness that Foucault (1973:26) said provides information, supervision, and constraint, all of which relates as much to the police as to the field of medicine proper. Government entered into a new and expansive contract with the medical profession by which medical space became one with social space. Medicine became irrevocably politicized. The doctors of the last century had a naive vision of themselves as the creators of a disease-free society. But, to do that, they had to reform society itself. In 1792, Lanthenas published an article on the influence of liberty on health in which he said, "At last, medicine will be what it must be, the knowledge of natural and social man," a statement Foucault dubbed as "brief, but heavy with history."

Instead of directing its attention to the alleviation of human infirmity, "the dubious negation of the negative," as Foucault (1973:34) explained, medicine "was given the splendid task of establishing in men's lives the positive role of health, virtue, and happiness; it fell to medicine to punctuate work with festivals, to exalt calm emotions, to watch over what was read in books and seen in theaters, to see that marriages were made not out of self-interest or because of a passing infatuation, but were based on the only lasting condition of happiness, namely, their benefit to the state."

No longer concerned with curing ills, medicine now focussed on the morally healthy man, the model man, the normal man. Medicine assumed a normative posture in the ordering of society, not only distributing advice on how to live a healthy life, but also dictating standards for the physical and moral relations of the individual and society.

As medicine and science proceeded in the conceptualization of same-sex behaviors, law applied the corrective forms. The rise of the industrial state, the consolidation and centralization of power, the breakdown of the community, and the advent of global conflict changed forever how people viewed sexual conduct.

As John Boswell (1980:271) noted in his work on Christianity and homosexuality, "Much of this codification and consolidation of power entailed loss of freedom for distinctive and disadvantaged social groups." Among the groups losing power during that time of emerging nationalism were the poor, Jews, and, of course, women. Erving Goffman (1963:7), writing on the increased demands for conformity in the modern state, also noted the new significance attached to normality:

The notion of the "normal human being" may have its source in the medical approach to humanity or in the tendency of large-scale bureaucratic organizations such as the nation state, to treat all members in some respects as equal. Whatever its origins, it seems to provide the basic imagery through which laymen currently conceive themselves. Interestingly, a convention seemed to have emerged in popular life-story writing where a questionable person proves his claim to normalcy by citing his acquisition of spouse and children and, oddly, by attesting to his spending Christmas and Thanksgiving with them.

The nineteenth century was, after all, the age of science, believed to be the solution to all the problems of society. The medical profession was keenly intent in classifying sexual behaviors, motivated by the desire to provide the state with new concepts of morality.

Shibutani (1961:19) wrote that sociologists in the last century, mimicking the biological sciences, often attempted to isolate common regularities found among different social problems as their underlying cause. There was the underlying assumption that "the things men do are manifestations of regular processes, and that the task of social scientists is to isolate and describe these uniformities."

Concerning the validity of this transference of biological science to the study of human behavior, Shibutani (1961:19) remarked: "It is unlikely that reliable generalizations can be formulated about acts that are superficially similar but basically different. Students of human behavior are just beginning to look beneath the apparent similarities which form the basis of many common sense concepts. In all probability men do act in an orderly manner, but most of these regularities are not yet discernible because of the faulty concepts being used."

What Barry Adam (1978:35) called "the logic of biologization," or Conrad and Schneider (1980) called the "medicalization of deviance," tended to deny the influence of individual choice as a cause of behaviors and preferred, instead, to place the cause in medical factors. Today we are more apt to see drug abuse and alcoholism not in terms of vice or wasteful habits (or possession by spirits, as did our ancestors) but in terms of a medical problem. By abstracting addiction from the *behavior* of ingesting addictive substances and referring it instead to the substances themselves, the state clears the way for medical intervention and control.

Carol Tavris (1982), in her book on anger, says that the legal system has abstracted the emotion of anger from behavior and is able to use it as a mentally disabling condition that reduces freedom of choice. In the "Twinkies defense" of Dan White's murder of San Francisco Supervisor Harvey Milk, low blood sugar joined "temporary insanity," "passion," and intoxication as restrictions on the legal competence required for the commission of a crime.

The medicalization of deviant behaviors found support in the new concept of *affinity* or *propensity*. Language previously made no distinction between the *pleasure* derived from an object and the acquired *taste* for the object. In Latin, one word, *gustus*, meant both. The new medical approach abstracted the pleasure from the act of being pleased and referred it now to a deeper taste or affinity for the object, something that could warrant medical attention.

David Matza (1969:90–93) remarked about the new paradigm of deviant pleasures:

> The idea of affinity has been the key element in the staple explanation of becoming deviant. It has been the ascendant conception at least since the rise of positivism. . . . Affinity is a simple and fairly useful conception. Persons, either individually or in aggregates, develop predispositions to [a] certain phenomenon, say, delinquency, as a result of their circumstances. . . . Thus, the underlying conception of those who utilize the idea of affinity is attractive force. This seems well-suited to the study of objects. . . . A human affinity does not exist as a force separate from the persons that harbor it. Instead, it may be regarded as a natural biographical tendency born of personal and social circumstance that suggests but hardly compels a direction of movement.

In medieval Europe, sexual behavior, like disease, was undifferentiated and undefined. Contemporary observers were rarely descriptive of sexual acts. Their comments merely referred to the "pleasures of gender" that took place in the public baths or the "unmentionable excesses" of the universities.

For centuries, sodomy — always vaguely defined — was outlawed on the same basis as onanism: They violated the demands of exogamy and patriarchy on which society was based. The wasting of the male "seed," believed to be the singular cause of conception and birth, was a particularly heinous offense among the Hebrews. Sodomy was condemned, not for its connotations of disorientation, but for violating the dignity of the passive male in treating him as a woman. The manner in which people then identified gender behavior with kinship alliances increased the abhorrence.

The significance that modern people attach to sexual desire would have been meaningless to their ancestors. What made sexual activity wrong to the Greeks was not the type of pleasure involved but any kind of excess. What made it wrong to Catholic theology was the violation of the norms of alliance. It had nothing to do with orientation, same-sexness, or feelings. On the contrary, emotional/erotic feelings between members of the same gender were generally regarded as normal and part of love, so ordinary as to rarely merit comment.

The Catholic church never outlawed homosexuality as such, nor did it ever ban any expression of affectivity between members of the same sex.

The various practices that we place under the term "homosexuality" were described and regulated with other terms.

Violations of gender norms were seen as "sins of the flesh," that is, as related to the earthly pleasures of gender, children, family, and kin. An appreciation of the familial connotations of sexual pleasures helps us to understand the uneven and contradictory attitudes of the church toward sexuality in the Middle Ages. Boswell (1980:269–302) claimed that both religious and civil attitudes towards homosexuality were rather lax during the Middle Ages. Greek sexual practices, in fact, enjoyed something of a revival during the tenth century in Europe. No one saw this development as a threat to the family or the social fabric. The legal and severe punishments for sodomy were rarely imposed. When they were, they were as apt to be imposed on heterosexual offenders as homosexual ones, and they were usually associated with charges of heresy or conspiracy against the state.

The scientific discourse of sex was unknown in the Middle Ages. The pleasures of gender were contained within the constraints of alliance and existed in a familial realm in which the needs of the commonweal had little significance. People did talk a lot about marriage and the scandal of children born outside of marriage. But sexual activities themselves were ignored, as we today maintain a collective ignorance about the functions of elimination.

This was to change in the self-consciousness of the Renaissance, with its studied glorification of ancient Greek culture and its individualism. It was the Age of Revolution, however, that marked the real beginnings of the new sexual discourse.

After the French Revolution, French jurists were determined to rid the law of its royalist and ecclesiastical vestiges. Since no one then knew of any social or medical justification for the ancient prohibition against sodomy—which had always escaped precise definition—the Napoleonic Code enacted on 22 February 1810 did away with not only the death penalty but all other punishments for private acts between consenting adults, establishing the same rights to privacy for the individual citizen that heretofore had been the privilege of royalty. For the first time, in Europe, homosexual crimes and heterosexual crimes—those involving youths and violence—were put on the same footing.

A whole new sexual technology appeared in which sex became a secular concern of the state. As we saw in the last chapter, the new technology centered on the sexuality of children, the medicalization of women's sexuality, and the regulation of births. As Foucault (1978:117) explained, the medicine of sex was set apart from the medicine of the body, abstracting a sexual "instinct" capable of many diseases of its own. Heinrich Kaan's *Psychopathia Sexualis*, published in 1846, was representative of the new medicine, an orthodoxy of sex that opened up a medico-psychological realm of sexual perversions, supplanting the old moral realm of debauchery and excess.

The doctors went even further to establish a link between sexual diseases and somatic diseases, a connection that was to dominate not only medicine and psychiatry but also jurisprudence, social work, and corrections almost until the 1940s. This theory of "degenerescence" associated the sexual excesses of one generation with the diseases of the next and vice-versa. Look into the genealogy of a homosexual, they said, and you will find a parent with emphysema or an uncle with psychosis. Or, one's sexual excesses will emerge as physical deformities in his own descendants. The theory of degenerescence conveyed a biological responsibility to the orthodoxy of orgasm. Although lacking in any scientific or moral evidence, the theory furnished an entire social practice with a form of state-directed racism. The medical focus on sexual perversions and government-sponsored programs of eugenics were the main occupations of the technology of sex in the latter half of the nineteenth century.

In the United States, this typology was the cause of the infamous Tuskegee Syphilis Study. Initiated by the Public Health Service in 1932 among 400 black sharecroppers in Alabama, the study sought to determine the effects of syphilis if left untreated and guaranteed that the men would never be treated for the disease. Allan Brandt (1985:158) reported: "During the forty years that the Tuskegee Study continued, it was widely reported in medical journals without raising any significant objections on the part of the professions. Indeed, only reports of the study in the general press in 1972 finally brought it to an end. . . . These assumptions about race and venereal disease, like syphilophobia, had the effect of making these infections a problem of morals rather than medicine."

Foucault (1978:120) pointed out that the only technology of Western medicine that stood up against the nonsense of degenerescence was the work of Freud. But his antidote—the medical classification of mental disorders—was almost as bad. While denying the function of heredity in most of the diseases of the mind and putting the emphasis on repression, Freud tended to classify the "health" of the emotion by its object. What turned a person on became more important than what he did. The net effect of Freud's teaching was to draw the attention away from homosexuality as a behavior and focus on the imaginary internal condition.

The enthusiasm for the classification of mental diseases focussed on the anomalies of sex, especially homosexuality. A typical example of the new enthusiasm was found in Carl Westphal (1833–1890), a professor of psychiatry at Berlin. In 1869, he published the case history of a young woman who, from her earliest years, liked to dress as a boy, cared more for boys' games than girls', and found herself attracted only to females. Westphal thought there was a congenital condition here, with no wrongdoing implied. He called the condition "contrary sexual

feeling." According to Bullough (1979:8), his work led the way to more
open discussion of such phenomena among scientists.

This more open discussion among scientists was matched, during the
latter half of the nineteenth century, by a repressive new legalism. In the
German states, the imposition of the Prussian Code nullified the
Napoleonic reforms, and sodomy again was recriminalized in Law #143.
German writers began to develop their own argot and to challenge the
new law. The beginnings of the homosexual discourse can be traced to
the arrest and trial of painter Karl Ernst von Zastrow in Berlin in 1869
for his alleged sex-murder of a 16-year-old youth and the attempted sex-
murder of a 6-year-old boy. Despite the questionable evidence, Zastrow
was sentenced in October of that year to 15 years of prison. Activists came
forward and began publishing a new defense of same-sex practices. Vern
Bullough (1979:6) notes in his history of homosexuality that

> One of the first to do so was Karl Heinrichs Ulrichs (1825–1895), who,
> under his own name and under the pseudonym Numa Numantius, poured
> out a series of polemical, analytical, and theoretical pamphlets about
> homosexuality in the years between 1865 and 1875. Ulrichs argued that the
> instincts he found in himself were not "abnormal" but were inborn and
> therefore natural. He was also concerned with attempting to find non-
> derogatory terms to describe individuals who had sexual preferences like
> his own. He coined the term *urning*, from an allusion to the god Uranus
> in Plato's *Symposium*, to describe homosexual individuals. Not content
> with this, he developed a whole vocabulary: a *Muningin* was a female
> homosexual; a *dioning* (after Dionysius) a heterosexual male; a homosex-
> ual who preferred effeminate males a *mannling*, and one who preferred
> powerful masculine types a *weibling*. There were many others.

Another writer to attack Law #143 at the time of the Zastrow trial
was Karl Maria Kertbeny (1824–1882), who published two pamphlets in
1869 in which he coined the words "homosexuality," "homosexual," and
"heterosexuality." He wrote:

> In addition to the normal sexual urge in men and women, Nature in
> her sovereign mood has endowed at birth certain male and female in-
> dividuals with the homosexual urge, thus placing them in a sexual bond-
> age which renders them physically and psychically incapable — even with
> the best intention — of normal erection. This urge creates in advance a
> direct horror of the opposite sex, and the victim of this passion finds it im-
> possible to suppress the feelings which individuals of his own sex exercise
> upon him (in Bullough, 1979:8).

While Ulrich viewed homosexuality as a normal condition, and
Kertbeny as a diseased condition, they were both caught up in the
medical beliefs of the day. If only the true "nature" of the behavior were
understood, they thought, society would drop its fearful attitudes. As

German writer Manfred Herzer (1985:13) commented: "The two pamphlets against #143 were not the first occasion for Kertbeny to express himself on what he named homosexuality. There is a fascination in reading the earlier passages and guessing at the difficulty he must have felt as he searched for the right expression for this condition." Kertbeny expressed on more than one occasion the conviction that the suppression of homosexuality was the result of the prevailing "confusion of ideas" and the lack of clear concepts about the "condition" which afflicts some people. If concepts were only clearly and rationally ordered, he felt, then rational order would be restored.

The fault of Kertbeny's reasoning was not so much that it was based on his "naive idealistic Enlightenment viewpoint," as Herzer claimed, but that he was taken in by the medical vogue of the time, obsessed with the naming of diseases. In his attempt to abstract the social opprobrium from the behavior and attach it to an internal condition, he both created and named the sexual disease the psychiatrists were looking for. He reduced the cause of a whole range of despised behaviors to a single, uncomplicated explanation: the "homosexual urge." Whether the "urge" referred to the pleasure itself, the perverse orientation of the appetite, or something else was not important then. The important thing was that it had been identified as a disease, offering the possibility of a cure.

Kertbeny's new term, "homosexual," was not taken seriously by the medical profession until the turn of the century, when it reappeared in psychiatric textbooks. This time, however, it was loaded not with Kertbeny's emancipatory appeal but with the weight of psychiatric pathology.

We should not think that Kertbeny was alone in creating the concept he named. He merely provided the word for which society was ready. His solution is an example of Foucault's theory of sexual discourse, in which the themes of liberation and oppression simultaneously serve the cause of power. The conceptualization of homosexuality as a disease did not take it out of the domain of law but instead invited the medical profession into the business of correction. The homosexual discourse stimulated at once new regulations and the intensification of pleasure.

Herzer concluded his discussion of Kertbeny's solution with comments on recent changes in the meaning of the German word "schwule" (now somewhere between "queer" and "gay"). He suggested that we continue to make the same mistake in believing that new refinements of expression and new words such as "gay" will somehow eliminate the oppression. The new, self-designated words, like the older words that preceded them, only confirm the fact of the oppression without eliminating it. Herzer (1985:20) wrote: "Words can only have the value that people attribute to their factual content. The euphemism that is intended to soften the ugly reality with beautiful new words is at best ineffective, and at worst a lie."

While gay activists of our day reject the disease concept of homosexuality, they have forgotten that the term itself was first conceived as a disease by the first gay activists in order to decriminalize the behavior. The gay community, however much it may protest the *disease* concept of homosexuality, still supports the concept of homosexuality as a *medical condition* that explains if not excuses the behavior.

The strategy can never work. The evil created by society is not cured by abstracting it from the behavior and attributing it to an internal condition. The problem is with society and the belief in homosexuality.

The medical concept of homosexuality is what gave birth to the new legal oppression. As Foucault (1973:163) pointed out, the church did not bother to condemn doctors opening up corpses until after they began doing it. "The moral obstacle was experienced only when the epistemological need had emerged," he wrote. "Scientific necessity revealed the prohibition for what it was: Knowledge invents the Secret." New knowledge of the homosexual condition intensified both the pleasure and society's oppression.

English diarists had reported the existence of what would now be called gay bars frequented by working-class clientele in large cities in the eighteenth century. Edward Ward, in the *History of the London Clubs* (1709), described the "Mollies Club," which met in a certain tavern of the city for "parties and regular gatherings." The members were described as adopting "all the small vanities natural to the feminine sex." The same club was later discovered and broken up by agents of the Reform Society. During the nineteenth century, policing of gay night spots later came under public control.

In 1828 a committee of the House of Commons in England was appointed by Sir Robert Peel, then Home Secretary, to investigate the causes of "vice" and the ineffectiveness of the constables in controlling it. The following year, as a result of that study, the famous Metropolitan Police Act was passed, which established in London a police force separate from the old constabulary and which served as a model for police forces throughout the whole United Kingdom.

A similar pattern of reform prevailed in the United States, where, in the early nineteenth century, the growth of cities called for daytime deployment of peace officers. Historical criminologist John Gillin (1926:263) wrote: "The constables might serve very well in the country for the serving of summonses and other papers, but they were men otherwise employed and could not give all their time to the work of preserving the peace and catching criminals."

Philadelphia and Boston were the first to establish a daytime police, and New York and Cincinnati soon followed. Somewhat later, the police were assigned to night duties and replaced the night watches. In 1844, New York became the first city to combine the day police and the night police into one force. This signaled the end of the watch system throughout the country. From that time on, all the leading cities of the country would have a unified police system under a chief or a commissioner.

The efforts by Sir Robert Peel in England to make the streets safe for people to go out at night, along with similar efforts in the United States, probably has as much to do with the development of the gay role as anything else. For the first time, cities had a way of enforcing the laws against unpopular sexual activities. The frequent raiding of gay establishments was to provide employment for the police right up to our own time.

In England, the year 1830 marked the last invocation of the old law against sodomy (which made no distinctions between men and women). In 1861, the Offences Against the Persons Act replaced the death penalty with ten years to life for the same offense. And in 1885, Henry Labouchere introduced his famous Amendment to the Criminal Law Act (which mainly had to do with prostitution). This revival of a dead-letter law against "gross indecency" was specifically aimed at male homosexuality by bringing males under the law with offenses punishable by two years hard labor. In 1898, the laws on solicitation for immoral purposes were extended to include males.

The discourse of law was matched by a new liberal sensibility within Western centers of learning. Spokespersons of the new sexual freedoms were the Oxbridge group in England, of which Oscar Wilde was a member, Stefan George-Kris in Germany, Walt Whitman, Edward Carpenter, Rimbaud, Verlaine, Proust, and later, Gertrude Stein, Cocteau, and Gide. This intellectual development was accompanied by the increasing visibility of unusual lifestyles. Mary McIntosh (1968) wrote of the manner in which male prostitutes became less feminine and more masculine during the eighteenth and nineteenth centuries in England.

On the top of all this came the highly publicized trials of Oscar Wilde. Their importance in the crystalization of the gay role can hardly be overstated. Oscar Wilde was condemned to two years in prison in 1895, and many of his academic friends were silenced or driven into exile. As one London newspaper editorialized the day after Wilde's conviction:

> England has tolerated the man Wilde and others of his kind too long. Before he broke the law of his country and outraged human decency he was a social pest, a centre of intellectual corruption. He was one of the high priests of a school which attacks all the wholesome, manly, simple ideas of English life, and sets up false gods of decadent culture and intellectual debauchery (in Adam, 1981:25).

What marks this event so well was the collaboration of Wilde himself in its execution. He had no need to parade his lifestyle before the public nor to bring Queensbury to trial. He could have easily avoided the case brought against him, as his friends advised him to do. He acted as if he had no idea of how depraved his lifestyle seemed to his contemporaries. When he saw the case going against him, he was rude to the court.

The whole of this episode, Wilde's subsequent self-exile in Paris, and the drinking which led to his early death are testimony to the role he had chosen. There is no question that Wilde's arrogant display of bad taste — and the discourse it stimulated throughout the English-speaking world — greatly enhanced the warrant of the state to further intrude into the lives of citizens.

Was it that the sexual freedoms — like the Jews, who had also been emancipated by the Napoleonic Code — had suddenly become "too visible" and triggered the new oppression? Or was it that, for the first time, people were beginning to identify same-sex behaviors as distinctive, a process to which the law, the professions, and the people all contributed?

Barry Adam (1978:25–27) traced this tandem development of the homosexual discourse and oppression:

> In Germany, a movement for gay emancipation formed in 1897 called the scientific-Humanitarian Committee which launched a petition campaign. Yet homosexuality proved a convenient charge when a Social Democrat newspaper sought to discredit the government. From 1906 to 1909, such charges led to purges in the aristocracy, civil service, and military. During the Weimar Republic, some thirty gay periodicals appeared and the gay movement enjoyed Communist support until the end of the Leninist period, when the Scientific-Humanitarian Committee and Wilhelm Reich's Sexpol movement fell from favor.
>
> The accession of the Nazi Party to power led to the immediate suppression of organized gay life and the destruction of the Committee's Institute for Sexual Science with a public burning of its books. The systematic extermination of gay people began with the "night of the long knives" when Hitler eliminated his rival, Rohm, and several thousand others, charging homosexuality. More than 200,000 died under a diet-and-work regimen designed for their extermination.
>
> The postwar period, however, did not bring emancipation for gay people, who were denied compensation for their camp experiences. In the United States, the McCarthy investigations of "un-American" activities purged suspected Communists and gay people from the civil service, cultural institutions, and the airline industry. Small-scale witchhunts recurred to terrorize gay people. John Gerassic documents the moral crusade of an American town in the 1950's, which led to numerous arrests, evictions, dismissals, and prison terms of five years to life, for vaguely supported accusations of consensual homosexuality.
>
> Psychiatric, social, and biological sciences declared homosexuality a hormonal imbalance, genetic disease, "mental illness with psychoses or feeble-mindedness," the result of "alcoholic indulgence," or "brain damage."...

Small gay societies for mutual support and legal reform formed during the late 1950's and 1960's. In 1969, the "Stonewall Rebellion," where New York gay people collectively resisted a two-day police assault, marked the beginning of the modern gay liberation movement.

The term "homosexuality" for a long time was not widely accepted in medical circles. Havelock Ellis used the term in 1937 (*Studies in the Psychology of Sex*, II, IV: 2) but observed that "'homosexual' is a barbarously hybrid word, and I claim no responsibility for it."

The term "homosexuality" did not appear in the official list of emotional disorders until the 1940s, when it appeared in a supplement. Even as the term "homosexuality" came more into use, however, it was heavily laden with the concept of gender inversion, as was the term "gay," which outdated the term "homosexuality" by several centuries and served as a popular catch-bag for ambiguous gender behaviors.

In Britain, an important chain of events was set off by the arrest and imprisonment of the young Lord Montagu for a homosexual affair. In 1954, as a result of the debate which ensued, a Royal Commission was set up under Sir John Wolfenden, vice-chancellor of the University of Redding, to study the problem of homosexuality. In 1957, after 62 meetings, the famous Wolfenden Report recommending the abolition of all laws against consenting adult sexual acts was made public. But it was not until 1967 that Parliament got around to making homosexuality legal.

A similar but much less publicized event took place in the United States when the American Law Institute proposed a Model Penal Code which legalized consenting adult sexual activity. The ensuing attempts in various states to implement the provisions of the Model Code did much to publicize the existence of the new homosexual: a person of ordinary dimensions, not a prostitute or transvestite, whose only distinction rests in his sexual orientation.

Ironically, it was Alfred Kinsey who did most to vindicate Kertbeny's solution. His pairing off of homosexuality against heterosexuality as opposite poles on the sexuality scale did more than anything else to identify them as two separate mental conditions. His protests against the medical use of the terms to describe an internal condition fell on deaf ears. His attempt to stretch the meanings of the terms to include only behaviors and not a medical condition was offset by a century of contrary usage.

John Marshall, in "Pansies, Perverts and Macho Men: Changing Conceptions of Male Homosexuality" (in Plummer, 1981), supported the claims of the gay liberation movement that a change took place in the conceptualization of homosexuality in the second half of the twentieth century. Before the 1960s, he wrote (p. 146), "The link between 'true' homosexuality, effeminacy in men and cross-dressing, which this account implies, suggests that the distinction between homosexuality and transvestism had not yet been clearly articulated."

Here we see Kertbeny's mistake repeated. It does no good to transfer the public disapproval of homosexuality from effeminacy to sexual orientation. The cause of gay oppression is not the mistaken belief that male homosexuals are like women or that lesbians are like men. The cause of gay oppression is public disapproval of homosexual activity. People may perceive homosexuals as mutants or confused as to gender, but only because they first regard homosexual behavior as abhorrent. Society does not condemn homosexual behaviors because it does not understand them, but because it sees them as a threat to important social values.

Kertbeny's mistake emerged again in "New Styles in Homosexual Manliness" in which Laud Humphreys (1971) wrote of the "masculinization of homosexuality." It would be more accurately described as the abstraction of pleasure from behavior and its assignment to the medical condition. The masculinization of male homosexuality has not relieved people of their fears of homosexuality in the least. It has only increased them by referring the cause to a hidden, often "latent," and vaguely conceived cause: sexual orientation.

The creation of the gay role followed the development of medicine and psychiatry in the last century. In the concern to identify sexual anomalies as specific mental diseases, the medical profession hit upon the term "homosexuality" as fitting their needs. Public officials, doctors, jurists, and professors directed their attention to the new definition in dramatic moves that served to redefine the function of the family as an agency of the state. The gay role was born, not out of the religious prohibitions of ancient societies, but out of the secular needs of the modern state.

By way of a medical footnote, we need to mention the work of Francois-Joseph-Victor Broussais, who, in his 1808 reexamination of the concept of fevers as diseases, struck the death knell for the essentialist view of disease. Foucault (1973:174–192) claimed that this work laid the foundation for the most remarkable revolution in modern medicine. Broussais' *Examen de la doctrine medicale* (1816) rejected the ancient medicine of diseases as specific entities and proposed a medicine of sick organs, one in which the disease follows the paths not of their own but of organs coping with stress. (We may draw comparisons with the interactive approach that was to follow nearly a hundred years later in sociology.)

Broussais' solution was not well accepted by his contemporaries, who launched frenzied attacks against his "physiological" medicine. Eventually, however, it vanquished all opposition, finally opening up the body to the gaze of medical science.

We wonder why psychiatry is taking so long in rejecting the concept of mental disorders as borrowed from classificatory medicine. The answer lies in the social mandate to define and enforce normality. Psychiatry, closer aligned to this normative mandate, is less free to investigate or cure. The essentialist concept of mental illness still dominates the field because of stigma, a technique of social control that predates psychiatry by many millenia. We now turn our attention to the first and most important component in the construction of the gay role, but the final component in our understanding of it.

VII. Stigma: The Making
of Strangers

*By transferring to the scapegoat his own inner craving for deviance
and promiscuity, the stigmatizer is cleansed of his evil desire. Once
again, the deviant's relationship to the group is to offer salvation
through pollution.* — S. Giora Shoham

*Of all vulgar modes of escaping from considerations of the effect
of social and moral influence on the human mind, the most vulgar is
that of attributing the diversities of conduct and character to inherent
natural differences.* — John Stuart Mill

While the sexual discourse reveals the content of the gay role, the
beliefs and behaviors that comprise it, it is stigma that defines the form
or structure of the gay role, attributing proscribed behaviors to the inherent differences of those who defy the norm. The analysis of the stigma
reveals to us how society uses stigmatized persons in its efforts to control
behavior.

Our society puts males into a double bind. On the one hand, we have
a high level of competition and hero worship that would seem to encourage erotic feelings of aspiration and emulation. On the other hand,
sanctions against that type of feelings are very high. The record shows the
sanctions are very effective, considering the high level of homosexual
motivation. Tripp (1975:77) pointed out:

> In America, for instance, at least fifty out of a hundred men admit
> being, or having been, sexually attracted to other males, and yet few of
> these "give in" to their response and only three or four of them turn out
> to be homosexual in the usual sense. Given this heterosexual success of the
> mores, the exceptions are what need to be accounted for: By what manner
> of individual psychology does a person in our society become predomi-
> nantly or entirely homosexual? — is something the matter with his back-
> ground, with his personality, with both, or with neither?

Much of the recent literature on homosexuality tends to ignore any
discussion of the ban, as if the authors were embarrassed to acknowledge

the human pain and suffering of their subjects. This attitude is also prominent in the gay press, whose business-as-usual promotion of gay entertainments, night spots, travel, and resorts reflects the siege mentality of the citizens of Beirut or Belfast. The human condition can tolerate the contemplation of only so much pain, and bunker diversions are necessary for survival.

The gay community is a country under siege. A number of states, nearly half, still have laws against adult homosexual conduct. Even in those areas where sex between consenting adults has been legal for some time, public attitudes regarding homosexuality have changed little. And there is every reason to believe that the AIDS crisis will serve only to escalate the fear of homosexuality.

The ban affects gay-identified persons so deeply that they take it for granted. Albert Memmi (1965:321–22) remarked that over time the oppression has a cumulative effect on the minds of the oppressed:

> The longer the oppression lasts, the more profoundly it affects him [the oppressed]. It ends by becoming so familiar to him that he believes it is a part of his own constitution, that he accepts it and could not imagine his recovery from it. This acceptance is the crowning point of oppression.

So thoroughly has the oppression become a part of what it is to be gay, gays are not so sure they are ready to pay the price of freedom.

In another work, Memmi (1968:88) wrote about the tendency to believe that new laws bring instant liberation:

> As for most social romantics ... the victim remains proud and intact through oppression; he suffered but did not let himself be broken. And the day oppression ceases, the new man is supposed to appear before our eyes immediately. Now I do not like to say so, but I must, since decolonization has demonstrated it: this is not the way it happens.

Barry Adam (1978:5–6) continued on Memmi's theme that we must not ignore the continuing casualties of oppression:

> A certain romantic liberalism runs through the literature, evident from attempts to paper over or discount the very real problems of inferiorization. Some researchers seem bent on "rescuing" their subjects from "defamation" by ignoring the problems of defeatism and complicit self-destruction. Avoidance of dispiriting reflection upon the day-to-day practice of dominated people appears to spring from a desire to "enhance" the reputation of the dominated and magically relieve their plight. Careful observation has been sacrificed to the "power of positive thinking."

Effective political strategy demands first of all the clear understanding of the dynamics of the ban, which subtly draws attention from the

98 Gay Identity

behavior and emphasizes, instead, characteristics of the oppressed person. In these next two chapters, we will look at the power of the ban to objectify homosexual experience by means of the gay role.

The ban works through the creation and implementation of deviant roles. ("Deviance" is used here not in a moral sense of right or wrong but in the sociological sense of socially outlawed behaviors.) Deviant roles are negative roles, anti-roles in the sense that they remove esteem rather than confer it; they are loaded with negative social meanings.

Deviant roles are not negative in function, however. They have an important purpose: They define the lines between acceptable and unacceptable behavior — lines which define the uniqueness of society.

The features that characterize each society and its special genius are due to something besides geography and the physical resources available. More than anything else, the distinguishing character of each society is determined by its list of forbidden behaviors, the "thou-shalt-nots." The general tendency of most laws governing personal conduct is not to tell us what we have to do but what we can't do.

Howard Becker (1963:9), in his famous work on stigma, said that deviance is defined not by a quality of the act or of the person who commits it but by what society defines as deviant. Deviance defines the inside and outside of a society, not only the good from the bad but what we stand for, the "us" from the "not us." In a very real way, the official regulatory systems in charge of defining deviance preserves the separateness of each society from all the rest.

But a society does more than make rules; it must also enforce them. Among the methods of enforcement, none is as ancient or as effective as stigma, the marking of outlaws. Even in our secular, unbelieving world, stigma retains its preeminent position as the enforcer of social boundaries. Instead of just disposing of offenders, stigma puts some of them to work by keeping them around as examples of what can happen if you don't behave. The special roles we create for offenders of social norms are called stigmatic or deviant roles. People so marked are called deviants. As Sagarin (1975:15) explained:

> One of the most effective methods of keeping most people in line is to throw some people out of line. This leaves the remainder not only in better alignment but at the same time in fear of exclusion. It is in this view of the world that deviance emerges as something that is useful to the continuity of an ongoing society. By reacting in a hostile manner to those who are not the good and proper, a majority of the people or a powerful group may reinforce the idea of goodness and propriety and thus perpetuate a society of individuals who are more conforming, more obedient, and more loyal to their ideology and rules of behavior.

A letter I recently received from a playful friend illustrates the social utility of deviant roles. Assuming the character of a minister in charge of a nationwide temperance campaign, my friend explained that he was aided in his soul-saving by an assistant, Clyde, "a pathetic example of a life ruined by over-indulgence in coffee, tobacco, whiskey, and women." This wretched figure would sit on the lecture platform to serve as an example of what such wicked ways could do to a person. The letter went on to say that Clyde had unfortunately passed away; the minister had been referred to me and wondered if I might "take Clyde's place for the remainder of the 1985 tour."

We can appreciate the minister's loss. The effectiveness of his hapless assistant is an object lesson in the function of stigma. There is a social truth in this tale, as if it follows a standard script, evoking images of drunks and winos from real life as well as literature, drama, and film. It also evokes images of fiery preachers, tent meetings, and the whole campaign for temperance. The two images seem to go together, the abject deviant and the self-righteous moral reformer, as if both of them came out of the same ancient archetype.

Indeed, the human brain may be anciently programmed for stigmatic images such as these. Perhaps in the brain there is a special place for storing the images of society's misfits and the proper way to respond to them. Whatever the biological mechanism, the practice of stigmatizing is universal. Stigma underlies and antedates the function of law. Louis Wirth (1931) wrote about the ability of some societies to get along without law altogether:

> The ethnological evidence ... seems to indicate that where culture is homogenous and class differences negligible, societies without crime are possible. A small compact, isolated, and homogenous group seems to have no difficulty in maintaining its group life intact, in passing on its institutions, practices, attitudes, and sentiments to successive generations and in controlling the behavior of its members.... The community secures the allegiance, participation, and conformity of the members not through edicts of law, through written ordinances, through police, courts and jails, but through the overwhelming force of community opinion, through the immediate, voluntary, and habitual approval of the social code by all.

In our modern dedication to individualism, we tend to ignore the sacral forces of stigma that we still exploit for the purposes of social control. These forces are often the subject of plays and films in which a community or a mob turns violently against an innocent stranger. Some writers have described the forces of stigma in mystical terms as having a personality and will of their own. Sociologist Leonard Matza gave the name Leviathan to society's intractable and powerful will, which is determined always to have its way.

For almost a century, the study of stigma has occupied a central place in sociology, not just because of its role in controlling human behavior but also because of its central role in defining society itself. The word "stigma" is borrowed from the practice in many societies of physically branding or marking those who break the law. The marking not only served as a kind of punishment, but it also reminded the community of the boundaries of acceptable behavior. As Erving Goffman (1963:3) explained:

> The Greeks used the term *stigma* ("mark") to refer to bodily signs designed to expose something unusual or bad about the moral status of the signifier. The signs were cut or burnt into the body and advertised that the bearer was a slave, a criminal, or a traitor — a blemished person, literally polluted, to be avoided, especially in public places. . . . Today the term is widely used in something like the original sense, but is applied more to the disgrace itself rather than to the bodily evidence of it. Furthermore, shifts have occurred in the kinds of disgrace that arouse concern.

In all societies, any kind of unusual appearance or behavior puts one at risk. The Greeks spoke of "chopping off the tallest heads of corn." If a person was too wealthy, too tall, disfigured, or handicapped in any way, he might be suspect and his social standing placed in jeopardy. But it was the violations of known regulations which brought the mechanisms of stigma into play most forcefully. The transgressor was seen to be *polluted*, spoiled by the violation. The concept of pollution is still dominant in the Christian concept of sin, which initiates a change in the person, the loss of grace, which can only be restored by reconciliation with the community. People still talk about feeling soiled by their misbehavior.

The idea of pollution is closely related to *xenophobia* or fear of strangers. There is an inherent need, not only to consider one's own culture the best, but also to regard the people of other cultures as inferior, even less than human. It is common among all peoples, not just primitive societies, to regard themselves "the real people" and refer to others as animals, dogs, ghosts, or otherwise lacking in humanity, grace, or sophistication. One of the first effects of stigma, whether it be the physical marking of ancient societies or the social marking of modern ones, is to confer the status of an outsider or stranger upon the accused offender.

Marvin E. Wolfgang (in Shoham, 1970:vii) emphasized the importance of the new *status* conferred by stigma:

> The social function of branding some segment of a society is as old as our knowledge of man's collectivity. Stigmata have been placed upon one or another group of deviants as a measure of segregating them in the minds of men in whose midst the branded are still permitted to dwell. The process of stigmatization can be physical, quick in time, permanent; it can also be subtle, informal, slowly developed. From the branding of the flesh to oral derogation, men have known the consequences of being denoted a

deviate. Stigma may be a form of retribution, of an untoward social classification that substitutes for more rigorous restraint of deviants, that replaces incarceration as a means of retaining social distance.

Books on the sociology of stigma are full of the examples of stigma, such as the ones pointed out by Shlomo Shoham (1970:130–137):

> Historically, the mark of Cain signified a *nonexpiated* murder, crime, or sin. . . .
>
> In England gunpowder was used to brand thieves, burglars and sodomites. Paint was used as a branding agent in Greece and ink in China. In the U.S., branding was employed for pirates, runaway slaves, and horse thieves. The common denominator seems the derogatory nature of the offenses so that the branding tends to perpetuate and formalize the pollution and turpitude of their perpetrators. The Roman *infamia* also highlights the pollution element in formalized stigma by inflicting it on persons of shameful trades, dismissal in dishonor from the army, and misconduct in family relations.
>
> In Florence the bankrupts, the financial failures, were the most hated and despised and a degrading public flagellation was meted out to them. Ranulf cites Berger that in medieval Europe, Jews, prostitutes, and the hangman were branded by the necessity to wear a particular dress. The common denominator of all three is presumably their turpitude and pollution.
>
> In the Jewish community of Castilia in the fifteenth century, the informers were branded with a hot iron and prostitutes in the Jewish community of Prague had to leave the community after the Day of Atonement; those who remained were branded on their forehead as a sign of pollution.
>
> In later days black signs of turpitude were posted in synagogues in Europe, naming persons who dressed extravagantly, spent conspicuously, or polluted themselves by drink and entertainment in non-Jewish houses. Here again conspicuity and pollution are represented in the formal stigma on the black signpost. . . . The heretic is formally stigmatized because his *acedia*, his standing apart, spells danger to the flock of unbelievers. . . .
>
> Maimonides grades the formal stigmata used against those who blasphemed or slandered the rabbinical authorities. The more severe was the *nidui*, by which an individual was publicly expelled from the synagogue. If the heresy was severe, and in fact it was measured by the individual's contrariness against the rabbinical power elite, he was branded with *shamta*, a personal sign of infamy. The *shamta* has been described as "a prison without a lock," as "iron chains which are invisible but a person feels them binding him." These are vivid and picturesque descriptions of the socially stifling effects of formal stigmata. . . .
>
> Excommunication in the ecclesiastical courts in England was what outlawing was to the temporal courts. As to the severe temporal consequences of excommunication we have Bracton's assurance that "an excommunicated person cannot do any legal act, so that he cannot sue any one, though he himself can be sued . . . for except in certain cases it is not lawful either to pray or speak or eat with an excommunicate either openly or secretly. He is a man who has *a leprosy of soul*. . . ."

The essence of outlawry has been properly described by Pollock and

Maitland as follows: "He who breaks the law has gone to war with the community; the community goes to war with him. It is the right and duty of every man to pursue him, to ravage his land, to burn his house, to hunt him down like a wild beast and slay him; for a wild beast he is."

From the descriptions of stigma certain common characteristics emerge. The concept of *pollution* arises from the idea that "there must be something wrong" with one who chooses to defy the will of the community. The person has "gone over the line" and is now outside the pale of social control, qualitatively altering the way others perceive him. The removal of legal rights and the denial of social esteem accompanies stigma in all societies. The person marked as an enemy of the community is stripped of the rights and protections normally offered to citizens.

If all this seems too far removed from modern society, we should consider the frequent abuse of offenders at the hands of the police and guards in the criminal justice system. Such abuse is often taken for granted and even defended as necessary by wardens, as society turns the other way in spite of the laws against such practices.

We also associate moral turpitude with a whole cluster of other unflattering attributes. We perceive public offenders as shorter, uglier, misformed, sick, disturbed, maladjusted, passive-aggressive, and annoying to be with. It is as if our esteem of the marked individual is altered by a filter inside our head that prompts automatic feelings of disgust, fear, or pity. Such is the power of deviant roles to influence our perceptions.

Becker (1963:33–34) wrote that the ban assigns a "master status" to the deviant role that overrides all the other roles and governs the way others perceive the labelled person. Whatever was the status of the person before being apprehended, whatever his talents or skills, the accused person now stands in a special way for the deviant behavior itself. His other attributes lose all significance.

We cluster deviance. Because the stigmatized offender is now an object of *mistrust*, we regard him as morally flawed and suspect of every wrong. People tend to perceive gay-identified persons as mentally ill, emotionally crippled, neurotic, sexually confused, promiscuous, unfulfilled, parentally fixated, unhappy, obsessed, lonely, depressed, and incapable of relationships.

In a remarkable study done at the University of California at San Francisco, Rodney Karr found that men who were labelled as homosexual were seen by others as significantly less masculine and less preferred as partners in experiments. Karr (1978:74) pointed out that so powerful is this effect that "fear of the label homosexual with its connotation of sex-role violation appears to function to keep men within their traditionally defined roles." He noted that when a male is accused of being homosexual, it often causes him to act in a more masculine manner.

In his classroom experiment, Karr (1978:79) found out that some people actually sit farther away from members of the experiment who were labelled as homosexual during a brief absence from class. Those who had difficulty relating to the one labelled homosexual also had more difficulty in solving the experiment "problem." Most significant were the verbal expressions of the way the participants felt about the one who did the labelling and the labelled. The primary labeller was seen as being taller, larger, stronger, more handsome, more powerful, more violent, more impulsive, more rugged, more active, more friendly, less sad, faster, and louder. The labelee was seen as being dirtier, softer, more womanly, more tense, more yielding, less rugged, more passive, and quieter.

We have here verification not only of the power of stigma to reduce status, but also its power to enhance the status of those who do the labelling. Karr stated (1978:81–82), "The experiment results reflect a difference in attribution by the perceivers, not any change on the part of the labelee.... That groups of men function less efficiently when they believe a homosexual man to be present speaks to the power that the homosexual label has for men."

The conversion of the homosexual role into a deviant identity is due in large part to this ability to cluster behaviors, assigning them to a single role serving as the shorthand for lazy minds. The gay role shares with other deviant roles the assignment of degrading differences that are seen as inherent, constitutional, and absolute. Barry Adam (1978:43–51) wrote about the similarities attributed to Jews, gays, and blacks in our society: They are considered subhuman ("medieval debates centered around the question of whether, like animals, Jews, sodomites, or savages could have souls..."); believed to engage in "uncivilized" behavior; "hypersexual"; "heretics and conspirators"; and overly visible ("all three groups have a reputation for offensive flamboyance").

Sociologists ask, "What distinguishes the offender from the rest of us?" Objectively speaking, it is not the impulse to do evil which is characteristic of the offender. There is no evidence that he "felt" any more like violating the law than anyone else did. We all have tendencies to do such things, at least in fantasy. What distinguishes the offender is not just that he got caught, but that he has been labelled and stigmatized as an offender.

A more revealing question is, "What distinguishes the stigmatizer from the rest of us?" Because some people spend a lot of energy repressing desires in the attempt to be social, they look for a release valve, a scapegoat onto which they can vent the inner aggression and negativity caused by the repression. There is a well-known correlation between righteous indignation and the repressed desire to violate the norm. People are loudest in demanding external controls and punishment for those norms that threaten them the most. As Shoham (1970:99–100) explained:

Stigma as an outlet for aggression and projection of guilt: inner aggression and the projection of guilt for the stigmatizer's own deviational tendencies are the subconscious sources of social stigma. On the subconscious level the urge to stigmatize is presumably linked to the inner aggression of individuals and groups.... The stigma is a subconscious substitute for the sanction that the stigmatizer wishes to inflict upon himself....

Albert Memmi (1968:191–193) stated that the self-accusation implicit in the act of stigmatizing is obvious in the need of the racist to justify the exploitation of his victims:

Why does the accuser feel obliged to accuse in order to justify himself? *Because he feels guilty toward his victim.* Because he feels that his attitude and his behavior are essentially unjust and fraudulent. Here, in fact, we must turn the racist's argument inside out: he does not punish his victim because his victim deserves to be punished; he calls him guilty because he is *already* punished or, at best, because he, the accuser, is preparing to punish him.

Proof? *In almost every case, the punishment has already been inflicted.* The victim of racism is *already* living under the weight of disgrace and oppression. The racist does not aim his accusations at the mighty but at the vanquished. The Jew is already ostracized, the colonized is already colonized. In order to justify such punishment and misfortune, a process of rationalization is set in motion, by which to explain away the ghetto and colonial exploitation.

And so the oppression perpetuates itself, sometimes long after the original reason for the domination has been lost. Because people are treated badly, they must be bad.

A notable feature of stigma is that it must be imposed by someone in *authority*. If culture or society is defined as a system of meanings and understandings about behavior common to a group of people, then the shaping and promulgation of those meanings engages those who speak for society itself. However we feel about what goes on in the halls of government or the acts of authority, it is in them that we are defined and created as a people.

The definition of social boundaries is a complex and formal affair. Usually, an educational process is necessary to convince the community that the old rules and values are no longer sufficient. Kinsey (1953:665) took note of the inherent problems that accompany such reformist campaigns:

The police force and court officials who attempt to enforce the sex laws, the clergymen and business men and every other group in the city which periodically calls for enforcement of the laws — particularly the laws against sexual "perversion" — have given a record of incidences and frequencies in the homosexual which are as high as those of the rest of the social level to which they belong. It is not a matter of hypocrisy which leads officials with homosexual histories to become prosecutors of the homosexual activity in the community. They themselves are the victims of the mores, and the public demand that they protect those mores. As long as there are such gaps between the traditional custom and the actual behavior of the population, such inconsistencies will continue to exist.

Reformist campaigns follow a familiar scenario. It may begin with a hideous act of violence or a revolting sex crime. Every sector joins in the outrage, demanding retribution. A suspect is produced, tried, and convicted. A moral entrepreneur arrives on the scene, campaigning for tougher laws and punishments. Politicians and editors rake over alternatives. After a period of public debate, the governor appoints a committee to study the matter and take it under advisement.

For months after the offender has been sent off to prison, meetings are held, experts are brought to testify, and the responses of other communities are studied. A report is drawn up and presented to the legislature. By the time the new law is enacted, the original clamor has been forgotten and the new law receives barely a line's notice in the press. But a new standard of public morality has been created. The police have been given new powers, which they will employ long after people have forgotten the outrage over the original incident.

Several authors have called our attention to the *political utility* of stigma. The defining of deviance is a *symbol of power* and often the object of intense political rivalry. The imposition of a new stigma—or its prevention—has often defined the limits of a political contest. Edwin Schur (1980:24–25) called this the "politicization of deviance" and wrote, ". . . the designation of deviance and the deviantizing of individuals involve the exercise of power and affect the subsequent distribution of power." Stigma is often "the object of conflict and disagreement, part of the political process of society. . . . Both sides . . . [seek] moral dominance; both may try to use political means toward that end."

Schur cited a wide range of modern "maladies" which have been successfully exploited by opposing groups for purposes of political gain, including homosexuality, abortion, dyslexia, hyperkinesis, and even the concept of mental illness. Today's examples would certainly include the political contest over the prohibition of abortion.

In the end, Schur (p.89) states, "society has the types of deviance with which it is preoccupied." Its attempts to "control" and "cure" deviance are rarely successful because they are merely different ways of describing the "problem." Prisons and mental hospitals do not eliminate crime nor cure mental illness precisely because they are not designed to. They are meant as concrete symbols of the boundaries of acceptable and negotiated standards of behavior peculiar to the community.

Others go beyond Schur's view and state that government is a participant in these contests as well as a mediator. Cynthia Enloe (1980:5) wrote about how both the police and the military use the issue of *ethnicity* in the creation and maintenance of power:

> Ethnic identifications can shape a state, but states more often than is recognized can and do shape ethnic identities and inter-ethnic relations. . . . The state, even highly centralized states such as France, Mexico, or the Soviet Union, derives its stability from a particular pattern of societal stratifications. If those stratifications shift, the state will be in jeopardy and state elites will attempt to adjust or re-entrench the stratification system.

Enloe (1980:11) cited recent studies which draw attention to the way in which "ethnically designed militaries are frequently used by governments to exert and maintain their authority." Such relationships are as significant in North America as in the Third World.

The modern creation of an ethnic group out of the concept of homosexuality serves to support the centralizing function of state-building. The elimination of homosexuals from both the military and the police are the "official" definitions of this process. As racial groups are being effectively integrated into these public services, a new "outside" group is being carefully defined to support the claims of the state.

Another characteristic of deviance is the *selectivity* of enforcement. Once the rule is effected, it must be enforced, but selectively. Effective execution of the ban demands a great deal of selectivity. Out of all the violations of a norm, only a few violators are publicly apprehended or accused. Bronislaw Malinowski, in *Crime and Custom in Savage Society*, told a story illustrating the selectivity of stigma enforcement among the natives of the Trobriand Islands in the Pacific near New Guinea. Malinowski related that one day during his stay in a particular village, there was a commotion, and he was told that a young man had committed suicide after he had been accused of having a secret affair which violated an exogamy taboo. That morning, the female partner's rightful boyfriend had accused him of the crime in public. The accused young man soon after climbed high into a coconut tree, and after addressing those gathered below, flung himself down to his death.

Malinowski (1926:80) wrote that it was obvious that the facts would not tally with the ideal of conduct. Public opinion was neither outraged by the knowledge of the crime to any extent, nor did it react automatically. Instead, it had to be mobilized by a *public statement* of the crime and by insults being hurled at the culprit by the offended party. This set in motion a dynamic so powerful that the culprit carried out his own punishment.

Malinowski commented that the breach of exogamy — as regards intercourse and not marriage—was by no means a rare occurrence, and public opinion was usually lenient, especially if the affair was carried on with a certain amount of decorum without stirring up a lot of public reaction. The same sort of "collective ignorance" often protects those engaging in homosexual behaviors. Members of the family, employers, or coworkers will often suspect or subconsciously know about such behaviors for long periods of time, but regard them with much tolerance. But open admission of such behaviors dramatically changes the situation, and such behaviors suddenly become a "problem," demanding some kind of sanction.

Becker pointed out, "The point is that the response of other people has to be regarded as problematic. Just because one has committed an infraction of a rule does not mean that others will respond as though it has happened."

Kinsey (1948:18) pointed out that our best efforts in arresting sex offenders will round up only a very insignificant number:

> The prodding of some reform group, a newspaper-generated hysteria of some local sex crime, a vice drive which is put on by local authorities to distract attention from defects in the administration of the city government, or the addition to the law-enforcement group of a sadistic officer who is disturbed over his own sexual problems, may result in a doubling—a hundred percent increase—in the number of arrests on sex charges, even though there may have been no change in the actual behavior of the community, and even though illicit sex acts that are apprehended and prosecuted may still represent no more than a fantastically minute part of the illicit activity which takes place every day in the community.

The reasons why all the known offenders are not always brought to justice are very practical. First of all, if everyone who had committed a crime were arrested, we would all be in jail at one time or other. Secondly, society needs the presence of deviants to justify itself and to objectify its values. In a real sense, it must engage the support of the deviants. Stigma doesn't work if the stigmatized offenders disappear.

Thirdly, the community must create the impression that deviant behavior is an *exceptional* occurrence in order to support the illusion that the system is effectively controlling crime. Enough people have to be arrested to maintain the illusion of public danger, but not too many. The public would stop supporting the police system if the actual extent of crime were widely known or appreciated. For example, the claim that 20 percent of the women in our society have been molested as children tends to give the impression that the problem is endemic and incapable of solution.

Selective enforcement also enters into shaping the content of the type of deviance involved. In an important essay on "The Ironies of Social Control," Gary Marx (1981) noted the manner in which the acts of officialdom often create new opportunities for deviance. Law-enforcement strategies such as surveillance, entrapment, and "covert facilitation" can actually encourage deviant conduct and make some forms of deviance more attractive than others.

A final reason for selective enforcement is the dramaturgical function of stigma. Confrontation between authorities and transgressors must be properly staged, especially for heinous crimes. Enforcement is selective because its main purpose is not the control of proscribed behaviors but the creation of warning signals and the enhancement of power.

The creation of stigma demands a certain amount of staging. Elements must take place successively in a prescribed order for the public scripting of the deviant role. Kai T. Erikson (1964:13-15) wrote that the transactions taking place between deviant persons and agencies of control—trials and punishment—in the past took place in the public market and gave the crowd a chance to participate in a direct, active way. Even today, an enormous amount of modern "news" is devoted to reports about crime and other forms of deviant behavior, constituting "our main source of information about the normative contours of society. In a figurative sense, at least, morality and immorality meet at the public scaffold, and it is during this meeting that the community declares where the line between them should be drawn."

The staging of the arrest, interrogation, booking, arraignment, trial, conviction, and imprisonment is designed not only to humiliate and depersonalize the suspect, but also to create the impression of gravity and dead seriousness about the "proceedings" for the benefit of the audience: the world beyond the courtroom.

The artificiality of these proceedings has been celebrated for as long as they have been around. The grave demeanor of judicial figures has never failed to entertain us—in medieval carnivals, Gilbert and Sullivan operas, and television's "Night Court"—precisely because it reveals the inherent artificiality of society itself. David Matza (1969:163) wrote about the *superficiality* of officialdom: "Being authoritative is the most superficial feature of authority. . . . Dressed properly and acting his part, the personification of authority, whether policemen, judge, or someone else less notable, impresses; by being impressive, he helps a bit to cast the deviant in the deviant part."

The gravity of being arrested is not to be denied. One's first arrest is often the cause of great depression and anxiety. The sudden removal from one's surroundings and friends, the loss of personal freedom, the humiliation of strip-searches, and the confinement to vile lodgings are aimed at the modification of identity and fashioning a new relationship between the accused and society.

The element of surprise usually characterizes the arrest. The offender must be caught off-guard and not be apprised beforehand about any hunt, warrant, or charges. Surprise is necessary not only to prevent escape, but to humiliate the suspect and create fear. When one is taken into custody, he is not told what is about to ensue. He is merely told, "You are coming with us."

The imposition of stigma takes on the propriety, ritual, and seriousness of a surgical amphitheater, complete with duly authorized officiants. As the violation of the intimacies of the body lend a certain magical solemnity to surgery, in the courtroom the sacred intimacies of one's social identity are incised, opened to view and manipulation, radically severed, and closed back up. With conviction, the judge imposes a new social identity.

The roles of transgressor and judge are endemic, written into the basic scripting of society. The actors could easily change roles and carry them off perfectly. We all know the scripts; they have been duly impressed upon us since birth. Those who gravitate towards the criminal justice system as clerks, policemen, detectives, judges, attorneys, guards, or criminals bring with them credits and notices earned in earlier theaters.

Matza (1969:147) observed that the inflictors of stigma, in using the language of condemnation, are usually not aware of the impact that their words can have upon their victims; in calling a person a criminal, they may not know that they are contributing to the creation of a deviant identity.

The highly *symbolic* nature of what is going on here is evident in the manner in which the action is quickly telegraphed to the rest of the community. The scene is enacted for the benefit of the whole community. We must all be able to feel the shame of the accused and the outrage of the judge for the drama to be effective. Symbols proceed out of the courtroom into that bar of authority we construct within our brains. We are refashioned by these remarkable events.

In marking the criminal, the judge casts a spell on all of us, radically altering the way we perceive the offender. Whatever our own crimes as a collectivity, we can now redeem ourselves by pointing to this symbolic danger object that embodies the "not us," from which we gain a renewed sense of moral worth and identity.

A society often lays much stress on the historical charters, conventions, battles, and institutions that define its character. It may be that those confrontations that take place daily in the courtroom may be equally, if not more, responsible for defining the limits of acceptable behaviors. For it is in these primeval confrontations that illusions of the state's legitimacy are established and maintained. As Matza (1969:196) wrote, the final product of the stigma is the "collective presentation of concentrated evil, or deviation, and pervasive good, or conformity." On top of this comes the paramount implication that only through the efforts of a benign society will the evil be extricated and the deviant cured. "In that manner every contingency is covered," Matza wrote. "The benevolence of society and the wisdom of the state — are affirmed."

In its avid concern for public order and safety, implemented through force and penal policy, the state produces the appearance of legality and concern, in spite of its own propensity for war and terror. We learn the dramas of stigma easily, absorbing them into our lives and then passing them down to the generations that follow through legend, lore, ritual, law, and liturgy. The creation of deviant roles is a technique by which society saves face as it brings judgment against offenders. By casting them as inherently deformed, it justifies its action and, at the same time, offers a powerful deterrent to others. In this remarkable drama, deviance is put to work on behalf of social stability and becomes an important part of how we think of ourselves as a people.

VIII. Stigma: Adopting the Role

I had this feeling of relief; there was no more tension. I had this feeling of relief. I guess the fact that I had accepted myself as being homosexual had taken a lot of tensions off me. . . .
And I said to myself, there was the realization, that not all gay men are dirty old men or idiots, silly queens, but there are some just normal-looking and acting people, as far as I could see. I saw gay society and I said, "Wow, I'm home." — from "Coming Out in the Gay World" by Barry Dank

The crucial factor in being gay is not one's sexual inclinations or behavior but the process of coming out: adopting the gay role. The gay-identified person is not a hapless victim of genetic or social circumstances, but rather a central actor in a remarkable social drama. In the dynamics of stigma, we find the explanation of why, among those who defy society's disapproval and engage in same-sex behaviors, some of them perceive of themselves as homosexual and others do not. There are a number of strategies that can be used for neutralizing the ban, and adoption of the homosexual role is only one of them.

As we saw in the last chapter, the public assignment of a deviant label to an offender has a profound effect on the way he is perceived by the community. Signification automatically strips him of *grace*: personhood, the esteem of one's fellows, legal rights, and social rank. The labelled person now stands for the act itself. Like an antisacrament, the signification is effective *ex opere operato*, by the operation of the act itself, not depending upon the intentions of the signifyer, but only on the rituals of gravity employed in the apprehension and judgment of the accused.

It is as if our brain provides us with a capacity for filtering or masking our perceptions of others and our reactions to them. This filtering function responds to social cues and labels, greatly affecting the degree of esteem we offer others. As soon as we suspect that someone is a drug addict or alcoholic, we begin taking certain precautions and acting on prejudgments whether they are warranted or not. These stereotyping filters also diminish our esteem of blacks, Jews, the deformed, and gay-identified persons.

111

In all of these responses in which esteem is scaled down, there is a projection of some internal fault in the object, as if some dignifying life-force were deficient or missing. The term "personhood" comes to mind in the attempt to describe this focus of our esteem. Those whom we esteem highly, such as notable celebrities, are described as larger than life and charismatic because their personhood seems overflowing. At the same time, we project a diminished personhood on those who have offended our standards. In anger we can treat others worse than animals because our hatred has deprived them of personhood entirely. We degrade people so that we can punish them.

How can a person apply to himself a label that is so loaded with negative meanings? The answer will provide us with the key to understanding the gay role.

The response of a person who is publicly condemned and labelled is by no means automatic and is highly problematic. As the object of the stigmatizing act, he often differs with the judgment of his accusers on just *who he is*. He can feel guilty and repentant for his act, but at the same time reject the insinuation that he is different from or worse than others. He can resist the spell under which others fall so readily, protesting that the label is highly inappropriate. He may proceed convinced that his relationship with the offensive behavior act is only *incidental* and not significant in the sense of *pointing to something different within him*.

The first thing that we note about the adoption of the deviant label — as opposed to the judicial and public act of labelling — is the intentional and voluntary nature of the task. Unlike public signification, the process is effective in the manner that theologians once attributed to prayer and good works, not automatically but *ex opere operantis*, by the operation of the actor.

One of the best explanations of this phenomenon is found in *labelling theory*, at one time one of the hottest and most controversial subjects in sociology. The debate has cooled down somewhat, and labelling theory is one of the foundation blocks of modern sociology, corrected and absorbed into the social construction school of sociology.

Labelling theory began in the classic work of French sociologist Emile Durkheim, who held that crime is not so much the violation of a penal code as it is an act which causes outrage in society. Durkheim was the first to suggest, in his classic work on suicide, that deviance satisfies that outrage and thereby fills an important social function.

Edwin Lemert, in his work on social pathology (1951), explained how some persons come to adopt a deviant role, which he described as *secondary deviation*. Like other interactionists, he described how all deviant acts are *social acts*, the result of a cooperation among a number of people.

While doing research on heroin addicts, he observed a very powerful and subtle force at work. Besides the physical addiction to the drug, and besides the influence of economic and sociological deprivation found in many histories, there was also an intensely *intellectual* process at work, involving the identity of the actor and his rationalization for the deviant behavior.

Lemert (1951:74) said it is easy to understand how a disadvantaged child may be "educated" in deviant behavior, growing up, as he does, in an alienated marginal group. How others are initiated into deviant behavior is a more intriguing process of constructing a *deviant role*:

> The importance of the person's conscious symbolic reactions to his or her own behavior cannot be overstressed in explaining the shift from normal to abnormal behavior or from one type of pathological behavior to another, particularly where behavior variations become systematized or structured into pathological roles. . . . But however it may be perceived, the individual's self-definition is closely connected to such things as self-acceptance, the subordination of minor to major roles, and with the motivation involved in learning the skills, techniques, and values of a new role.

Lemert claimed that students of human behavior have developed a myriad number of theories about the origins of deviant behavior, and that there are as many theories as there are authors. The confusion, he wrote, was the result of confusing the *original* causes with *effective* causes. There might be certain subjective and personal motives which might first lead a person to drink or shoplift. But the activity itself tells us little about the person's self-image or his relationship to the activity until, Lemert wrote (1951:75-76), the acts are repeated and

> . . . organized subjectively and transformed into active roles and become the social criteria for assigning status. . . . The deviations remain primary deviations or symptomatic and situational as long as they are rationalized or otherwise dealt with as functions of socially acceptable role. Under such conditions normal and pathological behaviors remain strange and somewhat tensional bedfellows in the same person. . . .
> However, if the deviant acts are repetitive and have a high visibility, and if there is a severe social reaction, which, through a process of identification, is incorporated as part of the "me" of the individual, the probability is greatly increased that the integration of existing roles will be disrupted and that reorganization based upon a new role or new roles will occur. . . . *When a person begins to employ his deviant behavior or a role based upon it as a means of defense, attack, or adjustment to the overt and covert problems created by the consequent societal reaction to him*, his deviation is secondary.

Lemert (1951:76) wrote that the adoption of a deviant role usually comes after a period of intense consideration: "Most frequently there is a progressive reciprocal relationship between the deviation of the individual and the societal reaction, with a compounding of the societal reaction out of the minute accretions in the deviant behavior, until a point is reached where ingrouping and outgrouping between society and the deviant is manifest." But, he wrote (1951:74), after that period of consideration and "negotiating" with society on the terms of the role, the actual adoption of the role can take place in an instant: "Self-definitions or self-realizations are likely to be the result of sudden perceptions and they are especially significant when they are followed immediately by overt demonstrations of the new role they symbolize."

A deviant role constitutes a *master status*, because of its tendency to encapsulate and dominate the other roles and priorities. Lemert (1951:77,89–90) explained:

> The most significant personality changes are manifest when societal definitions and their subjective counterpart become generalized. When this happens, the range of major role choices becomes narrowed to one general class. . . . After a person achieves, accepts, or is compelled to adopt an aberrant role, an integrational process comes into play wherein the other roles played by the individual are segregated out or subordinated to the major role. Subjectively a status personality materializes out of the unorganized or organized behavior which prevails during the transition from one role to another.

Sara Fein and Elaine M. Nuehring applied Lemert's doctrine to the case of gay identity in their article "Intrapsychic Effects of Stigma: A Process of Breakdown and Reconstruction of Social Reality." Applying labelling theory to the gay role (1981:4–6), they stated that the gay role assumes this master status and becomes the principle around which other roles are organized. This reorganization brings its own new set of problems and restrictions:

> To acquire a stigma, persons who consider themselves heterogenous must be placed with others in a single category and assumed to be homogenous with them; a widely held set of interpretations and negative valuations must be associated with that social category; and the typified characteristic must be seen as a master status, i.e., the most important of the individual's characteristics. . . .
>
> Placement in a social category constituting a master status prohibits individuals from choosing the extent of their involvement in various categories. Members of the stigmatized group lose the opportunity to establish their own personal system of valuation and group membership as well as the ability to arrive at their own ranking of each personal characteristic.
>
> This external challenge to individuals' freedom of choice sets the stage for a breakdown in their personal systems of valuations, producing a "crisis-in-thinking-as-usual." . . . The social interpretations and valuations

accompanying that category, although very different from one's own, impinge upon one's personal system of valuations. Stigmatized individuals are forced to question what was previously taken for granted and to doubt the validity of their personal systems of valuations or recipes for action (typical ways of bringing about typical ends). . . .

For example, newly self-acknowledged homosexual individuals cannot take for granted that they share the world with others who hold congruent interpretations and assumptions; their behavior and motives, both past and present, will be interpreted in light of their stigma.

Lemert emphasized (1967:48) that not only are deviant roles created by social stigma, but they are "assumed and sustained through antagonistic or degrading interactions with agents of respectable society. . . ." In other words, the negative interaction of stigma is interactive and current, not something dependent on values inherited from the past. Also, there is always some benefit gained in the adoption of a stigmatic role, which "may offer temporary or relatively stable solutions to life problems despite the fact that they offer a lower order of existence. . . . Thus becoming an admitted homosexual ('coming out') may endanger one's livelihood or his professional career, but it also absolves the individual from failure to assume the heavy responsibilities of marriage and parenthood, and is a ready way of fending off painful involvements with heterosexual affairs."

Lemert painted a picture of the world as a vast landscape of robust deviance, showing us all the ways in which human beings are violating social norms every day. How we symbolize and explain those acts to ourselves does not concern sociologists, he pointed out, until those acts are repeated and organized into observable social roles. So, the same deviant activities can have meanings that are quite different to individuals and to society.

A great deal of homosexual behavior goes on outside the gay community and without any reference to the stigmatic role. Those who are able to deny the stigma deny that their sexual activity violates their other roles or signifies that anything is different inside them. Fred Davis (in Becker, 1964) wrote about the extensive techniques employed by the visibly handicapped to remove the stereotype that people attempt to attach to physical deformity: "There is nothing wrong or different about us besides this physical problem," that is, physical difference has not diminished personhood. These techniques help others to normalize their perceptions of the visibly handicapped so as "to enforce a normalized projection of self." People don't like to multiply handicaps. The effort expended by the physically handicapped to deny the stigma is no surprise.

Laud Humphreys, in his work *Tearoom Trade: Impersonal Sex in Public Places*, revealed that a considerable number of married men regularly engage in homosexual activities in public restrooms. Humphreys was criticized much for his methods in this study, but most of all for failing to give us much information on the subjects' own accounts of their behavior. However, he did offer us (1970:119) one respondent's testimony:

> I guess you might say that I'm pretty highly sexed ... but I really don't think that's why I go to tearooms. That's not really sex. Sex is something I have with my wife in bed. It's not as if I were committing adultery by getting my rocks off—or going down on some guy—in a tearoom. I get a kick out of it. Some of my friends go out for handball. I'd rather cruise the park.

Among other examples of stigma denial are hustlers and prisoners. Albert Reiss wrote of an important study of young male homosexual prostitutes (hustlers) in "The Social Integration of Queers and Peers" (1961). Hustlers justify their activities by saying they are doing it merely for the money. Reiss stated that they are able to insulate themselves from homosexual identification through their social organization. Among the beliefs held by the peer group is the norm that sexual gratification cannot be actively sought, no affection is displayed, and the sexual transaction must be limited to fellatio. Other sexual acts are generally not tolerated. The hustler considers himself different from the "queer" client by adhering to these norms, by which his "masculinity" is preserved.

Prison is another place where extensive homosexuality can take place without adoption of the homosexual role. The homosexual activity in male prisons is often justified by the lack of female companionship. The sense of masculinity is preserved by configuring the activities that take place not as "homosexual," but as male and female, with the "male" taking the active role in anal intercourse or the passive role in fellatio. The "female" is whoever is taking the other role. Thus, the whole prison system is divided into "men" and "girls," the girls being anyone who is delicate, young or youthful-looking, the least bit effeminate, or a gay-identified individual.

There is a competition among deviant roles. As in the case of the physically handicapped, people choose not to multiply handicaps. One deviant role at a time is enough. Ned Polsky (1967:159), writing about the homosexual patterns among the beats in Greenwich Village, mentioned how they engaged in homosexual activities but avoided the role:

> In other words, an extraordinary number of male beats ... are fully bisexual or in some cases polymorphous perverse [an unusual clustering of Kinsey points two, three, and four]. They accept homosexual experiences almost as casually as heterosexual ones. Even beats with numerous and continuous post-adolescent homosexual experiences do not feel the need to define themselves as homosexuals and create some sort of beat wing of the

homosexual world. Beats not only tolerate deviant sex roles but, to a much greater extent than previous bohemians, display a very high tolerance of sex-role ambiguity.

Polsky's observation tends to confirm Donzelot's idea that the "social sector" of modern society is a leftover from the Middle Ages, with its polymorphous and patriarchal sexuality. Those with less stake in the family sector utilize values of a different age in which sexual behavior was not as socially significant. People in such levels of society go out of their way to minimize the sexual anomalies in order to give heightened meaning and strength to bonding forces.

We see the same bonding priorities in the upper levels of society, where patriarchal values remain dominant. Evelyn Waugh, in *Brideshead Revisited*, not once referred to the love affair that existed between Charles Ryder and Sebastian as homosexual. Evelyn Waugh was certainly aware of the term when he wrote the work in the early 1940s and was hardly constrained out of propriety. Terms such as "catamite" and "pansy" are found in the work, but not in reference to his young lovers. Rather Waugh resisted any temptation to label his subjects, probably because his well-to-do models in real life were able to avoid such labelling. Waugh explained this stigma denial in the words of lovely Cara, the "middle-aged, well-preserved, well-dressed, well-mannered" mistress of Lord Marchmain, Sebastian's father. "I know of these romantic friendships of the English and the Germans," she says in private conversation with Charles. "They are not Latin. I think they are very good if they do not go on too long. . . .

"It is a kind of a love that comes to children before they know its meaning. In England it comes when you are almost men; I think I like that. It is better to have that kind of love for another boy than for a girl." Waugh had no more to say on the subject other than that here were two young men deeply in love with one another.

As for the reactions of the Flyte family itself to the affair, they seemed to be considerably less embarrassed by it than by Charles' later affair with Julia, Sebastian's sister, when both of them were married to other partners. That scandal was so troublesome to the Catholic Flyte family that it dominated the rest of the story.

If it was Lemert who introduced the key concepts of labelling theory, then it was Howard Becker who became its recognized champion and began outlining the process of adopting a deviant role. Becker's first book was based on his study of professional dance musicians, with whom he once worked. He had recognized their tendency to separate themselves from the "straights" for whom they had to play regular dance music instead of the jazz they preferred.

Later, Becker studied the identity patterns of marijuana smokers.

This work resulted in the 1963 publication of *Outsiders*, which created a ferment of intellectual excitement. As Sagarin (1975:126) noted: "*Outsiders* was not merely a major theoretical contribution to the study of disvalued people; it was indeed a manifesto, and around its formulations there arose what came close to becoming, within sociology, a social movement."

Becker's opening manifesto (1963:9) set the stage for a theory of deviance that still dominates the human sciences:

> . . . *social groups create deviance by making the rules whose infraction constitutes deviance*, and by applying these rules to particular people and labelling them as outsiders. From this point of view, deviance is *not* a quality of the act the person commits, but rather a consequence of the application by others of rules and sanctions to an "offender." The deviant is one to whom that label has been successfully applied; deviant behavior is behavior that people so label.

Becker asked us to step outside the usual perception of the deviant as a person who has an unusual or abnormal need to commit a deviant act — as if he possessed some itch or impulse which the rest of us don't have. We have to look for, instead, "multivariate" causes of human behavior, with no one factor offering all the answers.

Secondly, we have to put the human being into a time dimension. Expanding Lemert's distinction between the original and the effective causes of deviance, Becker (1963:22) wrote: "All causes do not operate at the same time and we need a model which takes into account the fact that patterns of behavior *develop* in orderly sequence. In accounting for an individual's use of marijuana, as we shall see later, we must deal with a sequence of steps, of changes in the individual's behavior and perspectives, in order to understand the phenomenon." Becker introduced the concept of the deviant *career* as a dynamic and interactive process in which a person's commitment to deviance is subject to a wide assortment of changes over time.

In asking just what makes a person take the first step and commit a prohibited act, Becker (1963:26) reports:

> There is no reason to assume that only those who finally commit a deviant act actually have the impulse to do so. It is much more likely that most people experience deviant impulses frequently. At least in fantasy, people are much more deviant than they appear. Instead of asking why deviants want to do things that are disapproved of, we might better ask why conventional people do not follow through on the deviant impulses they have.

Becker (1963:26) suggested that people become normal exactly in the same way as others become deviant:

In fact, the normal development of people in our society (and probably in any society) can be seen as a series of progressively increasing commitments to conventional norms and institutions. (1963:26)

To put a complex argument in a few words: instead of the deviant motives leading to the deviant behavior, it is the other way around; the deviant behavior in time produces the deviant motivation. Vague impulses and desires—in this case, probably most frequently a curiosity about the kind of experience the drug will produce—are transformed into definite patterns of action through the social interpretation of a physical experience which is itself ambiguous. Marijuana use is a function of the individual's conception of marijuana and of the uses to which it can be put, and this conception develops as the individual's experience with the drug increases (1963:42).

Because everyone must defend his self-respect and integrity, the deviant actor must develop a rationale for his behavior that is at least convincing to himself. Becker (1963:2–3) explained:

Social rules define situations and kinds of behavior appropriate to them, specifying some actions as "right" and forbidding others as "wrong." When a rule is enforced the person who is supposed to have broken it may be seen as a special kind of person, one who cannot be trusted to live by the rules agreed on by the group. He is regarded as an *outsider*.

But the person who is thus labeled an outsider may have a different view of the matter. He may not accept the rule by which he is being judged and may not regard those who judge him legitimately entitled to do so. Hence, a second meaning of the term emerges: the rule-breaker may feel his judges are *outsiders*.

In spite of the great popularity of Becker's contribution to labelling theory, he and others supporting labelling theory were subject to a barrage of criticism. Sagarin (1975:129–142), summarizing the objections, wrote that labelling theory was accused of eliminating concerns about etiology and the personal responsibility of the deviant actor. Because of its emphasis on public labelling, it seemed to leave little room for secret deviance.

Instead of eliminating personal responsibility for deviance, labelling theory diminishes the importance of the original deviant impulse and puts the emphasis on meanings and the conversation explaining one's behavior, first to oneself and then to others. Sociology, as Lemert suggested, is not concerned so much with the etiology of an individual act so much as the causes of repeated acts that give rise to patterns of sociological significance. Becker (1973) answered his critics in a later edition of *Outsiders*:

Sociologists agree that what they study is society, but the consensus persists only if we don't look into the nature of society too closely. I prefer to think of what we study as *collective action*. People act, as Mead (1934) and Blumer (1966, 1969) have made clearest, *together*. They do what they do with an eye on what others have done, are doing now, and may do in the future. One tries to fit his own line of action into the actions of others, just as each of them likewise adjusts his own developing actions to what he sees and expects others to do. . . .

When we look at all the people and organizations involved in an episode of potentially deviant behavior, we discover that the collective activity going on consists of more than acts of alleged wrongdoing. It is an involved drama in which making allegations of wrongdoing is a central feature. Indeed, Erikson (1962) and Douglas (1970), among others, have identified the study of deviance as essentially the study of the construction and reaffirmation of moral meanings in everyday life.

Francis Cullen (1984:130), in appraising the fact that after 20 years labelling theory retains an unchallenged position in social theory, wrote that Becker was probably too generous here with his critics. While sociology after Becker has been increasingly concerned with deterministic manipulation of statistical research, his original insights about the contributions of labelling to the formation of deviant behaviors remain valid. Far from being supplanted, they have been corrected and absorbed into an expanded "structuring perspective."

Critics of labelling theory often object to its failure to explain secret deviance. How does one adopt a deviant role without having been publicly accused and labelled? The objection ignores the symbolic function of labelling. It is not necessary to apprehend every offender in order for society effectively to establish the signatory role. Public officials, striving to make "examples" of certain offenders, are much more effective at this than they realize. Their stigmatizing acts define and reinforce the stereotypical role, lodging it deep within the collective psyche. As we learn of a deviant activity, we have access to this collective psyche and become curious about our relationship to the behavior.

Those who are considering a secret deviant act are also placed in direct relationship with authority. David Matza (1969:163–164) is the writer who best described the transaction between the offender and authority:

> In shocked discovery, the subject now concretely understands that there are serious people who really go around building their lives around his activities — stopping him, correcting him, devoted to him. They keep records on the course of his life, even develop theories about how he got to be that way. So confident are they of their unity with the rest of society, so secure of their essential legitimacy, that they can summon or command his presence, move him against his will, set terms on which he may try to continue living in civil society, do, in short, almost anything of which only the mightiest are capable. What enormity has the deviant subject managed to uncover? Only the concrete reality of leviathan, armed with an authority more potent than his own.

Pressed by such a display, the subject may begin to add meaning and gravity to his deviant activities. But he may do so in a way not especially intended by agents of the state. . . . Impressed by the show of authority, persuaded of the gravity of his infraction, reminded of a unity of meaning, he may proceed inward. . . . Even without the explicit instructions of authority, implicitly he has already been turned in that direction: he has been made to feel self-conscious. He has been apprehended.

Burdened with the gravity of official judgment, the subject debates as to whether his behavior or his being is the source of concern. He can take this new gravity now applied to him and consider it as incidental to his personality. Or he can go the other way and begin to build identity: the gravity is located within one's being. Matza (1969:165–170) showed that it is in this internal dialogue with society that deviant identity is built:

The meaningful issue of identity is whether this activity, or any of my activities can stand for me, or be regarded as proper indications of my being. I have done a theft, been signified a thief; *am* a thief? To answer affirmatively, we must be able to conceive a special relationship between being and doing — a unity capable of being indicated. That building of meaning has a notable quality.

The subject discusses both the possibilities and consequences of becoming that danger symbol, what advantages such a state would allow him, what disadvantages. He goes through countless rehearsals of endless situations, stretching the responses of his imaginary audiences to the limit. Long before he reveals his new identity to real audiences, he knows what their responses will be.

It is an exciting though dangerous role that is being offered. Though filled with the imagery of defiance and power, it is a role that exacts a lock-step obedience. Matza (1969:157,174) explained the progressive nature of the servitude:

To be cast a thief, a prostitute, or more generally, a deviant, is to further compound and hasten the process of becoming that very thing. Because of ban, and his collaboration with *its* logic, more of the subject's character may be devoted to deviation that he could have reckoned initially. He has to be devious in order to be deviant. Consequently, he must become prepared for a more stunning spread.

Entering the role, the subject comes more and more to collaborate with his accusers' view of him. We all have this incapacity to *not* regard ourselves as others see us.

The process of building the deviant identity includes two opposing movements. The first is the conscious and intentional consideration of what is happening, a voluntary process which can be terminated at any time, the journey into deviant identity. It is a road anyone can take; no one has to. The second movement is one of *objectification*, becoming more and more an object-symbol of danger to society.

Matza (1969:119) insisted that the entry into the state of being object is a process intimately dependent upon choice:

> By being willing, the subject may begin a process that neither holds him within its grip nor unfolds without him. . . . As a person opens himself to the new phenomenon, he remains free and reconsidering throughout the process. He develops new meanings and sees the inherent problems in the project that are quite independent of what the social enforcers may say about it. He continues to ask, as Becker says in his essay, "How well-suited or attuned are phenomenon and subject to each other?" The key element in the subjective process of reconsideration is precisely that which is elevated and honored in the recipe: human consciousness. In becoming deviant, nothing happens behind the subject's back or despite him. Indeed, in order to be converted, he must be fully open to experience.

During this process, the subject utilizes his consciousness, and conceives himself as one who inhales marijuana, or who has homosexual feelings, or who engages in some other disvalued behavior. Throughout the entry process, the subject maintains authority.

But the further one proceeds into the deviant role, the less choice there is. For the process to take place, the capacity for resistance must diminish; one must reduce subjectivity and the opportunity for choice. The subject in creating identity does so with eyes wide open, but, as Matza explained (1969:93):

> The subject must become more like an object. That transformation occurs in the world and may be termed natural reduction. Once reduced, the subject is temporarily reconstituted. For a time he may become the kind of person who will choose not to choose. Periodically, thus the subjective capacity is forgotten or foregone. Being objectified, the subject behaves as if he were object.

The most dramatic moment in the work of building a deviant identity comes with the oftentimes sudden acceptance of that identity as "fact." This happens most distinctively, quite suddenly and with many of the same effects as suddenly realizing that one is "married," a widow, deformed, dying, or a hero. All of one's former relationships and activities now become radically altered as he begins to reorganize his world around the new identity.

As in any other identity overhaul, a heightened sense of identity occurs, not unlike the elation that accompanies a religious conversion or a marriage. This feeling of euphoria for a time masks present problems and future dangers. By incorporating the deviant act into one's constitution, one feels at home, safe.

The objections of some writers to the application of labelling theory to gay identity is based on their rejection of the idea that the gay identity is dependent on the external acts of authority instead of sexual orientation. They hold that a positive adjustment to the gay role somehow removes the dynamics of the stigma from the role and puts it "out there," back in society. They proceed in the hopeful assumption that the gay role is not really deviant. Included in this category are Carol A.B. Warren (1974), *Identity and Community in the Gay World*; Barry Dank (1971), "Coming Out in the Gay World"; Vivienne Cass (1979), "Homosexual Identity Formation: A Theoretical Model"; Thomas Weinberg's "On 'Doing' and 'Being' Gay: Sexual Behavior and Homosexual Male Self-Identity" (1978); Richard Troiden's "Becoming Homosexual: A Model of Gay Identity Acquisition" (1979); Shively and De Cecco's "Components of Sexual Identity" (1977); and Eli Coleman's "Developmental Stages of the Coming Out Process" (1982).

Rather than rejecting labelling theory outright, many of these authors came up with what can be described as a nondeviant labelling theory. Included in that group is Kenneth Plummer, for whom interactionism explains better than any other theory "why, when so many people are potentially available for homosexual experiences and identification, do so few enter stable homosexual roles?" (1975:137).

Plummer's model of the process or stages by which a person approaches the adoption of the gay role is generally shared by a large number of authors. Basically, it starts with the person making a connection between his own homosexual desires or experiences and the realization that there exist "out there" persons who are specially designated or labelled for that same type of behavior. It is in this *sensitization* that the first possibility of adoption of homosexual identity starts.

The next stage is that of *signification*, by which a person proceeds to a self-identification as homosexual (Plummer, 1975:141–142):

> It entails all those processes which lead to a heightened homosexual identity: subjectively, from the nagging inner feeling that one may be 'different' through to a developed homosexual identity, and objectively, from minor homosexual involvements through to the stage known as 'coming out'. For some these are passed quickly; for others they groan through the life span. For some, the awakening sense of homosexual identity comes as a positive relief; for others it is an issue to be constantly debated, challenged, and surrounded with ambiguity.

Finally there is the process of *stabilization*, by which the person both decides to stay gay-identified and adjusts his life accordingly. Plummer stated (1975:150–152) that many factors are responsible for holding a person in the gay role. Besides the sexual freedoms, gay lifestyles offer a range of supportive experiences. Cass (1979) and Coleman (1982) offered some refinements to Plummer's model, mostly referring to this last stage of stabilization, in which the commitment to the gay role is attenuated and a reintegration of other roles is achieved. Both Warren (1974) and Troiden(1979) claimed that the more stable gay coupling arrangements are the final stage of *commitment* to the gay role.

A noticeable feature observed in all these works is that, in spite of their attempts to accommodate labeling theory with their own views of gay identity, they always betray a positivist bias that points to an internal condition beyond the experience itself. Adherence to this positivist bias has led to basic conceptual flaws, mainly in the order of definition. Concepts such as "identity," "homosexuality," "sexuality," "sexual orientation," and "sexual feelings" are rarely defined and often used interchangeably, always with the implication that the recognition of an internal condition is the source of gay identity.

De Cecco's definition (1981:61) of sexual orientation as the "individual's personal activity with, interpersonal affection for, and erotic fantasies about members of the same or opposite biological sex," could as well serve as a description of "love," "intimacy," "sexuality," "sex," "eroticism," and a host of other related experiences.

Shively, Jones, and De Cecco (1983/84) got to the heart of the matter in their study of how sexual orientation was defined in 228 articles published in 48 different journals. Again, they found (1) the concept of sexual orientation not defined, (2) contradictory definitions, and/or (3) the concept used interchangeably with "sexual identity," "sex object choice" and "a lifelong process." Cass (1983/84) complained about the persistent refusal of writers to fit their theories of gay identity into the general literature on identity and about the failure to define the term "homosexuality." It is hard to define something the reality of which cannot be substantiated. If homosexuality refers to something beyond the social role or the personal experience, it just isn't there.

It merely repeats Kertbeny's error to say that the problem is one of failure of definition and attempting to transfer the object of social opprobrium to sexual feelings, orientation, or relationships. The triviality of this solution is seen in the attempt to consider the ominous force of stigma as external to the role itself. Built into the role, as Matza said, is the warrant to be told not to, in whatever terms authority wishes to dictate. It is the relationship with authority that makes the gay role different from nondeviant roles.

It is in the relationship of gay-identified persons themselves with authority that we observe the deviant nature of the gay role. One of the most significant factors proceeding the gay role is the *internalization of the norm*, which means not just going along with rules, but also regarding the labelled persons as personally diminished and inwardly polluted. Those who view homosexuals as "sick" are more apt to consider adoption of the role as a means of neutralizing the ban. The deeper the fear of homosexuality, the more elaborate is the neutralization technique, and the more compelling the gay role appears.

Gay males — often known for having been "the best little boys in the world" — have successfully internalized the moral values of their class, including those regarding homosexuality. The gay role offers them a radical solution to the conflicts between those values and their sexual desires.

Richard Troiden (1979:370), in his study of 150 gay-identified males, stated, "Before arriving at homosexual self-definitions, nearly all — 94 percent — of the respondents recalled having viewed homosexuality as a form of mental illness." This high figure supports the argument that commitment to the role is preceded by successful internalization of the norm. The internal condition of "being gay" legitimizes the behaviors and pleasures still regarded as socially deviant within the larger society.

Several authors have written about the manner in which gay-identified persons adhere to dominant cultural beliefs. Gregg Blachford, in his essay "Male Dominance and the Gay World" (1981:184), discussed the commitment of gay males to the core values of Western culture, including individual achievement, desire for consumer goods, age stratification, the worship of youth, and male dominance. Gordon Johnston, in *Which Way Out of the Men's Room?* (1979), discussed the manner in which today's gay males have embraced the modern worship of phallic sexuality. Few authors, however, have written about the manner in which their internalization of the social norms regarding *homosexuality* influences their behavior, even among those who claim to have a "positive gay identity."

The internalization of social norms may be the one factor which most clearly distinguishes the identity of gay males from that of lesbians. Unlike many other males, gay-identified males tend to be norm internalizers, "good boys," generally ill-at-ease with the defiant and ambiguous norms of "bad boys." Lesbians tend to be the opposite, more like mischievous boys (or tomboys) in defying social norms, especially those regarding appropriate female appearance and conduct. This means they are more apt to proceed in their lifestyle without, or with less need for, the role as a rationalization for their behavior. Being more publicly defiant of the norms, they are less apt to be encapsulated and bedevilled by the role itself. Lesbians also tend to regard their status more in relation to generalized feminine norms, while gay males see their status more in relation to sexuality.

Barbara Ponse (1978:6) wrote that the conversations she recorded in a lesbian center reinforced the concept of lesbianism not as a sexuality but as an *essence*. Everything, it seemed, turned upon this concept, reflected it, and was rooted in it: "The reduction of women-related women to an essence characterizes many theories of lesbianism and is a prevailing theme in religious pronouncements on lesbianism. Interestingly, the notion of essence is imbedded as well in the ways in which identity is conceived in the lesbian world."

As a result of this perspective, it is easier for some lesbians to dispense with the role altogether. Barbara Ponse (1978) quoted the testimony of two women who successfuly defied the ban:

> I reject the use of these labels to define a person; if she happens to have an interest in this person, it's not fair. If someone says a person is a lesbian, it's a critical word. I don't think that a private relationship between two people that are interested in each other has any social significance. They are simply expressing what they feel. I dislike such terms as *lesbian*. They imply a certain acceptance of a certain group. It's like we have a convert. It's a group rhetoric . . . I actually cannot function in a gay bar. I shake, I tremble, I am with a group of people who are not real. I have a strong sense of unreality. I certainly do not have gay identity (p. 146).

> I guess you might say I'm person-oriented, as opposed to being heterosexual or homosexual. I personally can't relate to the idea of being only with women or only with men. It depends on the person. One of the most important love relationships of my life was with a man, and I can only say that I would be with [L] whether she was a man or woman. It is her as a person I love. It doesn't matter to me what sex a person is, but what kind of person they are (p. 167).

The connection between norm internalization prompts the ironic conclusion that those who have the greatest commitment to the role are also those who have the greatest commitment to *innocence*. The story of convicted serial murderer Ted Bundy exemplifies the manner in which a deviant role serves to reconcile deviant behavior and a radical commitment to innocence. He was able to construct an *innocence-saving* role that allowed him to transfer the evil of his acts from the self to his psychological "problem." Bundy employed a very common technique of abstracting the evil of the deed from the self and attributing it to an internal compulsion.

Quentin Crisp took another approach altogether in dealing with his sexually ambiguous lifestyle. He readily took responsibility for his behavior, going so far as to admit the "depravity" of his sexual activities. Even though he may not have regarded the acts as offensive, he recognized they were offensive to society. He had no need to sanitize them for society's benefit, however. In his writings, he claimed that his identity was not built around his sexuality but upon a lifestyle skillfully crafted around his unusual physical appearance.

Internalization of the norm elicits attempts to *neutralize* the ban in consideration of the deviant activity. Gresham Sykes and David Matza (1957:667–669) offered a number of rationalizations that are used to launder and neutralize deviant acts:

(1) The "billiard ball theory," in which a person sees himself as helplessly propelled into new situations.

(2) Wrongfulness of the act turning on the question of whether or not anyone has suffered harm.

(3) Insistence that the injury in question may be neutralized in the light of circumstances: Some members of minority groups may have gotten out of hand.

(4) Condemnation of condemners. The accusers become accused of hypocrisy, being deviants in disguise, or acting out of spite or other motivations. The most important point is that deviation from certain norms may occur, not because the norms are rejected, but because other norms, held to be more pressing or involving a higher loyalty, are accorded precedence.

Sykes and Matza made the observation that the type and content of the neutralizations very often shaped the type and content of the deviant act. The denial of the status of the victim allows youths to beat up suspected homosexuals or members of other minority groups who seem to have gotten "out of place" (1957:688). Even more interesting is the manner in which crimes in the workplace are configured by the workplace environment itself. Workers can more easily pilfer company resources because they can deny injury: The company is large and is, after all, covered by insurance and tax write-offs. Stealing from a coworker is not so easily justified. Neutralization techniques protect corporation executives, not only from guilt, but also from prosecution. While workplace crime is rigorously prosecuted, corporate crimes involving enormous amounts of money, danger to lives, or social justice often go unpunished, mainly because of the neutralization techniques available.

Gay-identified persons utilize the gay role itself as their most favored neutralization technique. While some neutralization techniques focus on the status of the victim, the adoption of a deviant role focuses on the status of the actor: I can do this because that's how I am. This explains how one's gay behavior can pass so quickly into one's self-image: It has become the warrant to proceed in behavior regarded as unacceptable by society. For others, access to sexual pleasures is guaranteed by the mere status of being human. Gay-identified persons, however, secure that access by placing an emphasis on an internal condition: their sexual difference.

By displacing the social evil from the self to the internal condition of sexual orientation, one launders not only one's self-image but also the image of other labelled persons. The effect of adopting the role on one's perceptions of other gay-identified persons is immediate and profound.

Before adoption of the role, one regards such persons as sick, ugly, disturbed, mutant, and dangerous. After coming out, however, one sees them quite differently. Troiden (1979:370) commented: "When asked how these changes in attitudes were brought about, the vast majority (88 percent) claimed their favorable views stemmed from gaining the opportunity to meet homosexuals with interests and attitudes similar to their own—men who, like themselves, appear to be heterosexual."

Howard Becker (1963:37) said that moving into the deviant group is a final step in the adoption of the deviant role:

> When a person makes a definite move into an organized group—or when he realizes and accepts the fact that he has already done so—it has a powerful impact on his conception of himself. A drug addict once told me that the moment she felt she was really "hooked" was when she realized she no longer had any friends who were not drug addicts.
>
> Members of organized deviant groups of course have one thing in common: their deviance. It gives them a sense of common fate. From having to face the same problems grows a deviant subculture: a set of perspectives and understandings about what the world is like and how to deal with it, and a set of routine activities based on those perspectives. Membership in such a group solidifies a deviant identity....
>
> Most deviant groups have a self-justifying rationale (or "ideology"), although seldom is it as well worked out as that of the homosexual. While such rationales do operate, as pointed out earlier, to neutralize the conventional attitudes that deviants still may find in themselves toward their own behavior, they also perform another function. They furnish the individual with reasons that appear sound for continuing the line of activity he has begun. A person who quiets his own doubts by adopting the rationale moves into a more principled and consistent kind of deviance than was possible for him before adopting it.
>
> The second thing that happens when one moves into a deviant group is that he learns how to carry on his deviant activity with a minimum of trouble. All the problems he faces in evading enforcement of the rule he is breaking have been faced by others. Solutions have been worked out....
>
> Thus, the deviant who enters an organized and institutionalized deviant group is more likely than ever to continue in his deviant ways. He has learned, on the one hand, how to avoid trouble and, on the other hand, a rationale for continuing.

In Chapter 3 of *Outsiders*, Becker went through the initiation process of becoming a marijuana user. Because of the amorphous pleasures of marijuana, initiates often have to be instructed not only on how to use the drug, but how to recognize and value the "high" that comes with it. The initiate learns the techniques and values from those others who also show him how to get a good supply and stay out of trouble. Along with these helps, another process is taking place, that of dealing with the disapproval of society. As Becker (1963:59) wrote, another important function of affiliation is the resetting of the social norms by replacing the rules of the larger society with that of the deviant groups: "Important factors in the genesis of deviant behavior, then, may be sought in the processes by which people are emancipated from the controls of society and become responsive to those of a smaller society."

While affiliation has been given a positive interpretation by members of the gay community and many in the helping professions, Barry Adam (1978:93) defined it as a form of social withdrawal providing a coping strategy "which no longer requires a personal escape from identity, but externalizes the identity conflict into the immediate social world." Drawing on Goffman, Adam stated that inferiorized persons "develop repertoires of behavior" for different audiences. "Social withdrawal, then, presumes the possibility of alternative, in-group, or community audiences that permit a wider range of personal expression (or deviation) than in the larger society."

In spite of the sense of heightened identity that often accompanies coming out, the novitiate must face increasing inferiorization as he enters the role more fully. While he has secured a warrant for proceeding with the behavior, the basic conflict with society has been changed but not solved. The ghettoization of the deviant behavior compounds these conflicts. Adam (1978:94–95) explained that by allowing the gay ghettos to exist, the state is merely reorganizing the terms of the ban and extending its power under "liberal" restraints:

> The development of enclaves is precluded by the totalitarian state but becomes increasingly possible with the rise of the "bourgeois" or "liberal" socioeconomic formations. Domination evolves into new forms; outright destruction tends to give way to exclusion. . . .
>
> The ghetto frames the everyday life of inferiorized people, limiting even their expectations and aspirations. Life within this set of restricted possibilities draws back from the taken-for-granted privileges of superordinate groups. . . . An ideology which personalizes failure legitimizes the limitation of life possibilities. Inferiorization enforces the unhappy belief among its objects that their degradation is somehow "deserved."

While the deviant role provides a warrant for engaging in the behavior, it also entails a number of dangers and constraints that further define the special relationship between gay-identified persons and authority. Matza (1969:142,154), emphasizing the work relationship between authority and the deviant actor, wrote: "That anyone — sociologists especially — could write as if the authoritative fact of ban was of minor importance in the process of becoming deviant is hardly believable. . . . Right in the deviation is a warrant to be told not to in whatever terms and tone righteous authority chooses to speak. That is the meaning of deviation — what distinguishes it from merely 'being different'."

IX. Existing in the Project

Homosexual. I find the word hard to relate to because it puts me in a category which limits my potential. It also prescribes a whole system of behavior to which I'm supposed to conform which has nothing to do with the reality of my day to day living. I feel the same way about the word heterosexual. Our culture has created these artificial categories defining human sexuality, to protect and perpetuate the institutions and systems in power whose end result is only to dehumanize life. I reject the word homosexual. I reject a category that defines my central life thrust in limiting terms. I am a human being. — Jim Foratt in *Come Out!*, the gay radical newspaper

I remember the moment I decided I was gay. It was April 1971 and I was standing outside the newly opened gay community center in downtown Seattle, hesitating to go in. Somehow, going through those doors would mean joining the organization that made its home there, and life would never be the same. The thought came to mind that while I had done lots of work for other people's causes, it was time to do something for a cause that spoke for me.

It had been several years since a friend had introduced me to the idea—the possibility—that there was nothing wrong with gay people, they were only the victims of social injustice. I had quite recently come to connect the repression of my own sexual feelings with that phrase, "social injustice." There was not something wrong with me; the wrong was with society. Stepping through that door with heart pounding, I felt I was making a statement about myself and about the society in which I lived.

Within a few days, I had announced to my family, in-laws, and friends that I was gay. I jumped into the activities of the local gay community and soon found myself giving talks on gay liberation at local churches and schools. Working with the brassy gay organizations of Seattle was invigorating. Rowdy and fun-loving, they gave that hardworking town its gay money's worth, loudly parading down the streets, liberating skating rinks, bowling alleys, and dance halls, taking the message of sexual tolerance into churches, courtrooms, offices of government, and prisons.

130

Within two weeks of my coming out, I woke up to find myself in an all-gay world, where nearly all of my work and leisure was spent in the company of gay friends. I went to work in a halfway house for gays and lesbians who were alcoholic, drug abusers, or ex-offenders. It was a first attempt at running a publicly funded residential treatment center that regarded erotic feelings as an important factor in rehabilitation, a radical position to take in the field of corrections.

Such was the heady agenda of gay liberation. By the mid-1970s, however, it was evident that the agenda—encouraging people to come out and be proud of being gay—was not working. Reports of casualties—gay related suicides and beatings, illnesses and death from alcohol and drug use—were not declining. The mortality rate of gay people dying from hepatitis was staggering: 5,000 a year according to some accounts. New infectious diseases were appearing, including devastating intestinal parasites, that added to the already alarming incidence of other sexually transmitted diseases.

Worse, gay people did not seem to be coalescing into the productive lifestyle envisioned by the early leaders of the movement. Where was Whitman's vision of a land where men, women, and children would join in a continuous celebration of life and the body electric? What we saw instead was an escalating spread of promiscuity, prostitution, and pornography. Our liberated community was rapidly becoming an exploited community. Gay society found itself with less and less to be proud of. The march of gay rights seemed to slow down, and with the arrival of AIDS, was stopped dead in its tracks.

That was when many of us began questioning the assumptions of the movement. Some of us began looking at gay identity itself, which had been the cornerstone of the new movement. What we felt was going to be our salvation had become a Trojan horse. It was not an antidote but an instrument of the ban itself. It had not dealt a blow to the ban at all as we thought it would, but only reinforced stereotypes. Freedom seemed as far off as ever.

Matza (1969:147–148) explained that an innocent affiliation with the deviant role is difficult to retain. Being put to work as a marker of the boundaries of acceptable behavior, the new recruit is brought into the realm of deviance:

> Ban did not deter the wrong-minded; they did the activity anyway. But that incontestable failure hardly exhausts the consequences of ban. Leviathan may have its say even when disobeyed. In making the activity guilty, Leviathan bedevils the subject as he proceeds and thus is partly compensated for its gross failure to deter. . . .
> Ban bedevils the subject in a very concrete way. Working arduously, it virtually guarantees that further disaffiliation with convention will be a concomitant of affiliation with deviation; put slightly differently, that

the scope or range of disaffiliation will surpass or go beyond the amount implicit in the deviation itself. The logic of ban creates the strong possibility that the subject will become even more deviant in order to deviate....

A main purpose of ban is to unify meaning and thus to minimize the possibility that, morally, the subject can have it both ways. Either he will be deterred or bedevilled. And by bedevilled, I mean nothing mysterious — merely being made a devil as a result of being put in a position wherein more deviation and disaffiliation than was originally contemplated appears in the life of the subject.

Most writers on the subject of gay identity would have us believe that the ban is overcome by coming out. They ignore the manner in which people engage massively with the ban once they have adopted the role. Whatever the problems encountered previously, in terms of dealing with one's feelings, concealing one's gay behaviors, and the like, the problems of dealing with the ban are magnified immeasureably after adopting the role. It is not just feelings or behaviors that are the problem any more, but the role itself. As a highly elaborated warrant for proceeding in the behavior, it becomes in itself a management problem of enormous proportions.

Upon adoption, the role becomes a tremendous burden, the burden of a stigmatized identity. The subject immediately recognizes that he has a new secret that must be carefully managed. He is aware that society, if it knew of his gay identity, would regard not just his sexual behaviors as polluted but now his *being* as well. Of all the factors influencing the lives of gay-identified persons, nothing is more important than secrecy.

The person who revealed the influence of secrecy in deviant behavior was German sociologist George Simmel, who characterized deviant groups as *secret societies* (1950). Simmel saw two kinds of secret societies. The first is a society whose very existence is not known; the second, pertinent to the gay role, referred to those groups whose existence is known but whose members are not. In his analysis of secrecy, Simmel noted the conditions necessary for the emergence of secret societies: First, a secret society tends to arise under conditions of public oppression. Second, a secret society develops only within a society complete in itself; being a group which serves only some of the needs of its members, the secret society must depend on the larger society for satisfying other needs. In some ways, the secret society reflects the patterns of the larger community and in other ways opposes them. Third, secrecy tends to extend in importance beyond the secret itself and to permeate every feature of the secret world. Secrecy affects the relations between members of the gay community with one another as well as with the outside world.

Those newly initiated into the gay role often find secrecy a terrible, sometimes overwhelming, burden. This burden is not unlike the feeling of panic that often comes with one's first overt homosexual contacts with others. That concern is something else, created by an excruciating feeling of "transparency," the belief that one's transgression has become visible; one fears the possibility of discovery and shame. There are stories of people who, after their first sexual experience, examined themselves in the mirror for telltale signs of pollution. Only slowly did they convince themselves that they looked the way they used to.

Whether or not one has adopted the gay role, however, continued experience slowly removes the burden of transparency. As Erving Goffman (1963:80) explained:

> Where a differentness is relatively unapparent, the individual must learn that in fact he can trust himself to secrecy. The point of view of observers of himself must be entered carefully, but not anxiously carried further than the observers themselves do. Starting with a feeling that everything known to himself is known to others, he often develops a realistic appreciation that this is not so.

Matza (1969:150) added:

> Under the spell of the ban, the deviant subject almost surely senses himself as transparent, if only for a time. . . . Conscious of ban, and conscious that he has flaunted it, the subject becomes self-conscious. . . . The concerns underlying the fear of transparency are quite ordinary and based on the common understanding that social communication occurs through inadvertent cues, gestures, and expressions as well as plain talk, on the common sense that the subject will "give himself away."

The maintenance of opaqueness is much less of a problem for gay-identified persons than some other stigmatized persons, such as the physically handicapped. Gay-identified persons quickly become adept at maintaining opaqueness in non-gay situations. As Goffman noted (1963:75), nearly everyone faces these problems of concealing a secret at one time or another, and: "A woman who has had a mastectomy or a Norwegian male sex offender who has been penalized by castration are forced to present themselves falsely in almost all situations, having to conceal their unconventional secrets because of everyone's having to conceal the conventional ones."

Because gay-identified persons share a stigma that is most often invisible, they rarely have the day-to-day dangers of many other stigmatized individuals such as epileptics, stutterers, and the physically deformed. But the gay role also has its dangers: Its very invisibility adds to the threat that homosexuality already poses, making the dangers of exposure all the more feared and life-threatening.

Experienced persons can develop a sense of opaqueness about their gay behaviors long before the adoption of the gay role. But new concerns with secrecy arise with the adoption of the gay role itself, concerns that may or may not overlie the problems of concealing one's gay behaviors. The stigma attached to the role is not only distinct, it is much greater than that attached to the behaviors, which often can be explained away as being regarded as incidental to one's being. A married man, for example, can engage in discreet homosexual liaisons for many years without ever feeling the need to disclose the secret to anyone. But the burden of the role is much greater, in spite of its invisibility.

The management of a deviant identity is at once complex, demanding both keeping the role secret and sharing it with others. So great is the burden that absolute secrecy becomes an impossibility. To whom does one disclose? First of all, to one's sexual partners, especially if they are also gay identified.

Sharing the secret often becomes an important condition of the negotiations leading up to sexual contacts, and not just for reasons of personal safety. This cruising disclosure, "laying one's cards on the table," as one makes a sexual proposition, illuminates the central function of the gay role itself as a social license to proceed in the behavior: "*Because I am gay* it's all right for me to ask you to have sex with me." Many gay-identified persons come to regard sexual contacts with those not gay-identified as less satisfying if not actually dangerous.

People who regularly have sex with "trade" (non–gay-identified persons) learn to reduce the risks by skillful management of the secret. They sometimes present themselves as degraded "queers" with the compulsive need to service others. This suppliant pose has its risks, but usually evokes cooperative interest by supporting the dominant masculine status of one's partners. Another approach is to come off as *more* masculine than one's partners, assuring them that "it's all right for straight males to do this on occasion." In all cases, it is important *to shield trade from the stigma* less they become threatened by it.

The shared knowledge of the role is the foundation of the gay community. Affiliation with other gay-identified persons not only serves as a source of role models and sexual contacts but also provides release from the burden of maintaining secrecy. The release from secrecy, more than any other bond, is the cause of the special piquancy and camaraderie found in gay meeting places. As Ponse commented (1978:63):

> In line with Simmel's observations about the intensity of relations among secret-sharers, the gay audiences before whom the straight mask is dropped assume great importance for the hidden lesbian (Simmel, 1950:360). Correspondingly, gay time and gay space are given a greater accent of reality than is the straight world. The gay subculture becomes the real world, where the authentic self is revealed. Lesbians whose world of sociability is exclusively gay describe themselves as living a "totally gay life."

Goffman wrote (1963:81) that deviants carefully divide their world into different parts: forbidden places where discovery means exposure; civil places where people of that kind are carefully and painfully tolerated; and then there are the "back places where persons of the individual's kind stand exposed and find they need not try to conceal their stigma, nor be overly concerned with cooperatively trying to disattend it."

While members of the gay community and some professionals advise "coming out" to others as a means of developing a "positive gay identity," they exhibit considerable ambiguity about the audience of this disclosure. While emphasizing the need to embrace one's own gay "nature" and feel good about sharing that information with other gay-identified persons, disclosing to others becomes much more problematic, creating a problem that never goes away.

Erving Goffman's best writing (1963:13–15) is found in his descriptions of the intense complexities created by this ambiguity:

> When normals and stigmatized do in fact enter one another's immediate presence, especially when they attempt to maintain a joint conversational encounter, there occurs one of the primal scenes of sociology; for, in many cases, these moments will be the ones when the causes and effects of stigma must be directly confronted by both sides. . . .
>
> This uncertainty arises not merely from the stigmatized individual's not knowing which of several categories he will be placed in, but also, where the placement is favorable, from his knowing in their hearts the others may be defining him in terms of his stigma. . . . Thus in the stigmatized arises the sense of not knowing what the others present are "really" thinking about him.
>
> Further, during mixed contacts, the stigmatized individual is likely to feel that he is "on," having to be self-conscious and calculating about the impression he is making, to a degree and in areas of conduct which he assumes others are not.
>
> Also, he is likely to feel that the usual scheme of interpretation for everyday events has been undermined. His minor accomplishments, he feels, may be assessed as signs of remarkable capacities in the circumstances. . . .
>
> At the same time, minor failings or incidental impropriety may, he feels, be interpreted as a direct expression of his stigmatized differentness. Ex-mental patients, for example, are afraid to engage in sharp interchanges with spouse or employer because of what a show of emotion might be taken as a sign of.

Some people have expressed the notion that gay liberation has invalidated the applicability of Goffman's descriptions to gay-identified persons. Would that it were so! It would indeed be fortunate if a "positive adjustment" to the gay role would automatically eliminate the need to be concerned about the reactions of others to one's gayness. The fact is that very few gay-identified persons go around disclosing their gay status to everyone without being aware of the variety of reactions it causes in others, sometimes highly dangerous ones.

Most gay-identified persons are very selective in their choice of audiences for such disclosure, for no other reason than to avoid publicizing the central concern of one's gayness. It is one thing to tell others that you are gay. It is quite something else to tell them you think about it all the time and you want them also to always be aware of it. What Goffman (1963:88) wrote is still true: "What are unthinking routines for normals can become management problems for the discreditable. . . . The person with a secret failing, then, must be alive to the social situation as a scanner of possibilities, and is therefore likely to be alienated from the simpler world in which those around him apparently dwell."

It is because of the complex risks involved that friends and advisers are ambiguous about *how far* one should come out. As Goffman wrote (1963:123): "The individual is told that if he adopts the right line (which line depending on who is talking), he will have come to terms with himself and be a whole man; he will be an adult with dignity and self-respect. And in truth he will have accepted a self for himself; but this self is, as it necessarily must be, a resident alien, a voice of the group that speaks for and through him." This is a remarkable admission that disclosure of the role is a requirement of the ban itself. The role hardly does Leviathan any good if it is not made public. If gayness were merely a sexual feeling and not a role, such a disclosure would hardly be thinkable.

Goffman (1963:108–111) explained that the requirement is filled with contradictions: On the one hand, the gay-identified person is told that he is no different from anyone else, and on the other hand he is told that he must declare his status as a resident alien who stands for his group. In order to solve this dilemma, he is generally warned against any attempt at *normification*, defined as "passing too completely," and he is "encouraged to develop a distaste for those of his fellows who, without actually making a secret of their stigma, engage in careful covering, being very careful to show that in spite of appearances, they are very sane, very generous, very sober, very masculine, very capable of hard physical labor and taxing sports, in short, that they are gentlemen deviants, nice persons like ourselves in spite of the reputation of their kind."

At the same time, however, he is warned against *minstrelization*, "whereby the stigmatized person ingratiatingly acts out before normals the full dance of bad qualities imputed to his kind, thereby consolidating a life situation into a clownish role."

It is a thin line which gay people must walk: One must not hide, but neither must one be too obvious. One must be committed to the role, loyal to his "group," and at the same time act like everyone else. Nowhere are these contradictions more prominent than in the general prohibition against males holding hands, embracing, kissing or other expressions of bonding.

Goffman (1963:121–122) stated that since the "good adjustment" code has its origins in the liberal beliefs of the larger society, its true nature is evident:

> It requires that the stigmatized individual cheerfully and unselfconsciously accept himself as essentially the same as normals, while at the same time he voluntarily withholds himself from those situations in which normals would find it difficult to give lip service to their similar acceptance of him. . . . It means that the unfairness and pain of having to carry a stigma will never be presented to them; it means that normals can remain relatively uncontaminated by intimate contact with the stigmatized, relatively unthreatened in their identity beliefs. The stigmatized individual is asked to act so as to imply neither that his burden is heavy nor that bearing it has made him different from us; at the same time he must keep himself at that remove from us which ensures our painlessly being able to confirm our belief about him. . . . A *phantom acceptance* is thus allowed to provide the base for a *phantom normalcy*.

Connected to the issue of disclosure is the gay political strategy of altering stereotypes by the public presentations of gay-identified individuals, based on the theory is that if people could only see more real gay people, they would become more accepting of them. But the results do not support such a strategy, as Goffman (1963:52–53) warned:

> In spite of this evidence for everyday beliefs about stigma and familiarity, one must go on to see that familiarity need not reduce contempt. . . . In our society, to speak of a woman as one's wife is to place this person in a category of which there can be only one member, yet a category is nonetheless involved and she is merely a member of it. . . . Thus, whether we interact with strangers or intimates, we will find that the fingertips of society have reached bluntly into the contact, even here putting us in our place.
>
> For one thing, the individual's intimates can become just the persons from whom he is most concerned with concealing something shameful. The situation of homosexuals provides an illustration: even some of those who behave fairly openly in public are most careful to avoid arousing suspicions in the family circle.

Activists who attempt to eliminate "gay stereotypes" with the presentation of masculine-looking gay males and feminine-looking lesbians not only succeed in supporting sexist stereotypes but heighten the threat: "It can even happen to the most normal-looking people."

The gay role is itself the most formidable obstacle to political consciousness and change. The problem of the acceptance of homosexuals gets in the way of the acceptance of gay behaviors. People are not more accepting of gay behaviors because of their exposure to those who have

138   Gay Identity

adopted the role. The strategy results not in the expansion of tolerance
of homoeroticism but in its restriction to the gay community. To be effective, the movement must appeal to the affectionate roots of human
solidarity, and not to the involuntary differences that are more imaginary
than real.

Much of gay political strategy is aimed at the "denominationaliza-
tion" of homosexual behaviors, the attempt to define homosexuals as a
minority or class of persons, a kind of religious enclave enjoying special
protections for unpopular behaviors. The policy of defining religions as
denominations in our society worked as a means of reducing tensions and
allowing different religions to co-exist. As Reinhold Niebuhr pointed out,
becoming a denomination meant giving up any claims to monopoly.

But religious beliefs are not moral beliefs. Emile Durkheim taught
us that society is first of all a moral community and demands a consensus
on everyday behavior. We can agree to disagree on religious beliefs but
not on moral issues, as we learned in the case of slavery, polygamy (in the
case of the Mormons), prohibition, and now abortion. The only way to
legitimize homosexual behaviors will be to change society's mind. That
means, first of all, finding some common ground. The gay role and the
idea of a separate gay society offer no common ground.

What is the solution to the problem of disclosure? As Goffman and
others have suggested, under the present ban, there is no solution. One
can never reveal one's gay activities or feelings to others without seriously
altering the relationships. People can overcome the force of the stigma
only with the most concerted efforts.

What should be the norm for disclosing one's gay feelings? Goffman
(1963:122) was inspired to write:

> If in fact he desires to live as much as possible "like any other person,"
> and be accepted "for what he really is," then in many cases the shrewdest
> position for him to take is this one which has a false bottom; for in many
> cases the degree to which normals accept the stigmatized individual can
> be maximized by his acting with full spontaneity and naturalness as if the
> conditional acceptance of him, which he is careful not to overreach, is full
> acceptance. But of course what is a good adjustment for the individual can
> be an even better one for society.

This statement is surprising as it carries the implication that people
can easily isolate and define their "true nature" that can be spontaneously
expressed. We have no roles for unselfconscious gay behavior in our
society. Because of the ban, spontaneity is just not possible. But we can
wing it, and one of the few public persons to do so is Quentin Crisp. As
affected as his presentation is, it presents possibilities to us of how people
might live in a society without the ban.

How can we spontaneously express a sexuality in a society that strives constantly to present it as something unnatural and grotesque? The very concept of "sexuality," in fact, smells of something manipulated and political, as if it is more a creation of power than of our own individual needs. When told to be "spontaneous" in the expression of sexuality, some persons think of throwing themselves into a lifestyle dedicated to orgasm and openly cruising (or having sex) in public places.

Crisp's solution of constructing a lifestyle directed around what he perceived to be his unacceptable appearance suggests a broader strategy: deflecting the focus from "sexuality" to more meaningful and concrete differences. Many others have employed this technique and have organized their gay lifestyle not around sex but their other sensibilities and aspirations. It may be art, music, science, dance, physical culture, or even business.

If gay-identified persons are ambivalent about disclosure, it is because they are ambivalent about the role itself. Because of the ban, it is never worn very comfortably. Like an ill-fitting suit, even in the best of circumstances, one is always aware of having it on. As one proceeds through a gay career, its disadvantages become more and more apparent. It has to do with deficiencies in the role itself as a strategy for dealing with the ban. Kertbeny's solution did not expunge the evil, only refocussed it on sexual orientation. It stays there, slowly infecting everything.

This may be the reason that there is no honor among thieves: They still regard one another as polluted. The adoption of the gay role removes the stigma from the behavior, allowing gay-identified persons to freely engage one another on the level of sexual behavior, but they still have great difficulties in dealing with one another on other levels. This difficulty is not unrelated to the problems of relationships with outsiders. The deviant role obstructs normal interactions.

This results in the tendency to stratify the gay community as Goffman (1963:107) described:

> Whether closely allied with his own kind or not, the stigmatized individual may exhibit identity ambivalence when he obtains a close sight of his own kind behaving in a stereotyped way, flamboyantly or pitifully acting out the negative attributes imputed to them. The sight may repel him, since after all he supports the norms of the wider society, but his social and psychological identification with these offenders holds him to what repels him, transforming the repulsion into shame, and then transforming ashamedness itself into something into which he is ashamed. In brief, he can neither embrace his group or let it go.

Ambivalence is a function of one's reservations about the role, rising from the realization that evil has not been fully expunged in the adoption of the role. Kurt Lewin, in his work on ambivalence among Jews and blacks in *Resolving Social Conflicts* (1948:186–200), took the position that ambivalence is a form of self-hatred, referring not to the individual's hatred for himself, but for the group to which his stigma assigns him. Lewin understood this self-hatred as the residue of internalized social attitudes toward the role. Since self-hatred is a psychological impossibility, the stigmatic pollution is projected on one's own kind.

Ambivalence arises from the perception that the social constrictions one suffers are attributed to one's sexual orientation, now both a license and a burden. The role carries a built-in alienation from full participation in the life of society, something for which all people naturally yearn. Ambivalence represents the pain of being put outside one's own history. That is what stigma is all about.

Memmi (1965) wrote that free men and women are able to rise out of their lethargy, take pride in their traditions of liberty, and revolt, "upsetting the politicians' little calculations." Dominated peoples, however, are forbidden access to the political system, and this kills their ability to function as a community:

> The most serious blow suffered by the colonized is being removed from history and from the community. Colonization usurps any free role in either war or peace, every decision contributing to his destiny and that of the world, and all cultural and social responsibility . . . (p. 91).
> The colonized . . . feels neither responsible nor guilty nor skeptical, for he is out of the game. He is in no way a subject of history any more. Of course, he carries its burden, often more cruelly than others, but always as an object. He has forgotten how to participate actively in history and no longer even asks to do so. No matter how briefly colonization may have lasted, all memory of freedom seems distant; he forgets what it costs or else he no longer dares to pay the price for it . . . (pp.92–93).
> Colonized society is a diseased society in which internal dynamics no longer succeed in creating new structures. Its centuries-hardened face has become nothing more than a mask under which it slowly smothers and dies. Such a society cannot dissolve the conflicts of generations, for it is unable to be transformed (pp.98–99).

Self-hatred also emerges in a residual *guilt* that Barry Adam (1978:71, 73) explained results from the pain caused by the restrictions of one's life options:

> The oppressed subject tends to reflect guiltily upon his biography when presented by his systematically constricted life chances. . . . Guilt is the crampedness of the powerless subject in dialectical relation with the powerful object. It is the symptom of the aborted project and frustrated intention. "This *instinct for freedom* forcibly made latent — we have seen it already — this instinct for freedom pushed back and repressed, incarcerated within and finally able to discharge and vent itself only on itself: that, and that alone, is what the bad conscience is in its beginnings," wrote Nietzsche.

In other words, it is not that we lead unsatisfying lives because we are guilty, but we are guilty because we lead unsatisfying lives.

Self-hatred is expressed not only in guilt but also in *mimesis*, the slavish imitation or mimicking of social norms. Mimesis is sometimes manifested in the physical behavior of inferiorized persons. Among gay males, it can take the form of affected feminine mannerisms or in the rigid adherence to norms of masculine conduct and appearance. Altman (1971:19) remarked, "It is a strange paradox that homosexuals, who suffer from the opprobrium of 'respectable' society, are often its most stalwart defenders." Nothing is more customary in man than to recognize superior wisdom of the larger society.

Barry Adam traced the way in which the self-hatred becomes institutionalized and second nature, developing "a logic of its own." The demands of the social order cause a masochism which exists "in reification of the dominator and repetition of the guilt response" (1978:74). The masochist is motivated by a strongly idealistic belief that justice governs the world, suffering is the result of sin, and goodness is rewarded.

Self-hatred combines with the bedevilling lure of the ban to swallow the soldiers of Leviathan into a widening vortex of deviance. Living on the edges of society, gay-identified persons become used to the casualties of the ban. As they become familiarized with promiscuity, prostitution, pornography, and drugs, they become easier prey for more exotic forms of deviance. The sexual activities of those who knowingly expose themselves to the risk of AIDS testify to the forces of bedevilment.

The enormous problems created by ambivalence have prompted the formation of several institutions to deal with them. The most notable of such institutions are the gay community centers, which not only serve as a bridge between the gay community and the rest of society, but are mainly concerned with fighting ambivalence and the maintenance of the deviant role. There is a great labor going on here, "identity work," which Ponse (1978:92) said is directed at the *normalization* of the gay world, "the process of making gayness routine." Many of the activities center around effective techniques of affiliation aimed at the presentation of "role models of proud gays, explanatory rationales, and positive interpretations of gayness, accounts of other gay people's experiences, as well as the opportunity for the novice to talk about her own experience of lesbianism" (1978:106).

Heightening the *essential* differences between homosexual and heterosexual persons plays a large part in identity work.

An effective indicator of one's commitment to a homosexual identity is the degree of alienation one feels from the larger community, including family, parents, and former friends. Ponse (1978:63) explained that some women preferred to avoid straight people altogether, their only point of contact being work:

For these women, the world of work provides the single avenue of contact with straight people. Relationships with work associates are maintained at an instrumental level only. In a very special sense, the "real lives" of these secretive lesbians are spent with gay people in gay places that demarcate the gay subculture: the time, places, and people that are significant to these women are all gay.

In spite of the best efforts of the gay community, one's commitment to the role is often shaken by the casualties of the ban. The deviant nature of the role slowly emerges and becomes more and more threatening. Gay writers often appeal for more discretion, but at the same time call for a greater commitment to gay identity.

The increase of experience in sexual matters, however, makes retention of the role less important as a sexual license. The process of disaffiliation from the role begins as the person starts to restrict more and more his contacts with the gay community. Secretly, he looks for a way to become himself and at the same time subvert the ancient ban, to have the best of both worlds. Attenuation of commitment to the role, "being gay," proceeds as new roles are given a new prominence in one's self-image, challenging the dominance of the deviant role. A reaffiliation with old friends and family occurs. The self is de-objectified as the person learns to take on a new responsibility for sexual behavior. He learns to see his homosexual feelings as more of an option than an internally programmed mandate. Other sexual options take on more reality and interest.

Some may never drop their gay role entirely. They have been able to marshall sufficient forces on their side to restrain the forces of bedevilment: family, lovers, friends, career, community standing, and a wide circle of friends. They have reduced the demands of the role to a minimum level, mainly through the prominence given to other roles. Through strict discipline, they have deactivated the parasite without excising it, and have achieved a life about as comfortable as one can expect.

Others, taking a more direct approach, manage to escape the role entirely. Accomplishing the forbidden, they are neither gay nor straight. Again learning to choose, they develop the ability to make the ban ambiguous, taking responsibility, refusing explanations for their behaviors. Incredibly, Leviathan can no longer use them, has no power over them. They have surrendered the license and gone home.

The new integration of gay and straight behaviors often takes the form of new living arrangements and bonding behaviors. In spite of the failure of many of the large-scale alternative families and communes in the 1960s, sociologists today have noted a steady rise in such experiments, mainly of a smaller scale. Even in small towns, we can observe the successful formation of new family structures that resemble the kinship arrangements of other societies. They include both children and a wide assortment of adults, related and unrelated, some in heterosexual relationships, some in gay ones, some in neither. These groups sometimes include senior citizens, young workers, students, and the handicapped. Their success is predicated on the effective bonds that are established that make better use of resources over time.

This development suggests an answer to the genital primacy that has dominated family life in our society. These alternatives clearly represent a return to a situation in which nongenital bonding alliances determine the parameters of living arrangements. As friends of mine have said, a good roommate is worth much more than a good lover. It may well be that society's fears of homosexuality may be best answered in expanding the definition of the family to include nongenital bonding and affectivity.

X. The Homosexual Discourse II: The Rhetoric of Domination

If men define situations as real, they are real in their consequences. —W.I. Thomas

In spite of the overwhelming tide of support for Kertbeny's solution—much of it coming from within the gay community itself—there was a small but growing body of dissent from within the academic community. The cross-cultural anthropological studies on human sexuality did most to point up the inadequacies of Kertbeny's solution. The publication in 1952 of *Patterns of Sexual Behavior* by Ford and Beach illuminated the new possibilities promised by an anthropological investigation into reproductive behaviors. Questions posed by such studies were: "How could homosexuality be an inherent factor if it is so culturally variable?" "Does homosexuality really exist or is it merely a cultural artifact?" and even, "Is sexuality, a term so significant in our society, itself a cultural artifact?"

Attacking the validity of the gay role was its variability in some societies and its absence in others. In some cultures, same-sex activities were common but not isolated within any particular role. In other cultures, same-sex activities were scarce or not observed at all.

Alfred Kinsey, although not a sociologist, had a good grasp of the social realities affecting human sexuality and was one of the first persons to call attention to the stigmatic effects of the medical paradigm. Kinsey claimed there was no clinical explanation to account for the homosexual response, that is, the explanation is not found in anything different within the individual but in the individual's interaction with his environment.

Besides Kinsey, there were others who proposed the theory that homosexuality was a social construct, not an individual one. G.H. Mead of the Chicago school of social psychology insisted that the self is the sum of social roles an individual plays. In California, the sociology of Lemert and Matza clarified the mechanisms of social stigma and deviant roles in the building of identity. Investigators such as Lester Kirkendall (1960) asked important questions about how sex is learned and the influence of peers upon one's sexual activities. These ideas were applied to homosexuality in the social psychology of Evelyn Hooker (1956, 1958, and 1969) and in the sociology of Leznoff and Westley, who published (1956) the first contemporary study of the gay male community. Sociologists Howard Becker and Erving Goffman used the everyday experiences of gay-identified persons to expound theories of labelling and symbolic interaction.

In the same tradition, Simon and Gagnon (1967:179, 181) explained that later events in a person's life are as important in understanding homosexuality as original causes and the "patterns of adult homosexuality are consequent upon the social structures and values that surround the homosexual after he becomes or conceives of himself as homosexual. . . . It is necessary to move away from an obsessive concern with the sexuality of the individual, and attempt to see the homosexual in terms of the broader attachments that he must make to live in the world around him."

One of the clearest statements of the problem came with the publication of "The Homosexual Role" by Mary McIntosh (1968), which marked the enthusiasm of European investigators for interactionist theory. She defined the manner in which social labelling (1) defines good and bad behavior for the cultures and (2) creates the possibility of deviant identities and subcultures. Then she wrote:

> It is proposed that the homosexual should be seen as playing a social role rather than having a condition. The role of "homosexual," however, does not simply describe a sexual behavior pattern. If it did, the idea of a role would be no more useful than that of a condition. For the purpose of introducing the term "role" is to enable us to handle the fact that behavior in this sphere does not match popular beliefs; that sexual behavior patterns cannot be dichotomized in the way that the social roles of homosexual and heterosexual can (p. 184).
>
> The term [homosexual] is, of course, a form of shorthand. It refers not only to a cultural conception or set of ideas but also to a complex of institutional arrangements which depend upon and reinforce these ideas. These arrangements include all the forms of heterosexual activity, courtship, and marriage as well as the labeling process — gossip, ridicule, psychiatric diagnosis, criminal conviction — and the groups and networks of the homosexual subculture. For simplicity we shall simply say that a specialized role exists.
>
> How does the existence of this social role affect actual behavior? And, in particular, does the behavior of individuals conform to the cultural conception in the sense that most people are either exclusively heterosexual or exclusively homosexual? It is difficult to answer these questions on the basis of available evidence because so many researchers have worked with the pre-conception that homosexuality is a condition, so that in order to study the behavior they have first found a group of people who could be identified as "homosexuals." Homosexual behavior should be studied independently of social roles, if the connection between the two is to be revealed.

146		Gay Identity

> This might not sound like a particularly novel program to those who
> are familiar with Kinsey's contribution to the field. . . . But, although
> some of Kinsey's ideas are often referred to, particularly in polemical
> writings, surprisingly little use of has been made of his actual data
> (p. 189).

Those who warned about the dangers of labelling did not seem to
deter other members of their professions from proceeding headlong in
their commitment to the gay role. The manner in which investigators
were able to ignore the stigmatic nature of the role was exemplified in a
series of studies on homosexuality emanating from Kinsey's own Institute
of Sex Research.

Colin Williams and Martin Weinberg, in *Homosexuals in the
Military* (1971), compared gay-identified persons who received a less than
honorable discharge to those who received an honorable discharge.
Claiming that a dishonorable discharge did little to affect the
"psychological adjustment" of those who received it, they missed the
whole point of labelling theory, namely that the primary effect of
stigmatic labelling is not maladjustment or distress, but the deviant role.
The fact that most, if not all, of the subjects of this study had already
adopted the gay role long before discharge is an indication of the authors'
misrepresentation of the symbolic nature of labelling. While official acts
of labelling contribute to the social maintenance of the deviant role, the
main source of personal stress is the role itself. To properly test labelling
theory, we have to instead measure the amount of psychic reorganization
that takes place upon adopting the role and the reduction of life options
that follow.

We notice, in this work and others that followed, a general confusion about the definition of "homosexuality." This confusion can be attributed to the mythical fundament of the gay role itself. Sexual orientation and behaviors do not provide a consistent explanation for the adoption of the role; stigma does. Denying this, the authors are unable to
perceive the social and deviant nature of the role.

In "Homosexual Identity: Commitment, Adjustment and Significant Others," Sue Hammersmith and Martin Weinberg (1973) tested the
interactionist theory that the more a person is committed to a role, the
more his significant others will support it, and the better will be his
psychological adjustment. The authors' data was taken from questionnaires completed by 2,497 gay-identified persons contacted through
homosexual organizations from the United States, the Netherlands, and
Denmark. The conclusions of the study were hardly surprising: Yes, people are better adjusted if they regard their identity in a positive fashion
than if they do not; and yes, the positive social support of the gay community helps in making that commitment.

Here, again, the authors failed to define their terms, confusing "homosexuality," "sexual orientation," and "identity." At the outset, they used "identity" in the sense of an adopted role: "Thus deviant identities may reflect not personal disintegration or failure, as is often supposed, but rather success in establishing an identity" (p. 56). But following statements indicated a progressively positivistic meaning: ". . . Homosexuality is a sexual orientation that emerges despite contrary social expectations and cultural condemnation and which, if not merely a transitory stage, the person must reckon with as a stable part of his social and psychological being. . . . Accepting one's homosexuality may involve redefining one's self as a homosexual rather than as a temporarily variant heterosexual" (p. 58). The term "sexual orientation" is left undefined, because, as we have seen, it is undefinable. If it is not a "transitory stage," the authors said that it must be reckoned with.

Nowhere do the authors consider the possible alternative of enjoying homosexual pleasures without "reckoning" with sexual orientation — or any other explanation of the behavior. They leave the reader to conclude that refusing to define one's feelings in terms of "sexual orientation" is the same as denial of one's feelings. They made the obligation clear: If your homosexual feelings are dominant, you must adopt the deviant role and accept our explanation. They imposed this obligation without the slightest clinical evidence that such a condition as sexual orientation even exists.

In the second work (1974) based on this same study, *Male Homosexuals: Their Problems and Adaptations*, Weinberg and Williams (1974) compared the psychological adjustment of homosexuals in San Francisco and New York (purportedly intolerant societies) with that of homosexuals in Amsterdam and Copenhagen (purportedly tolerant societies).

The sampling was puzzling enough. Plummer (1981:23) complained, "Even on empirical grounds one is at a loss to see why Weinberg and Williams believe that San Francisco (traditionally a homosexual 'mecca') should be more intolerant than Copenhagen."

Again, we cannot help noting the same confusion regarding definition. The authors admitted the need for a sociological approach to homosexuality and gave due credit to Kinsey and the interactionist position that homosexuality should be considered as a social, deviant role. In the same instance, they proceeded to write of "homosexuals" as if they were a different kind of human being without defining the nature of that difference. We were not told in what manner their homosexual subjects came to be defined as homosexuals.

Alan Bell and Martin Weinberg (1978) committed the same mistake again in *Homosexualities: A Study of Diversity Among Men and Women*. They begin with the required nod toward Kinsey, citing his insistence that homosexuality is an activity that appears along a continuum of

various human sexual behaviors. But having said that, they betrayed
their commitment to the stigmatic role in the presentation of their
findings gleaned from interviews of a thousand *homosexuals* in the San
Francisco area. At what point on the Kinsey scale their subjects became
"homosexual," we can only guess.

They alluded to the difficulties created by their position, however,
in the second volume based on that same study, *Sexual Preference: Its
Development in Men and Women*, authored by Alan Bell, Martin
Weinberg, and Sue Kiefer Hammersmith. In a footnote in the chapter on
"Making Sense of the Data" (1981:9), their attempt to clear up the confu-
sion only compounded it:

> Since a principal concern of the present study is to test theories and
> others' findings that have contrasted homosexuals on the one hand with
> heterosexuals on the other, we divided our respondents into two broad
> goupings—homosexual versus heterosexual—instead of allowing for
> various degrees. The criterion we used for assigning respondents to one
> group or the other is described on page 32. Occasionally we use "homosex-
> ual" and "heterosexual" as nouns, reflecting popular usage. It should be
> noted, however, that some persons disapprove of this usage and argue that
> since these words do not wholly define a person, they should be used as
> adjectives only.

On page 32 the authors explained their reasons for going along with
the popular usage:

> The classification of respondents as homosexual or heterosexual was
> obtained as follows. Repondents were asked to rate their sexual feelings
> and behaviors on the seven-point Kinsey scale, which ranges from "ex-
> clusively heterosexual" (a score of 0) to "exclusively homosexual" (a score
> of 6). Respondents' sexual feelings scores were then averaged with their
> sexual behaviors scores. Those with a combined score of 2 or more were
> classified as homosexual; those with a combined score of less than 2
> heterosexual. As it turned out, most of the heterosexual respondents had
> a combined score of 0, meaning that they rated themselves as exclusively
> heterosexual in both behaviors and feelings. Most of the homosexual
> respondents had a combined score of 5-4, considering themselves
> predominantly or exclusively homosexual in both sexual feelings and sex-
> ual behaviors.... Thus, the placement of respondents into two boldly
> defined groups—homosexual versus heterosexual—represents a natural
> division between respondents as well as the distinction most theoretically
> important for our study.

The first item to grab our attention is the manner in which the
Kinsey scale was stretched to accommodate the "natural division" between homosexual and heterosexual. Although most of those defined as
homosexual had a combined score of 4 or 5, the standards applied
allowed for the possibility that a person with a "2" rating ended up in the

"homosexual" category. According to Kinsey's explanation (1948:641), the "2" rating refers to basically heterosexual but with more than incidental homosexual experience. It always refers to those whose psychic preference is decidedly heterosexual. Making room for the corrections that have been made in Kinsey's figures, and allowing for the fact that a person in the "homosexual" category could have a combined rate of 2 in both psychic and behavioral outlet, we conclude that nearly one-third of our adult white male population in the United States would have qualified for the homosexual label in this study. Such a definition suggests that there is more *variety* in sexual expression within the gay community than outside it, and that sexual experience (not to say "sexual orientation") is *not* what gay-identified persons have in common.

The difficulty of such an approach illustrates the fallacy of attributing gay identity to such a confusing and ambiguous element as sexual orientation. The fact that such a large study had to expand the description of the "homosexual" respondents to include the outlets of nearly one-third the adult male population of the United States put the relationship of homosexual orientation and gay identity into proper perspective: Orientation is not the determinative factor in gay identity. Because of its spurious clinical status, it is not even a *descriptive* factor. Stigma is.

We are even more puzzled by the statement that "predominantly or exclusively homosexual in both feelings and behaviors" creates a "boldly defined" group representing a "natural division" between people. The fact that the authors had to stretch the Kinsey scale out of recognition to accommodate the self-definitions of their subjects as belonging to one camp or the other is indication enough that the two groups are not "boldly defined," nor do they represent any "natural" divisions between people. The difference between a "1" (a person with insignificant homosexual experience) and a "0" (one with no homosexual experience) can hardly be considered basis for a "natural" division, any more than the difference between liking and not liking coffee.

Kinsey and others have objected strongly to the distinction as "natural." The presence of both the homosexual and heterosexual in the history of so many of the respondents—in spite of their current self-definition—indicates that such a division has nothing to do with "nature" but is the product of social labelling.

The site of the study (San Francisco) and the sampling methods heavily biased the findings towards those persons who were heavily committed to the gay role. The sampling conveniently eliminated most of the casualties of the stigma, people who suffered depression, anxiety, and suicidal impulses, or those who later found reasons to attenuate or abandon the gay role.

Barry Adam singled out these studies because of their avoidance of the realities of inferiorization. He wrote (1978:66) that, although there was an increased interest in the subject of self-hatred among inferiorized peoples in the late 1940s, "by the 1970s the analysis had become arrested in an ill-defined psychological state divorced from the original problem and abstracted from the situation which made it meaningful." Soon, he writes, "the concern had been drained of meaning by positivist distortions and mangled by the romantic liberalism which found it an embarrassment at best."

Adam (1978:67) wrote that the surveys conducted to measure the self-esteem of gay-identified persons were contradictory, ambiguous, and nonsignificant: "By 'freezing' individuals at different stages in their personal evolutions and failing to consider their marginality or their centrality in the group, the dialectical movement from internalized oppression to emancipation is 'averaged' and 'balanced out'." The reliance on questionnaires which solicited self-reporting of psychological states was not only a poor indicator of self-esteem, but said nothing of the degree of domination experienced in terms of alienation of family, difficulties in relationships, constriction of life options, and the like. The strictures imposed by the gay role can, in fact, bring out the best survival instincts in many people, giving them a high level of emotional adequacy. Adam (1978:68–69) explained:

> Measures of "general self-esteem" by vague indices often run aground in a conceptual fog. All assume a common absolute standard of esteem and anxiety. Questions addressed to individuals about general psychological states ignore the general level of anxiety tolerance of the group of which the individual is a part.... Research interest in the "self-esteem" of minorities makes sense only in relation to the mechanisms by which dominating groups preserve inequality and reproduce behavior functional to the status quo.

In other words, a good adjustment to a deviant status is still a deviant adjustment.

We see in all these studies a tremendous effort within the academic world to reinforce acceptance of the deviant role. The attempt to neutralize the term as referring to a nonpathological sexual orientation merely perpetuates Kertbeny's mistake. Serving no clinical purpose, the designation of people as homosexual cannot be imposed without severely stigmatic consequences. Whatever implies the notion of an internal condition as distinctive only reinforces the pollution projected upon the victims of social stigma. If there is anything that explains the continuing support for the concept of sexual orientation as the basis for gay identity, it is the mechanisms of the ban. The confused status of sexual orientation fits the dynamics of pollution just fine.

Some authors directly attacked the application of labelling theory to gay identity. "A Critique of Labelling Theory from the Phenomenological Perspective," by Carol A.B. Warren and John M. Johnson (1972), took advantage of a lull in the enthusiasm for labelling theory, which they described as an example of the "fads and foibles" (p. 72) that often appear to overcome the social sciences. Denying the element of stigma in the gay role, they repeated a common objection to the position that gay identity could be subject to the chanciness of social, historical, and political processes.

The authors claimed that "the conception of man as partially governed by a series of abstract rules or norms" only partially recognizes the "phenomenological view of man as an actor."

In their attempt to abstract the deviance from the gay role, the authors (p. 77) attempted to deny the connection between the official acts of society and the "informal, and amorphous process of *being labelled*, or having an identity infused with the cognizance of its public opprobrium," implying that the social stigma can be abstracted from the role it creates and sustains. It is indeed unfortuate that this position is not more than a velleity. It would be so nice if we could dissolve the stigmatic nature of the role simply by denying its existence! Again, the authors misrepresent the symbolic nature of labelling. The ban does not consist of "a series of abstract rules or norms," but in rules and norms that have been embodied in roles and those who adopt them. Leviathan does not issue rule books; he recruits soldiers to serve as object lessons on the banned behavior.

Frederick Whitam, (1977:1–11) in "The Homosexual Role: a Reconsideration," attacked the tendency of aligning the adoption of a gay identity with affiliation with the homosexual community. His fieldwork among gay-identified persons in Mexico made him realize that people experience homosexual feelings and behaviors quite independently of the gay community. He also claimed that homosexuality cannot be a role since it is not taught to children like other roles. "Homosexuality is neither a pathological condition nor a role," he wrote (p. 2), "but rather a sexual orientation and no useful purpose can be served by regarding it as anything else."

He is right in that, without knowledge of the role, one can hardly adopt it. But the role is alive and well in Mexico, in spite of the reduced visibility of the gay community. Here again, we have a misunderstanding of the symbolic nature of labelling. It is not so necessary that people *see* other gay persons in order to affiliate with them as long as one knows that they are there. People in Mexico (and Japan and the U.S.S.R. and most other industrialized nations) don't live in a vacuum and are influenced by developments elsewhere, including the rise of the gay role in Europe and the United States.

In Mexico, male roles are taught even more unambiguously than in

the United States. Part of that teaching includes clear descriptions of
negative values surrounding same-sex behaviors. Even though the gay
role in Mexico is construed more in terms of gender rather than orientation, its effect upon behavior is still the same. The fact that many males
in Mexico can engage in homosexual conduct without identifying
themselves as homosexual only clarifies the real distinction that people
there make between the behavior and the role: Some males may not conceptualize their homosexual feelings as such — and are still able to enjoy
them without adopting the gay role.

The gay community busies itself with rewriting history to enhance
the status of the gay role. Anything that has to do with tender relations
between people of the same gender is quickly expropriated as an example
of the gay role.

The ambiguity regarding the role is evident in the works of serious
scholars who tried to achieve some accuracy in definition. K.J. Dover
(1978:vii) stated in the preface to *Greek Homosexuality*: "Established
linguistic usage compels me to treat 'heterosexual' and 'homosexual' as antithetical, but if I followed my inclination I would replace 'heterosexual'
by 'sexual' and treat what is called 'homosexual' as a subdivision of 'quasi-
sexual' (or 'pseudo-sexual'; not 'parasexual')." While Dover's approach
has been criticized for not being sufficiently accepting of homosexuality,
the real problem is not with his treatment (his paradigm would have
avoided modern stigmatic connotations had he used it) but with the fact
that the Greeks were unfamiliar with the role.

Dover sensed this problem but proceeded resolutely with his theme.
In a footnote on page one he explained again: "The Greeks were aware
that individuals differ in their sexual preferences, but their language has
no nouns corresponding to the English nouns 'a homosexual' and 'a
heterosexual'." For the Greeks, "(a) virtually everyone responds at
different times to both homosexual and heterosexual stimuli, and (b) virtually no male both penetrates other males and submits to penetration by
other males at the same stage of his life."

Dover said that Greek norms regarding sexual behaviors had more
to do with avoidance of excess of any kind and were indifferent to sexual
feelings. He also described the failure of the Greeks to relate to the
modern concept of sexual orientation as divorced from sex roles (p. 62).

A more flagrant imposition of the medical concept of homosexuality
on ancient history is found in the works of theologians attempting to explain the church's traditional proscription of same-sex practices. D.S.
Bailey of England, in *Homosexuality and the Western Christian Tradition* (1975), and the United States Jesuit John McNeil, in *The Church and
the Homosexual* (1976), both attributed the rigor of the ancient proscriptions to the fact that the founders of the church were not familiar with
the concept of "true homosexuals," the discovery of which waited until

our own time (!). They argued that both Paul and the Old Testament writers had no concept of homosexuality as an internal and given condition, and did not actually condemn those "who had no choice" about their sexual orientation. What the sacred writers were condemning, instead, were heterosexuals who were using their bodies in an unnatural way. It is all right, these authors concluded, for "true homosexuals" to use their bodies in such a way, though others may not. It did not occur to these men of the cloth that people always have the option of not acting on their sexual feelings.

The creation of separate rules for homosexuals and heterosexuals stretches Christian doctrine to the breaking point, violating the church's teaching on the universal efficacy of "the means of salvation." Nothing is gained by abstracting sin from the activity and referring it to as an internal condition over which one has no control. Such a solution would be unthinkable in traditional theology. By attempting to replace the concept of sin with one of an inherent condition that excuses errant behavior, Bailey and McNeil have placed gay-identified persons even further outside the pale of salvation by making them *inherently* sinful. It would be simpler for the church to declare that, while there may or may not have been reasons for outlawing homosexual behaviors in the past, there is no reason for doing so now. The church can change its mind on sin, as it has on several occasions.

Historian John Boswell (1980:109) unfortunately exploited Bailey's view in his discussion of the highly controverted passage in Romans regarding homosexuality:

> Although the idea that homosexuality represented a congenital physical characteristic was widespread in the Hellenistic world—and undoubtedly well known to Chrysostom—it is not clear that Paul distinguished in his thoughts or writings between gay persons (in the sense of permanent sexual preference) and heterosexuals who simply engaged in periodic homosexual behavior. It is in fact unlikely that many Jews of his day recognized such a distinction, but it is quite apparent that—whether or not he was aware of their existence—Paul did not discuss *gay persons* but only homosexual *acts* committed by heterosexual persons.

If Paul was not aware of the difference between homosexuals and heterosexuals, how could he have made this distinction? Boswell expressed his own difficulties with the role (1980:58):

> Few classicists have doubted that homosexuality occupied a prominent and respected position in most Greek and Roman cities at all levels of society and among a substantial portion of the population. Indeed familiarity with the literature of antiquity raises one very perplexing problem for the scholar which will not have occurred to most persons unacquainted with the classics: whether the dichotomy suggested by the terms

"homosexual" and "heterosexual" corresponds to any reality at all. Terms
for these categories appear extremely rarely in ancient literature, which
nonetheless contains abundant descriptions and accounts of homosexual
and heterosexual activity. It is apparent that the majority of the ancient
world were unconscious of any such categories.

This fact is disturbing. How can a dichotomy so obvious to modern
society, so morally troublesome, so urgent in the lives of many individuals,
have been unknown in societies where homosexual behavior was even
more familiar than it is today?

Boswell's discomfort betrayed his own support of the gay role.
Taking the resulting straight-gay dichotomy as "normal," he mistakenly
attempted to impose it upon those of other societies, wondering why they
never embraced it. The teachings of Paul and the ancient church accurately reflect the prevailing attitudes of those times regarding forbidden sexual behaviors, which were associated with laws of exogamy, not
orgasm. The people of the ancient world were not only unfamiliar with
the concept of "homosexuality," they would have been equally puzzled
the concept of "sexuality." Indeed, we can legitimately question whether
either of these terms has any clinical validity at all. The Greeks were
aware that some people enjoyed tender relations with their own sex and
others did not. Period.

What are we to make of all the above studies and others like them?
In the face of scientific evidence to the contrary, their authors had a profound effect on the sexual scripting of our times and did much to
legitimize the homosexual role. They made the tragic mistake of attempting to legitimize homosexual behavior by attempting to legitimize the gay
role. As a deviant role, created and maintained for the purposes of social
control, it cannot be corrected or legitimized by just declaring it so.

In spite of their definitions of gay identity as a social construct and
their allusions to the findings of sociology, their easy use of the term
"homosexual" as referring to sexual orientation only confirmed the concept of homosexuality as an internal condition. They forgot that words
do more than communicate data; they also serve as constructive symbols
of social realities that profoundly affect behaviors. In their attempts to
deny the realities of stigma, they end up being co-opted by it.

Unfortunately, studies which made a clear distinction between the
gay role and factual descriptions of gay experience are few and far between. Erving Goffman's *Stigma: Notes on the Management of Spoiled
Identity* was one of these. In it, he gave us one of the most practical definitions of "homosexual," remarkable for its avoidance of the medical
concept:

> The term "homosexual" is generally used to refer to anyone who
> engages in overt sexual practices with a member of his own sex, the

practice being called "homosexuality." This usage appears to be based on a medical and legal frame of reference and provides much too broad and heterogenous a categorization for use here. I refer only to individuals who participate in a special community of understanding wherein members of one's own sex are defined as the most desirable sexual objects, and sociability is energetically organized around the pursuit and entertainment of these objects (1963:143–144).

The definition is all the more brilliant for its modest restraint. Perhaps scholars of a future age will define homosexuality in a similar manner as "a mid-twentieth century social movement organized around a stigmatized sexual role."

Among the other authors supporting interactionist explanations of gay identity, Sara Beck Fein and Elain M. Huehring (1982) described the processes by which adoption of the gay role alters one's perceptions. The subjects of this study were primarily young and urban university students or professionals. The results were much the same as the study done by Barbara Ponse (1976), whose sample included many older and more secretive gay-identified persons. The intrapsychic effects of stigma detailed by Fein and Huehring (1982:3) were found to be identical with those in other stigmatized groups and included:

> . . . a *breakdown* of the person's system[s] of interpretation and valuation, which may lead to reality shock; and a *reconstruction* of those systems that take into account the stigmatized characteristic. The latter aspect is associated with frequently noted sequels to stigma, including identity reconstruction, changes in affiliative patterns, and revisions of long-range plans and goals. Key elements in both major aspects are the master-status of stigma, or, in other words, its being a status that takes precedence over all others; the widespread knowledge of stereotypes associated with a given stigma; and the actual and imagined responses of others.

The Fein-Huehring report associated this breakdown and reconstruction of one's world with the coming out event itself. It is not precipitated by something that happens to the individual or by some latent condition that is triggered into actuality at some point in life, but by a process of events and choices taken by the individual.

In France, Guy Hocquenghem used the teachings of Foucault in developing a New Left explanation of homosexual oppression and moving away from the medical model. He pointed out (1978:134) that by gathering so many varied behaviors and emotions under the umbrella of the concept "homosexuality," society has made it especially dangerous and threatening by reason of not being able to avoid its myriad manifestations: "The 'heteroclite' nature of homosexual desire makes it dangerous to the dominant sexuality. Every day a thousand kinds of homosexual behavior challenge the classifications imposed on them. The unification of practices of homosexual desire under the term 'homosexuality' is as imaginary as the unification of the component drives of the ego."

Hocquenghem stumbled in his attempt to combine Freud and Marx. He claimed that society's separation and isolation of the homosexual impulse is the result of the Oedipal repressiveness of the modern nuclear family. He saw capitalism — and not the modern industrial state — as supportive of these Oedipal needs.

The support of gay academics for the gay role was strikingly demonstrated in their opposition to Edward Sagarin's interactionist explanation of the gay role. Sagarin had written some gay novels under the pseudonym of Donald Webster Cory. According to some reports, he later abandoned his gay identity and used his position as a sociologist to attack gay labelling and promote an interactionist perspective. For this, a caucus of gay-identified sociologists bitterly attacked him. They seemed as upset by his alleged abandonment of his gay identity as by his argument attacking the gay role.

In *Deviants and Deviance*, Sagarin (1975:150) described his position: "There are no homosexuals, transvestites, chemical addicts, suicidogenics, delinquents, criminals, or other such entities, in the sense of people having such identities." In the following imaginary dialogue between a counselor and student, Sagarin (1975:155) described possible other alternatives to the adoption of the gay role as a means of dealing with one's sexual feelings:

> STUDENT: (on first visit to college counselor):   I want to tell you, Dr. Smith, I'm gay.
> DR. SMITH: What does that mean?
> STUDENT: You know, I'm a homosexual.
> DR. SMITH: No, you're not.
> STUDENT: But I am. I admit it. How can you say I'm not?
> DR. SMITH: Because there's no such thing. There are some people who, at some stages of their lives, want sex with their own sex. But the minute they call themselves homosexuals they become trapped. Instead of thinking that that is what they do, they think that is what they are.
> STUDENT: What's the difference? Whatever I do, that is what I am. When I play tennis, I am a tennis player. And when I finish school, I'll be doing chemical work, I'll be a chemist.
> DR. SMITH: Yes, that's precisely the fact. You were not a tennis player until you started to play tennis, and nothing forced you to choose the path. At any time, you can stop playing tennis, and you will not be a tennis player, you will be an ex-player. You can give it up because you have other interests, you're bored, disappointed with your game, not in good health, or for a few million other reasons. You have decided that you want to do chemical work, and you are taking a voluntary step to become a chemist. And you can do that as long as it is worthwhile, if it pays okay, if you like the work, or you can give it up because it's boring or because

you inherit a million dollars and want to spend your life travelling. Now, you put your finger right on it: you should start thinking of people as homosexuals the way people are tennis players and chemists. It is something they do, not something they are, and as soon as they realize this they will not feel that they *have* to be this.

STUDENT: I thought it was something that I was all along, that I just made the discovery, when I had this first affair, and knew that that's what I was all along.

DR. SMITH: You weren't that all along, and you don't have to be that if you decide that it's not for you.

While we can congratulate Dr. Smith for his good sense in rejecting the gay role, we can hardly expect the explanations of this short session to have much of an effect. He does not deal realistically with the compelling force of the ban. The student has most likely wrestled with the realities of that role for some time before making his decision to be gay and is not apt to abandon it lightly. There is a naivete in the comparison of the gay role with the roles of a chemist or a tennis player, as if they were different kinds of the same thing.

In *The Making of the Modern Homosexual*, Plummer regretted that pitifully few scientific studies addressed the oppression that surrounds the gay role. Yet he failed to indict the gay role itself as an instrument of that oppression. He wrote (1981:26–27):

> Does "homosexuality" as currently defined lead to a reinforcement of sexual divisions — passivity among women, dominance among men — or does it lead to a glimpse of the future where equal relationships are possible — where contemporary women may engage one another in equal but "objectificatory" sex for pleasure because both are equal in a way that men-women relationships are not?
> This book is actually lodged in that twist. It persistently strains to debunk the category of "homosexual," to show its relativity, its historical sources, its changing meaning and — overwhelmingly — its damaging impact on human experience. Yet *at the current moment* it also tacitly finds it hard to believe that "liberated, joyful homosexuals" could ever have attained their "liberation" without that label. It is a theme which haunts this book and will probably haunt inquiries to come.

Among all the works applying interactionist theory to homosexuality, there is none so perplexing as Kenneth Plummer's *Sexual Stigma*. In many ways the inspiration for this book, it fails at the point of analyzing the deviant nature of the gay role. Plummer reflects the excellent scholarship of the Europeans and their enthusiasm for interactionist thought, but is ambivalent about its conclusions. Perhaps this ambivalence is caused by the need to avoid dealing with what Barry Adam called the sociologist's tendency to deny the "systematic restrictions of life's chances."

Many critics of labelling theory have claimed that the works of those

158   Gay Identity

such as Lemert, Goffman, and Becker no longer apply to the gay community since the beginnings of the gay movement with the Stonewall
riots in Greenwich Village in 1969. Like Kertbeny, they made the
mistake of believing that the new conceptualization of homosexuality
(this time in terms of sexual orientation) would liberate us from the need
to speak of homosexuality in terms of stigma or deviance.

Far from equipping the gay movement with a well-founded theology of liberation that would help reduce the levels of bias regarding
same-sex behaviors, support of the gay role only made matters worse.

During the 1960s, the sexual discourse took a new direction,
centered on challenging the definitions of the modern nuclear family. A
convenient date for the beginning of this attack was 1963, when Betty
Friedan's *The Feminine Mystique* was published, arguing that women
should expand their horizons by getting jobs out of the home. Of course,
women had been in the industrial workforce since its beginning, but in
the 1960s people were beginning to conceptualize the phenomenon
differently by questioning the patriarchal structure of industry itself.

Student uprisings, the New Left, and lesbian and gay organizations
augmented the feminist position on the family, which began demanding
that alternate lifestyles be given the same public advantages as the
family. Although various sectors of this coalition tried not to appear antifamily, their support of casual sex, abortion, and child-care centers
clearly supported the state's new agenda of breaking down what was left
of ancient bonding structures.

Supporting this political thrust were the helping professions — the so-
called "knowledge class," made up of middle-class, college-educated
communicators ready to take on the "establishment," which they identified as business and industry (Berger and Berger:1984). The high level
of support for genital primacy observed in the halls of the academe and
the ranks of the New Left was an embarrassment to feminists and gay
activists.

The modern gay liberation movement grew, not out of a new insight
into sexual behaviors (Kertbeny was fully in command), but in this
misguided attack on the middle-class family. As a result, the gay movement, already a mutant hobbled by stigma, became further implicated
in this antifamily environment.

Activist and writer Dennis Altman played a typical role in this
development. A Fulbright scholar from Australia and a gay-identified
political scientist, he eloquently defended the adoption of the gay role.
Altman was intimately associated with the early gay liberation
manifestos, such as that published in *Come Out*, New York's first publication of gay liberation. His *Homosexual: Oppression and Liberation* (1971)
aligned the new homosexual with the counter-culture, which he believed
radically challenged capitalism and offered a higher awareness. "The

counter-culture has been," he wrote (1971:152), "the most significant development in America over the past decade, and we need first to examine it as a general phenomenon before examining its relation to gay liberation."

Altman gleaned theory from authors such as Norman O. Brown, Paul Goodman, and Theodore Roszak to attack the institutions of the nuclear family, capitalism, Christianity, and psychiatry as the enemies of a liberated sexuality. While he envisioned a time in the future when liberation will bring an end to the heterosexual-homosexual dichotomy (p. 101), he strongly urged homosexuals to develop their own political groups separate from the rest of the New Left (of which it was never a part) and "get their shit together first" (p. 222). Along with other mentors of the counter-culture, Altman has reductively used the gay movement to attack the family (in Germaine Greer's sense of the capitalized, extended Family with its strong support for bonding alliances) rather than win support for same-sex practices.

One of the most vocal critics of both the gay role and the New Left was Don Slater of the Los Angeles Homosexual Information Center. Slater claimed: "There is no such thing as a homosexual lifestyle. There is no such thing as gay pride or anything like that. Homosexuality is simply based on the sex act. Gay consciousness and all the rest are separatist and defeatist attitudes going back to centuries-old and outmoded conceptions that homosexuals are, indeed, different from other people" (Leopold, 1975:27).

Writing in a 1971 issue (p. 28–29) of *Vector* magazine, Slater protested the alignment of gay politics with the New Left:

> The homosexual movement must continue to have room for difference and diversity. To permit a posse of New Left militants to pressure the movement into putting all its eggs in one basket is a tactical mistake, especially since no politically radical group or country has shown the slightest inclination to be more tolerant of homosexual behavior than middle class America.

Slater blasted the organizers of gay liberation as being insensitive to the goals and accomplishments of the earlier gay organizations:

> Homosexuals who had been in hiding for one reason or another despised themselves — like a stream of pentecostal witnesses — appeared to confess their guilt and affirm their salvation — and then excoriate the "pre-revolutionary" homosexual leaders who persisted in contending that homosexuals should not be organized into an anabaptist sect and that the "concern of the movement," as the Mattachine founders had perceived, is with the problems of sexual variation.

Referring to the negative effects of labelling, Slater asked:

> Is it the purpose of the movement to try to assert sexual rights for everyone
> or create a political and social cult out of homosexuality?... Persons who
> perform homosexual acts or other non-conforming acts are sexually free.
> They want others enlightened. They want hostile laws changed, but they
> resent the attempt to organize their lives around homosexuality just as
> much as they resent the centuries-old attempt to organize their lives
> around heterosexuality.

Such complaints as Slater's became fewer and fewer as the cause of labelling was taken up more and more by professionals supporting the goals of the gay movement—so much so, in fact, that to question the labelling perspective within gay intellectual circles is now considered a form of heresy. All of this represents the vindication of the state's agenda to confine homosexual behaviors to the gay community. This agenda, of course, is but a part of the state's larger agenda of reducing the family to its smallest components.

Central to our theory of gay identity is the claim that gay identity is not based on something different—an erotic condition—found within gay-identified people, but instead on a role created by society for the purpose of social control. But why is the modern state so constrained to construct a role for gay behaviors? The answer is found in the state's influence on the structure and function of the family. In its need to extend and consolidate its power, the state moves to replace the functions of the family with its own services and agencies, reducing the family to the reproductive dyad.

The first element of eroticism to be identified and eliminated in this process is homoerotic bonding. In its discourse of power, the state exploits issues of genital sexuality as a smokescreen attempt to cover its actual agenda of the suppression of erotic bonding, which it regards as the real threat.

The origin of the gay role is also an object lesson in the philosophy of behavior. Conduct is not the result of social modification of aimless drives but rather the product of the individual's unique ability to construct, configure, and manipulate his own environment for the purpose of maintaining biological identity. Or, as Maturana and Varela (1980:45) stated in their extraordinary work on the biology of cognition, learning is not a process of accumulation of representations of the environment, but a continuous process of transformation of behavior through the continuous change in the capacity of the nervous system to synthesize it.

The unique feature of all life is not genetic coding, the transfer of information, evolution, or even reproduction, but the maintenance of identity by means of the ability of the living system to transform new materials into its own productive components, the process that defines both cognition and life.

What impresses us first about the process of coming out is what most tend to ignore: a revolutionary and often disruptive change in behavior. More than just a recognition of one's "tendencies," it is often accompanied by a social uprooting of the most primary nature. The whole phenomenon of coming out is basic evidence of the way in which human behavior is always the result of the brain's ability to synthesize behaviors in a manner consistent with the demands of identity.

Society's current view of homosexual behaviors represents a zeitgeist taken up with genetic coding, evolution, and reproduction. As long as we regard reproduction, and not the nurturing claims of identity, as the primary function of human love and sexuality, we will continue to place little priority on the tender relations between members of the same sex.

Bibliography

Adam, B.D. *The Survival of Domination*. New York: Elsevier, 1978.

Altman, D. *Homosexual: Oppression and Liberation*. New York: Outerbridge & Dienstfrey, 1971.

Aries, P. (Baldick, R., tr.) *Centuries of Childhood: A Social History of Family Life*. New York: Random House, 1962.

Bailey, D.S. *Homosexuality and the Western Christian Tradition*. Hamden, Conn.: Archon Books, 1975.

Becker, H.S. *Outsiders: Studies in the Sociology of Deviance*. New York: Free Press, 1963 (rev. ed. 1973).

Bell, A.P., and Weinberg, M.S. *Homosexualities: A Study of Diversity among Men and Women*. New York: Simon and Schuster, 1978.

_____, _____, and Hammersmith, S.K. *Sexual Preference: Its Development in Men and Women*. Bloomington, Indiana: University of Indiana Press, 1981.

Berger, B., and Berger, P. *The War Over the Family: Capturing the Middle Ground*. Garden City, N.Y.: Anchor Books, 1984.

Berger, P., and Luckman, T. *The Social Construction of Reality*. Garden City, N.Y.: Doubleday, 1966

Blackwood, E. "Breaking the Mirror: The Construction of Lesbianism and the Anthropological Discourse on Homosexuality." *Journal of Homosexuality* 11(3/4), Summer 1985:1–17.

Blumer, H. "Sociological Implications of the Thought of George Hubert Mead." *American Journal of Sociology* 71, March 1966:535–44.

_____. *Symbolic Interactionism*. Englewood Cliffs, N.J.: Prentice-Hall, 1969.

Boswell, J. *Christianity, Social Tolerance and Homosexuality*. Chicago: University of Chicago Press, 1980.

Brandt, A. *No Magic Bullet*. New York: Oxford University Press, 1985.

Braudel, F. *Civilization and Capitalism, Vol II. The Wheels of Commerce*. New York: Harper & Row, 1982.

Briggs, J.L. *Never in Anger: Portrait of an Eskimo Family*. Cambridge: Harvard University Press, 1970.

Brown, G. *The New Celibacy*. New York: McGraw-Hill, 1980.

Bullough, V. *Homosexuality: A History*. New York: Meridien, 1979.

Cass, V. "Homosexual Identity Formation: A Theoretical Model." *Journal of Homosexuality* 4(3), Spring 1979.

_____. "Homosexual Identity: A Concept in Need of Definition." *Journal of Homosexuality* 9(2/3), Winter/Spring 1984:105–126.

Coleman, E. "Developmental Stages of the Coming Out Process." *American Behavioral Scientist* 25(4), March/April 1982.

Conrad, P., and Schneider, J.W. *Deviance and Medicalization*. St. Louis: C.V. Mosby, 1980.

163

164 Gay Identity

Cucchiari, S. "The Gender Revolution and the Transition from Bisexual Horde to Patrilocal Band." In Ortner and Whitehead, 1981:33–79.
Cullen, F.T. *Rethinking Crime and Deviance Theory*. Totowa, N.J.: Rowman & Allanheld, 1984.
Curle, A. *Mystics and Militants*. London: Tavistok, 1972.
Dank, B.M. "Coming Out in the Gay World." *Psychiatry* 34, May 1971:180–197.
de Becker, R. *The Other Face of Love*, New York: Bell, 1964.
De Cecco, J.P. "Definition and Meaning of Sexual Orientation." *Journal of Homosexuality* 5(4), Summer 1981:51–67.
Donzelot, J. (Hurley, R., tr.) *The Policing of Families*. New York: Pantheon, 1979.
Douglas, J. (ed.) *Deviance and Respectability*. New York: Basic Books, 1970.
Dover, K.J. *Greek Homosexuality*. New York: Vintage Books, 1978.
Ellis, H. *Studies in the Psychology of Sex, Vol. II*. New York: Random House, 1937.
Enloe, C.H. *Police, Military and Ethnicity*. New Brunswick: Transaction Books, 1980.
Erikson, E.H. *Young Man Luther: A Study in Psychoanalysis and History*. New York: Norton, 1958.
_____. *Identity and the Life Cycle*. New York: International Universities Press, 1959.
_____. *Identity: Youth and Crisis*. New York: Norton, 1968.
Erikson, K.T. "Notes on the Sociology of Deviance." *Social Problems* 9, 1962: 307–14.
Fein, S., and Huehring, E. "Intrapsychic Effects of Stigma." *Journal of Homosexuality* 7(1) 1981:3–13.
Flandrin, J. *Families in Former Times*. New York: Cambridge University Press, 1979.
_____. "Repression and Change in the Sexual Life of Young People in Medieval and Modern Times." In Wheaton and Hareven, 1980:27–48.
Ford, C.S., and Beach, F. *Patterns of Sexual Behavior*. London: Methuen, 1952.
Foucault, M. *The History of Sexuality, Vol. I: An Introduction*. New York: Pantheon Books, 1978.
_____ (Sheridan Smith, A.M., tr.) *The Birth of the Clinic: An Archeology of Medical Perception*. New York: Pantheon Books, 1973.
Frank, L.K. "Tactile Communication." *Genetic Psychology Monographs* 56, 1957:241.
Freud, S. (1905). "Three Essays on the Theory of Sexuality." *Standard Edition* 7:125–243. London: Hogarth, 1953.
_____ (1908). "Civilized Sexual Morality and Modern Nervous Illness." *Standard Edition* 9:177–204. London: Hogarth, 1959.
_____ (1920). "Beyond the Pleasure Principle." *Standard Edition* 18:7–64. London: Hogarth, 1961.
_____ (1923). "The Infantile Genital Organization." *Standard Edition* 19:14–145. London: Hogarth, 1961.
_____ (1940). "An Outline of Psychoanalysis." *Standard Edition* 23:144–207. London: Hogarth, 1964.
Gagnon, J., and Simon, W. *Sexual Conduct: The Social Sources of Human Sexuality*. Chicago: Aldine, 1973.
Gillin, J.L. *Criminology and Penology*. New York: Appleton-Century-Crofts, 1935.

Goffman, E. *Stigma: Notes on the Management of Spoiled Identity.* Englewood Cliffs, N.J.: Prentice-Hall, 1963.

Goody, J. *The Development of the Family and Marriage in Europe.* New York: Cambridge University Press, 1983.

Gordon, S., and Libby, R.W. (eds.) *Sexuality Today and Tomorrow.* North Scituate, Mass.: Duxbury Press, 1976.

Gottleib, B. "The Meaning of Clandestine Marriage." In Wheaton, R., and Hareven, T., 1980:49–83.

Greer, G. *Sex and Destiny: The Politics of Human Fertility.* New York: Harper & Row, 1984.

Hammersmith, S.K., and Weinberg, M. "Homosexual Identity." *Sociometry* 36(1), 1973: 56–79.

Henry, J. *Jungle People.* New York: Random House, 1964.

Herdt, G.H. *Guardians of the Flutes: Idioms of Masculinity.* New York: McGraw-Hill, 1981.

Herzer, M. "Kertbeny and the Nameless Love." *Journal of Homosexuality* 12(1), Fall 1985:1–23.

Hocquenghem, G. *Homosexual Desire.* London: Allison & Busby, 1978.

Holleran, A. *Dancer from the Dance.* New York: Wiliam Morrow, 1978.

Holt, L.E. *The Care and Feeding of Children.* New York: Appleton-Century, 1935.

Hooker, E. "A Preliminary Analysis of Group Behavior of Homosexuals." *Journal of Psychology* 42, 1956:217–25.

_____. "Male Homosexuality in the Rorschach." *Journal of Projective Techniques* 22, 1958:33–54.

_____. *Final Report of the Task Force on Homosexuality.* Washington, D.C.: National Institute of Mental Health, 1967.

Humphreys, L. *Tea-room Trade: Impersonal Sex in Public Places.* Chicago: Aldine, 1970.

_____. "New Styles in Homosexual Manliness." *Transaction*, March/April 1971:38–46.

Imperato-McGinley, J., et al. "Androgens and the Evolution of the Male Gender-Identity among Male Pseudohermaphrodites with 5a-reductase Deficiency." *Biology of Reproduction* 22, 1979:66–72.

Johnson, G. *Which Way Out of the Men's Room?* New York: A.S. Barnes, 1979.

Karr, R.G. "Homosexual Labelling and the Male Role." *Journal of Social Issues* 34(3), 1978:73–83.

Kinsey, A.C., Pomeroy, W.P., and Martin, C.E. *Sexual Behavior in the Human Male.* Philadelphia: Saunders, 1948.

_____, _____, _____, and Gebhard, P.H. *Sexual Behavior in the Human Female.* Philadelphia: W.B. Saunders, 1953.

Kirkendall, L.A. "Circumstances Associated with Teenage Boys' Prostitution." *Marriage and Family Living* 22, 1960.

Konner, M. *The Tangled Wing.* New York: Holt, Rinehart and Winston, 1982.

Kuhn, M.H. "Kinsey's View on Human Behavior." *Social Problems* 1, 1954:119–25.

Langbaum, R. *The Mysteries of Identity: A Theme in Modern Literature.* New York: Oxford University Press, 1977.

Lemert, E.M. *Social Pathology.* New York: McGraw-Hill, 1951.

_____. *Human Deviance, Social Problems and Social Control.* Englewood Cliffs, N.J.: Prentice-Hall, 1967.

Leopold, A. "The Angry Men: Broadsides from the H.I.C." *In Touch*, June/July 1975:26.

Lewin, K. *Resolving Social Conflicts*. New York: Harper, 1948.

Leznoff, M., and Westley, W.A. "The Homosexual Community." *Social Problems* 3, 1956:257–263.

Lichtenstein, H. *The Dilemma of Human Identity*. New York: Jason Aronson, 1977.

Lindesmith, A.R., and Strauss, A.L. *Social Psychology* (3rd ed.). London: Holt, Rinehart & Winston, 1968.

Lindholm, C. and Lindholm, C. "The Erotic Sorcerers." *Science Digest*, 90(9), September 1982.

McCall, G.J., and Simmons, J.L. *Identities and Interactions*. London: Collier-Macmillan, 1966.

McIntosh, M. "The Homosexual Role." *Social Problems*, 16(2), 1968:182–192.

McNeil, J.J. *The Church and the Homosexual*. Kansas City: Sheed Andrews & McMeel, 1976.

Malinoski, B. *Crime and Custom in Savage Society*. New York: Humanities Press, 1926.

Marcuse, H. *Eros and Civilization*. Boston: Beacon, 1966.

Marx, G. "Ironies of Social Control." *Social Problems* 28, February 1981:221–246.

Maturana, H., and Varela, F. *Autopoiesis and Cognition: Realization of the Living*. Dordrecht, Holland: D. Reidel, 1980.

Matza, D. *On Becoming Deviant*. Englewood Cliffs, N.J.: Prentice-Hall, 1969.

Mead, G.H. *Mind, Self, and Society*. Chicago: University of Chicago Press, 1934.

Mead, M. *Male and Female*. New York: William Morrow, 1949.

_____. *Sex and Temperament in Three Primitive Societies*. New York: New American Library, 1952.

Memmi, A. *The Colonizer and the Colonized*. New York: Orion Press, 1965.

_____. *Dominated Man*. New York: Orion Press, 1968.

Money, J. (ed.) *Sex Research, New Developments*. New York: Holt, Reinhart and Winston, 1965.

_____, Hampson, J.G., and Hampson, J.L. "Hermaphroditism." *Johns Hopkins Bulletin* 97, 1955:284–300.

_____, _____, and _____. "Sexual Incongruities and Psychopathology." *Johns Hopkins Bulletin* 98, 1956:43–57.

Montagu, A. *Touching: The Human Significance of Skin*. New York: Harper & Row, 1978.

Ortega y Gasset, J. (1939) "The Self and the Other." In *The Dehumanization of Art and Other Writings*. New York: Doubleday, 1956.

Ortner, S.B., and Whitehead, H. (eds.) *Sexual Meanings: The Cultural Construction of Gender and Sexuality*. New York: Cambridge University Press, 1981.

Parker, S., and Parker, H. "The Myth of Male Superiority." *American Anthropologist*, 81(2), June 1979.

Plummer, K. *Sexual Stigma: An Interactionist Approach*. London: Routledge & Kegan Paul, 1975.

_____ (ed.) *The Making of the Modern Homosexual*. Totowa, N.J.: Barnes & Noble, 1981.

Polsky, N. *Hustlers, Beats, and Others*. Chicago: Aldine, 1967.

Pomeroy, W.B. *Dr. Kinsey and the Institute for Sex Research*. New York: Harper & Row, 1972.

Ponse, B. *Identities in the Lesbian World*. Westport, Conn.: Greenwood, 1978.

Raisman, G., and Field, P.M. "Sexual Dimorphism in the Neuropil of the Preoptic Area of the Rat and Its Dependence on Neonatal Androgen." *Brain Research* 54, 1973:1–29.
Reiser, S.J. *Medicine and the Reign of Technology.* New York: Cambridge University Press, 1978.
Reiss, A.J. "The Social Integration of Queers and Peers." *Social Problems* 9, 1961:102–119.
Rossiaud, J. "Fraternités de Jeunesse et Niveaux de Culture dans les Villes à la fin du Moyen Age." *Cahiers d'Histoire*, 21(1–2): 67–102
Sagarin, E. *Deviants and Deviance.* New York: Praeger, 1975.
Schur, E.M. *The Politics of Deviance.* Englewood Cliffs, N.J.: Prentice-Hall, 1980.
Shibutani, T. *Society and Personality.* Englewood Cliffs, N.J.: Prentice-Hall, 1961.
Shively, M.G., and De Cecco, J.P. "Components of Sexual Identity." *Journal of Homosexuality* 3(1), Fall 1977:41–48.
_____, Jones, C., and _____. "Research on Sexual Orientation." *Journal of Homosexuality* 9 (2/3), Winter/Spring 1983/1984: 127–36.
Shoham, S. *The Mark of Cain.* Jerusalem: Israel Universities Press, 1970.
Simmel, G. (Wolf, K.H., ed.) *The Sociology of George Simmel.* New York: Free Press, 1950.
Simon, W., and Gagnon, J.H. "Homosexuality: The Formulation of a Psychological Perspective." *Journal of Health and Social Behavior* 8 September 1967:177–85.
Slater, D. "Don Slater." *Vector*, 8(7), 1971:29
Spitz, R.A. "Hospitalism." *Psychoanalytic Study of the Child*, 1945:53–57.
Sykes, G.M., and Matza, D. "Techniques of Neutralization: A Theory of Delinquency." *American Sociological Review* 22, 1957:664–670.
Tavris, C. *Anger: The Misunderstood Emotion.* New York: Simon and Schuster, 1982.
Tripp, C.A. *The Homosexual Matrix.* New York: McGraw-Hill, 1975.
Troiden, R.R. "Becoming Homosexual: A Model of Gay Identity Acquisition." *Psychiatry* 42, November 1979:362–373.
Ward, E. (1709). *The Secret History of the London Clubs.* London: Dutton, 1896.
Warren, C.A.B. *Identity and Community in the Gay World.* New York: Wiley-Interscience, 1974.
_____, and Johnson, J.M. "A Critique of Labelling Theory." In Scott, R.A., and Douglas, J.D., eds., *Theoretical Perspectives on Deviance.* New York: Basic Books, 1972.
Watson, J.B. *Psychological Care of Infant and Child.* New York: W.W. Norton, 1928.
Waugh, E. *Brideshead Revisited.* Boston: Little, Brown, 1945.
Weinberg, M.S., and Williams, C.J. *Male Homosexuals.* New York: Oxford University Press, 1974.
Weinberg, T. "On 'Doing' and 'Being' Gay." *Journal of Homosexuality* 14(2), Winter 1978.
Wheaton, R., and Hareven, T.K. (eds.) *Family and Sexuality in French History.* Philadelphia: University of Pennsylvania Press, 1980.
Whitam, F.L. "The Homosexual Role: A Reconsideration." *Journal of Sex Research* 13(1), February 1977.
Whitehead, H. "The Bow and the Burden Strap: A New Look at Institutionalized Homosexuality in Native North America." In Ornter and Whitehead, 1981.

Williams, C.J., and Weinberg, M. *Homosexuals in the Military*. New York: Harper & Row, 1971.

Wirth, L. "Culture Conflict and Misconduct." *Social Forces* 9, January 1931:484–92.

Yeats, W.B. *Collected Poems*. New York: Macmillan, 1963.

Index

169